Bestselling Books by
Robert T. Kiyosaki & Sharon L. Lechter

Rich Dad Poor Dad
What the Rich Teach Their Kids About Money
that the Poor and Middle Class Do Not

Rich Dad's CASHFLOW Quadrant
Rich Dad's Guide to Financial Freedom

Rich Dad's Guide to Investing
What the Rich Invest In that the Poor and Middle Class Do Not

Rich Dad's Rich Kid Smart Kid
Give Your Child a Financial Head Start

Rich Dad's Retire Young Retire Rich
How to Get Rich Quickly and Stay Rich Forever

Rich Dad's Prophecy
Why the Biggest Stock Market Crash in History is Still Coming...
And How You Can Prepare Yourself and Profit From it!

Rich Dad's Success Stories
Real-Life Success Stories from Real-Life People
Who Followed the Rich Dad Lessons

Rich Dad's Guide to Becoming Rich Without Cutting Up Your Credit Cards
Turn "Bad Debt" into "Good Debt"

Rich Dad's Who Took My Money?
Why Slow Investors Lose and Fast Money Wins!

Rich Dad Poor Dad for Teens
The Secrets About Money – That You Don't Learn In School!

Rich Dad's Escape from the Rat Race
How to Become a Rich Kid by Following Rich Dad's Advice

Rich Dad's Before You Quit Your Job
Ten Real-Life Lessons Every Entrepreneur Should Know
About Building a Multi-Million Dollar Business

Rich Dad's Increase Your Financial IQ
Get Smarter With Your Money

www.richdad.com

Bestselling Books by
Rich Dad's Advisors

Sales Dogs
by Blair Singer
Reveal the Five Simple but Critical Revenue - Generating Skills

Own Your Own Corporation
by Garret Sutton
Don't Climb the Corporate Ladder, Why Not Own the Corporate Ladder?

How To Buy & Sell A Business
by Garrett Sutton
Strategies Used by Successful Entrepreneurs

The ABC's of Real Estate Investing
by Ken McElroy
Learn How to Achieve Wealth and Cash Flow Through Real Estate

The ABC's of Building A Business Team That Wins
by Blair Singer
How to Get Rich Quickly and Stay Rich Forever

The ABC's of Getting Out of Debt
by Garrett Sutton
Strategies for Overcoming Bad Debt, as Well as
Using Good Debt to Your Advantage

The ABC's of Writing Winning Business Plans
by Garrett Sutton
Learn to Focus Your Plan for the Business and Format Your Plan to Impress
About Building a Multi-Million Dollar Business

The Advanced Guide to Real Estate Investing
by Ken McElroy
How to Identify the Hottest Markets and Secure the Best Deals

Own Your *Own* Corporation

*Why the Rich Own Their Own Companies
and Everyone Else Works for Them*

REVISED EDITION

GARRETT SUTTON, ESQ.

**BUSINESS
PLUS**

NEW YORK   BOSTON

E B   E|B
S I   S|I

Business Plus
Hachette Book Group USA
237 Park Avenue
New York, NY 10017

Visit our Web sites at www.HachetteBookGroupUSA.com and www.richdad.com.

Business Plus is an imprint of Grand Central Publishing.
The Business Plus name and logo are trademarks of Hachette Book Group USA, Inc.

Printed in the United States of America

First Revised Edition: June 2008

10 9 8 7 6 5 4 3 2 1

Library of Congress Cataloging-in-Publication Data

Sutton, Garrett.
    Own your own corporation : why the rich own their own companies and everyone else works for them / Garrett Sutton.
        p.   cm.—(Rich dad's advisors)
    ISBN-13: 978-0-446-53906-7
    ISBN-10: 0-446-53906-6
    1. Small business—Management.   2. Home-based businesses—Management.
3. Self-employed.   4. Small business—Law and legislation.   I. Title.

HD62.7.S977   2008
658.02'2—dc22
                                                              2008007662

Acknowledgments

This book is dedicated to my wonderful wife, Jenny, and our terrific kids, Teddy, Emily, and Sarah. Thank you for your understanding as this book was being written.

I would like to acknowledge the assistance of Mona Gambetta, Leila Porteous, and, of course, Robert Kiyosaki in the revision and updating of this book. Thank you.

And thanks to all the readers of the first version of this book. Your comments and suggestions have led to an even better revision.

Contents

Foreword by Robert Kiyosaki

When I was ten years old and in the fifth grade, I began to read about the great explorers, such as Columbus, Magellan, Cortéz, da Gama, Cook. I dreamed of someday traveling the world in a wooden ship, in search of treasures in unexplored lands. I read every book I could about their lives and adventures. In the fifth grade, I often had the highest scores on the tests and quizzes about the great explorers.

"You read about the explorers who were successful," said rich dad. "What about the explorers who failed?" Rich dad was helping me prepare for my final exam in the fifth grade.

"The ones who failed?" I asked.

"Yes, the ones who failed," said rich dad. "In school they teach you about the successful explorers or the famous explorers. There were many more explorers who were not successful and not famous whom we have never heard about, nor will we ever hear about them."

"Why is studying about the explorers who failed so important?" I asked.

"Because you need to know how the owners and the investors in those failed voyages protected themselves against the repercussions from such failures," said rich dad.

"Repercussions?" I asked. "What kind of repercussions?"

"Such things as the loss of life," said rich dad. "The owners and investors wanted to protect themselves and their fortunes from the families of the explorer and his crew in the event there was a loss of life on the voyage."

"You mean the men on the ship risked and sometimes lost their lives, and all the owners and investors on land wanted to do was protect themselves from losing money? That's one of the repercussions you're talking about?"

Rich dad nodded his head. He then began to tell me about the Dutch East India Company and the British East India Company, two of the more powerful and famous corporations behind some of those explorers. Some of these corporations even had their own navy and army to control access to their nation's overseas wealth. He told me how these corporations in many ways took over whole countries, such as New Zealand, Hawaii, Australia, Malaysia, Indonesia, South Africa, and other parts of the world. One of those countries was one day to become the United States of America. Rich dad pointed out to me that the flag of the United States was originally the flag of the British East India Company, reportedly modified by Betsy Ross. While England may have lost control over its colonies, the British East India Company simply changed its name—a simple d.b.a.—and kept on trading.

The more rich dad told me about the corporations behind these great explorers and how they shaped world history, the more interested I became in global business and doing business through a corporation. When I was sixteen, I began applying for a congressional appointment to the U.S. Merchant Marine Academy, the federal military school that trains young men to sail ships of the merchant marine. Kings Point, which the school is also known as, continues to train young people to replace the great seafaring explorers. Only two students from Hawaii are admitted to this little known federal academy each year, so I felt fortunate to be accepted after passing rigorous exams and interviews. At age eighteen, I began sailing as a student onboard ships carrying cargo along the same trade routes established by Ferdinand Magellan and Captain James Cook. I quickly realized that although the early explorers are gone, some of those corporations rich dad talked about still exist today, and the U.S. government funds the education of these corporations' leaders. I began to understand why rich dad told me years ago, "Don't just study the explorer and his ships, study the power of the corporations behind the explorer and his ships."

747 Replaces Cargo Ships

Today I travel by 747 rather than by cargo ship. Although my mode of transportation has changed, I have heeded rich dad's advice and learned my lessons well. Today I travel as a representative of several corporations—the difference is that I control those corporations rather than simply work for them.

As I stated in *Rich Dad Poor Dad*, my poor dad thought it was a good idea to be a good employee and climb the corporate ladder, while my rich dad said, "Don't climb the corporate ladder, why not own the corporate ladder?" Rich dad also said, "The problem with climbing the corporate ladder is that when you look up, you see somebody's big fat butt above you." On a more serious note, he said, "The two main reasons you need to own your own corporation are for protection against lawsuits and against excessive taxes, yet there are many other reasons and other strategies. The point is, if you are serious about being rich and keeping your wealth, understanding corporations and other legal structures is an important part of your ongoing financial education."

Introducing Garrett Sutton

I am pleased to introduce Garrett Sutton to you. Often in my classes, students ask me questions about corporations and legal structures. My standard reply is, "I did not go to law school and I am not an attorney, so I do not give advice on that subject. I suggest you do as I do: Find a good attorney and use him or her as your advisor on this very important subject." I am pleased to introduce to you my advisor in these matters, Garrett Sutton. He is a pleasure to work with, and he is more than a great advisor, he is a great teacher. As rich dad said to me years ago, "If you are serious about being rich and keeping your wealth, understanding corporations and other legal structures is an important part of your ongoing financial education."

Introduction

Congratulations. You are about to undertake a powerful and enlightening journey. By reading this book you will learn quickly and easily the legal secrets and strategies that the rich have used to run their businesses and protect their assets. In short order you will clearly understand exactly how certain entities—corporations, limited liability companies, and limited partnerships—can not only save you thousands and thousands of dollars in taxes but can also save your house and savings and family assets from the attacks of creditors.

These are the same lessons that Robert Kiyosaki's rich dad taught him. Own nothing and control everything. Use the techniques of the rich to improve your financial standing and protect your family. And above all, work smarter instead of harder.

By the time you finish this book you will have the legal savvy of an experienced entrepreneur and the knowledge necessary to immediately implement your own custom legal strategy.

Let's begin . . .

Own Your *Own* Corporation

Chapter 1

Your Entity Menu

- C corporation
- S corporation
- Limited Liability Company (LLC)
- Limited Partnership (LP)
- General Partnership
- Sole Proprietorship

As legal business systems and traditions have developed over the last five hundred years, several structures for running a business have evolved. Each structure (or entity) has its own advantages and drawbacks, which we will explore.

As a frame of reference for making your selection, it is important for you to clarify your strategy in this planning. The purpose of this chapter is for you to clearly understand and choose the best entity for your unique and specific purpose. To that end, the following checklist should be considered:

1. Protection of family assets and investments
2. Management control
3. Avoiding family disputes
4. Flexibility of decision making
5. Succession of children and other family members to management
6. The nature of the business to be operated
7. The nature of the asset to be held

8. The number of owners involved
9. Estate planning and gifting of assets
10. Who may legally obligate the business
11. Effect upon an owner's death or departure
12. The need for start-up funding and raising of capital
13. Taxation
14. Privacy of ownership
15. Consolidation of assets and investments

These and other issues will become apparent as we review your choices. And please note, your decision does not have to be made alone. It is recommended that these issues be discussed with your attorney, accountant, or other professional advisor. An individual well versed in these areas will provide excellent insight into which entity is right for you.

By reading this book you will be better able to work with your professional advisors. They won't have to spend time explaining all of the tax issues and limitations of liability strategies to you. By reading this book you will have a leg up. When you meet with your advisors you won't be stepping up to the plate for the first time. Instead, you'll be at second base, ready to score. (Fear not, our first sports analogy is also our last one.)

It is important to know that in entity selection one size does not fit all. If your attorney or accountant suggests only one entity, a general partnership for example, for each and every business venture you have him or her review, you will want to question why they believe one entity fits all situations. Or you may want to seek out a new professional advisor.

We will discuss which entities work well in various business and asset holding scenarios. But before doing so, we must point out which entities do not work well in any situation. For as important as knowing which entity to use for running your business, protecting your assets, and limiting your liability is knowing which entity NOT to use.

Bad Entities

- Sole proprietorships
- General partnerships

In my legal practice I represent various businesses, from small and basic to large and complicated. I enjoy helping entrepreneurs and business owners make money, provide for their families and employees, and secure a stable future.

I cannot do my job if a client insists on using a bad entity. Sole proprietorships and general partnerships provide no asset protection. One lawsuit against your business, and your house, savings, and personal assets can all be lost. Our first case is illustrative.

Case No. 1—Johnny

Johnny was a plumber. He had been at it for five years and was starting to succeed. His customers were satisfied with his work and the word of mouth for Johnny's Ace Plumbing was good.

While Johnny was a good plumber, he felt intimidated by legal matters. Lawyers and accountants were supposed to be smart, so the work they did must be difficult. When Johnny was a young boy his father had been unfairly treated by a lawyer. He remembered it to this day, and wanted nothing to do with them.

So instead of consulting with a professional on how best to conduct his business, Johnny let his part-time bookkeeper select an entity off the menu. The results were disastrous.

Johnny's part-time bookkeeper knew only that forming a corporation required filing special documents with the state but did not know how to file them. He knew that a corporation needed to file a separate tax return but was not sure of the ins and outs of preparing one. And so he suggested Johnny use a sole proprietorship because he knew how to handle one and always suggested one for his clients. One size fits all.

The problem was that a sole proprietorship provides absolutely no asset protection. By operating as a sole proprietorship Johnny has unlimited liability for the debts, claims, and obligations of the business. This unlimited liability meant that his house and savings and personal assets were exposed to the claims of others.

Of course, as in all horror stories, a demon entered Johnny's business. He had hired Damien as an employee to assist with his growing workload. Damien seemed like a decent guy and appeared to know the plumbing business. Johnny did not bother to do a background check on Damien. Johnny was new to the business world and not aware of the need to do so.

After one week on the job, Damien assaulted one of Johnny's customers while they were alone in her house. Without going into the sordid details, this woman was so severely traumatized by what Damien did to her in her own home that she and her family had to move away.

Within three weeks of the incident Johnny's business was sued. Because Johnny was a sole proprietor, this meant that he, and not the business itself, as with a corporation, was sued and had to defend himself.

The lawyers suing for the woman did the background check of Damien that Johnny did not do. Damien was a recently released ex-convict with a history of sexual assaults. Johnny did not have the insurance to cover such a claim. The case went forward. The lawyers argued to a jury that Johnny's business was irresponsible for failing to check up on Damien and was responsible for the consequences. They presented to the jury what was true—a business is vicariously liable, or responsible, for the acts of its employees. The jury was horrified by the whole case and awarded damages of $10 million.

Johnny was wiped out. As a sole proprietor he was completely and personally responsible for every claim the business incurred. And he had attorneys with a one-third contingent interest in the collection of $10 million after him.

Johnny lost his house, his savings, and his family. The stress of it all resulted in his wife divorcing him, obtaining custody of the children, and moving away. Johnny declared bankruptcy. He ended up a broken man despising lawyers and our legal system all the more.

The irony, of course, is that by consulting with a lawyer and using the legal system to his advantage, Johnny could have prevented the disastrous consequences that resulted from relying on a part-time bookkeeper with a one-size-fits-all mentality for entity selection.

A competent lawyer would have told Johnny that there were risks—known and unknown—in running any business. To protect yourself from such risks you need to limit your liability by establishing a corporation or other good entity.

A good entity is one that shields and protects your personal assets from business risk. A bad entity is one that provides you no protection whatsoever. By using a good entity Johnny could have used the legal system—which has evolved to encourage business activity and limit the liability of risk takers—to his advantage.

Other Sole Proprietorship Disadvantages

As if personal liability was not bad enough, there are two other disadvantages to using a sole proprietorship:

• *Owners.* There can only be one owner of a sole proprietorship. If you later want to bring on owners you will have to switch to another business entity.

• *Sale.* It is hard to sell a sole proprietorship since its value is based on the owner and not the business.

• *Death.* When a sole proprietor dies, the sole proprietorship terminates. The sole proprietor's successors can only sell assets, not the business as a going concern.

• *Audit Risk.* Because sole proprietors report their business profits and losses to the IRS on Schedule C, there is a much higher risk of IRS audit. Schedule C returns are audited at a five times greater rate than corporate tax returns.

A general partnership is also a bad entity. In fact it is twice as bad as a sole proprietorship because you have twice the personal exposure: personal liability for your acts *and* your partners' acts. This will be illustrated in Case No. 2 ahead.

Whenever two or more persons agree to share profits and losses a partnership has been formed. Even if you never sign a partnership agreement, state law provides that under such circumstances you have formed a general partnership.

A written partnership agreement is not required by law. A handshake is acceptable for formation. In the event you do not sign a formal document, you will be subject to your state's applicable partnership law. This may not be to your advantage, since such general rules rarely satisfy specific situations. As an example, most states provide that profits and losses are to be divided equally among the partners. If your oral understanding is that you are to receive 75 percent of the profits, state law and your handshake will not help you. Instead, against your wishes, state law may have you sharing 50-50. You are better advised to prepare a written agreement addressing your rights and rewards. But again, you are better off not using a general partnership in the first place.

Unlike a sole proprietorship, in which only one individual may participate, by definition, a general partnership must consist of two or more people. You cannot have a one-person partnership. On the other hand, you may have as many partners as you want in a general partnership. This may sound like a blessing but it is actually a curse.

The greatest drawback of a general partnership is that each partner is liable for the debts and obligations incurred by all the other general partners. While you may trust the one general partner you have not to improperly obligate the partnership, the more general partners you bring aboard the greater risk you run that someone will create serious problems.

And remember, just as with a sole proprietorship, your personal assets are at risk in a general partnership. Your house and your life savings can be lost through the actions of your partner. While you may have had nothing to do with the decision that was made and you may have been five thousand miles away when it was made and you may have voiced your opposition to it when you found out it was made, you are still personally responsible for it as a general partner.

As such, a general partnership is much riskier than a sole proprietorship. In a sole proprietorship, only the proprietor can bind the business. In a general partnership, any general partner—no matter how wise or, unfortunately, how ignorant—may obligate the business. By contrast, limited liability companies, limited partnerships, and corporations offer much greater protection. All of them offer owners limited personal liability for business debts and the acts of others.

It should be noted that because of these unlimited risks the last thing you want to do is become a general partner of an enterprise in which you do not have day-to-day management control. If you do not thoroughly know what is going on in the company you should not put your future on the line as a general partner.

Case No. 2—Louise

Louise had worked for someone else all her life. For the last ten years she had worked in the gift section of a large department store. She did not like the floor manager insisting she do things a certain way when she knew her way would generate more sales for the company. It was all petty politics. She looked forward to the day when she could open her own business and make her own decisions.

Then one day, Maxine came to work at the department store. The two of them hit it off immediately. Maxine had a certain style and attitude that appealed to Louise. They had similar interests, the same feel for what the customers wanted, and the same desire to escape working for a faceless corporation filled with narrow-minded managers who stifled their every idea for improvement. Soon they were talking about opening their own gift boutique.

Louise had managed to save $10,000 to pursue her dream. Maxine did not have any money to contribute, but convinced Louise that she would contribute her first $5,000 in profits back into the business.

Louise was not aware that agreeing to form a partnership with Maxine without getting a written agreement as to distributions meant that they were automatically 50-50 partners. While Louise put up all the money and Maxine orally agreed to put her profits back later, the law treated them as each owning 50 percent of their new business, L&M Gifts.

In nine businesses out of ten there are problems when only one partner puts up all the money. L&M Gifts was no exception.

Maxine wanted the store to have the right atmosphere. She decided on leasing a storefront in a nice area and obligated the partnership to a three-year lease at an above-market rate. She decided on stylish tenant improvements to achieve the right look for her dream store. She then obligated the partnership to buy a large quantity of gifts in order to stock the store.

Before L&M Gifts opened its doors the partnership had obligated itself to spend $12,000 on improvements. They were also obligated to pay $1,500 per month in rent for the next three years. Louise was not aware of these transactions. However, as general partner, Maxine could obligate the partnership without informing or getting the approval of her other partner.

Louise wanted to announce their grand opening by placing an ad in the newspaper. Because they were a new business, the paper wanted a check up front. When Louise went to write a check it hit her. They were out of money. Maxine had spent Louise's entire $10,000, and then some, to open the store.

When Louise confronted Maxine with this Maxine was unconcerned. She asked Louise if she could put up any more cash. But Louise did not have any more money. Her life savings, her dream of her own business and control of her future, was the $10,000 that Maxine had already spent.

Maxine said she did not have a credit card but asked if Louise had or could get a credit card to help them get over this hump. Maxine said that if they could just get the doors open together they would be rolling in profits. It was with this comment that Louise realized that she was putting up all the money and taking all the risk so that Maxine could share in all the profits.

Louise was shaken by this realization but remained composed. She said she did not have a credit card nor did she have good enough credit to get one.

At this, Maxine flew off the handle. She said that she had invested all her ideas of style and atmosphere into the business. All Louise had to do was put up the money. She was furious that her creative vision for L&M Gifts was to be dimmed by Louise's refusal to put in more money.

Louise was stunned by her partner's reaction. She had put her life savings into the business. Maxine, without telling her, had squandered it. And now Maxine was angry that she could not put in more.

As one would expect, things soured very quickly between the two. As soon as Maxine learned that no more money was forthcoming, she reignited a relationship with an old boyfriend who lived two thousand miles away. She picked up and left town within forty-eight hours. No one heard from her again.

Louise was left with all the bills. Because Maxine had obligated the partnership, even though Louise had no knowledge of such obligations, Louise as the remaining general partner was personally responsible.

The landlord, the contractor who did the tenant improvements, and the suppliers of the inventory all sued Louise. While Maxine was equally responsible (if not more so) for these debts, the creditors did not even bother to pursue her. She had no money and she was on the other side of the country. Why would someone spend the time and money to chase her? The sole burden of the partnership's debts fell upon Louise.

With her life savings gone and her vision of her own business dashed, Louise unhappily went back to work at the department store.

As Case No. 2 illustrates, with a general partnership you have double the exposure of a sole proprietorship. Not only you—but your partner—can put your personal assets at risk. All of the risk and double (or triple or more

Other General Partnership Disadvantages

As if all of the risk and double the exposure were not bad enough, there are other disadvantages to operating as a general partnership:

- *Termination.* A partnership terminates when one partner dies, leaves, or goes bankrupt. You may be surprised by some unexpected event.
- *Sale.* Most sophisticated buyers do not want the risk of being in a general partnership. This will hinder the ability to sell your interest in a general partnership.
- *Self-employment taxes.* We will be discussing those darn Social Security and Medicare taxes throughout this book. Please note here that all general partners (even those not considered employees of the partnership) must pay self-employment taxes on their share of partnership income. Several good entities ahead offer ways to reduce such taxes.

depending on the number of general partners you have) the exposure is not a good way to do business.

As our first two cases point out, it is important to select the correct entity at the start. (And, please note, not all of our stories will be so dire. It is just that right now we are dealing with bad entities.)

Rich Dad Tips

- The longer you operate as a sole proprietorship or general partnership the longer you are going to be personally responsible for every bad thing that can happen in your business.
- If you are currently operating as a sole proprietorship or general partnership, see a professional or visit www.corporatedirect.com about switching to a good entity.
- If you are considering getting into a business, do not start out on the wrong foot by using a bad entity.

Good Entities

- C corporations
- S corporations
- Limited liability companies (LLCs)
- Limited partnerships (LPs)

To succeed in business, to protect your assets, and to limit your liability, you will want to select from one of the good entities listed above. Each one has its own advantages and specific uses. Each one is utilized by the rich and the knowledgeable in their business and personal financial affairs. And, depending on your state's fees, each one can be formed for $800 or less so that you can achieve the same benefits and protections that sophisticated businesspeople have enjoyed for centuries. But beware of promoters claiming they can incorporate you for $99 or less. We will discuss the consequesces of using such services in Chapter 17.

Before we discuss the relative strengths of corporations, LLCs, and LPs, it is important to know the language of each. While their basic structure is similar, the terms for each structural facet are different. Here then is the language for the good entities.

The Language of Corporations, Limited Liability Companies, and Limited Partnerships

Term	Corporation	Limited Liability Company	Limited Partnership
Owner	Shareholder	Member	General and limited partner
Senior management	Chairman of the board; chief executive officer (CEO); president	Manager(s)	General partner(s)
Organizational document filed with state	Articles of incorporation	Articles of organization	Certificate of limited partnership
Operational road map	Bylaws	Operating agreement	Limited partnership agreement

Corporations

The best place to start the discussion of good entities is with corporations. They have evolved over the last five hundred years to become the most commonly used entity for conducting business.

As Robert Kiyosaki learned during his study of admiralty law, corporations came into common usage in the 1500s to protect investors in maritime ventures. Prior to the popular use of corporations, investors would come together as a partnership, outfit a ship, and send it out for trading purposes. If the ship was lost at sea, the investors could not only lose everything but also be personally sued by various creditors. Of course, this exposure deterred people from risk taking and discouraged economic activity. Seeing this, the English Crown and courts allowed for the charter of corporations whereby risks and liabilities could be limited to the corporation itself.

The shareholders, the investors in the corporation, were liable only to the extent of their contribution to the business. This was a significant development in world economic history.

Case No. 3—The *English Rose*/Sir Richard Starkey

In the late 1500s maritime activity was increasing. The New World beckoned with the promise of riches and opportunity. The then small segment of Europeans with money were investing in sailing ships to pursue trading opportunities. If your ship could make it across the Atlantic with supplies, sell them or trade them for commodities, and return with a valuable cargo, you could make a fortune. This scenario was the origin of the phrase: "When my ship comes in."

During this time, two groups of London promoters were soliciting investors to outfit a ship and send it to the Caribbean in search of trading opportunities. A ship known as the *Royale Returne* had just recently arrived at the London docks and its investors had reaped profits of 1,000 percent. Investors were excited by these opportunities. The first group was outfitting a ship known as the *English Flyer*. The promoters brought investors in as general partners, offering 10 percent of the profits in exchange for £250. In Elizabethan England, as today, there was no special requirement to get permission to operate as a general partnership.

Two British gentlemen, Sir Richard Starkey and Master John Fowles, were potential investors. Master John Fowles was astounded by the profits the *Royale Returne* had generated for its investors. He wanted to invest in the very next ship set to sail. It didn't matter that the *English Flyer* was a partnership. The personal liability of a general partnership did not trouble him—not when huge profits were in sight. Fowles invested £250 in the *English Flyer* as soon as he could.

The second group of promoters was outfitting the *English Rose*. They wanted the limited liability of a new entity called a corporation. The problem was that, like today, it cost extra money to form and you had to wait for the Crown to give you a charter. But the second group of promoters was more careful than the first. They did not want to put themselves or their investors at risk in case the ship never returned. Sir Richard Starkey, being prudent and cautious, chose to invest in the *English Rose*. He knew there was risk in venturing across the Atlantic. He wanted to limit his exposure to just £250.

As it turned out, the *English Rose* and the *English Flyer* left London for the Caribbean at about the same time. As they set sail the risks to the investors in each enterprise were as follows:

	The English Flyer	**The English Rose**
Business entity	General partnership	Corporation
Investment	£250 for 10% of general partnership interests	£250 for 10% of corporation's shares
Liability	Unlimited joint and several	Limited to £250
If ship does not return	Each investor personally liable for all debts and obligations	Each investor's liability limited only to the £250 put into corporation

As luck would have it, the *English Flyer* was lost near the Bermuda Triangle. The promoters had leased the ship, provided their own captain, and were now responsible to the owners for its loss. The promoters and 90 percent of the general partners did not have as much money as Master John Fowles did. As we learned in Louise's case, and as has been the case for centuries, creditors will go after the easiest target with the deepest pockets. And so Master John Fowles, only a 10 percent general partner, was sued and held responsible for the entire loss of the *English Flyer*. He learned the hard way what happens when your ship does not come in, and you are responsible for it.

As Sir Richard Starkey's luck would have it, the *English Rose* did well on each side of the Atlantic and provided a huge return to its investors. Unlike Master John Fowles, Sir Richard Starkey was willing to lose £250 and no more. By using a corporation instead of a partnership he was able to establish his downside risk, while allowing for his upside advantage to be unlimited.

Sir Richard Starkey and other knowledgeable and sophisticated investors have used corporations, and other good entities, to limit their liability for centuries.

Forming a corporation is simple. Essentially, you file a document that creates an independent legal entity with a life of its own. It has its own name, business purpose, and tax identity with the IRS. As such, it—the corporation—is responsible for the activities of the business. In this way, the owners, or shareholders, are protected. The owners' liability is limited to the monies they used to start the corporation, not all of their other personal assets. If an entity is to be sued it is the corporation, not the individuals behind this legal entity.

A corporation is organized by one or more shareholders. Depending upon each state's law, it may allow one person to serve as all officers and directors. In certain states, to protect the owners' privacy, nominee officers and directors may be utilized. A corporation's first filing, the articles of incorporation, is signed by the incorporator. The incorporator may be any individual involved in the company, including, frequently, the company's attorney.

The articles of incorporation set out the company's name, the initial board of directors, the authorized number of shares, and other major items. Because it is a matter of public record, specific, detailed, or confidential information about the corporation should not be included in the articles of incorporation. The corporation is governed by rules found in its bylaws. Its decisions are recorded in meeting minutes, which are kept in the corporate minute book.

When the corporation is formed, the shareholders take over the company from the incorporator. The shareholders elect the directors to oversee the company. The directors in turn appoint the officers to carry out day-to-day management.

The shareholders, directors, and officers of the company must remember to follow corporate formalities. They must treat the corporation as a separate and independent legal entity, which includes holding regularly scheduled meetings, conducting banking through a separate corporate bank account, filing a separate corporate tax return, and filing corporate papers with the state on a timely basis.

Failure to follow such formalities may allow a creditor to disregard the corporate veil and seek personal liability against the corporate officers, directors, and shareholders. This is known as "piercing the corporate veil"—a legal maneuver in which the creditor tries to establish that the corporation failed to operate as a separate and distinct entity; if this is the case, then the veil of corporate protection is pierced and the individuals involved are held personally liable. Adhering to corporate formalities is not at all difficult or particularly time-consuming. In fact, if you have your attorney handle the corporate filings and preparation of annual minutes and direct your accountant to prepare the corporate tax return, you should spend no extra time at it with only a very slight increase in cost. The point is that if you spend the extra money to form a corporation in order to gain limited liability it makes sense to spend the extra, and minimal, time and money to ensure that protection is achieved.

One disadvantage of utilizing a regular (or C) corporation to do business is that its earnings may be taxed twice. This generally happens at the end of the corporation's fiscal year. If the corporation earns a profit it pays a tax on the gain. If it then decides to pay a dividend to its shareholders, the shareholders are taxed once again. To avoid the double tax of a C corporation, most C corporation owners make sure there are no profits at the end of the year. Instead, they use all the write-offs allowed to reduce their net income.

The potential for double taxation does not occur with the other good entities, a limited liability company or a limited partnership. In those entities profits and losses flow through the entity directly to the owner. Thus, there is no entity tax but instead there is a tax obligation on your individual return. Depending on your situation, an LLC or LP with flow-through taxation may be to your advantage or disadvantage. Again, one size does not fit all.

It should be noted here that a corporation with flow-through taxation features does exist. The Subchapter S corporation (also known as the S corporation or S corp), named after the IRS code section allowing it, is a flow-through corporate entity. By filing Form 2553, "Election by a Small Business Corporation," the corporation is not treated as a distinct entity for tax purposes. As a result, profits and losses flow through to the shareholders as in a partnership.

While a Subchapter S corporation is the entity of choice for certain small businesses, it does have some limits. It can only have one hundred or fewer shareholders. All shareholders must be American citizens or resident aliens, who are foreign citizens working and paying taxes in America. Individuals may list their revocable living trust as a shareholder. That said, corporations, limited partnerships, limited liability companies, and other entities, including certain trusts, may not be S corporation shareholders. A Subchapter S corporation may have only one class of stock.

In fact, it was the above-named limitations that led in part to the creation of the limited liability company. Because many shareholders wanted the protection of a corporation with flow-through taxation but could not live within the shareholder limitations of a Subchapter S corporation, the limited liability company was authorized.

The Subchapter S corporation requires the filing of Form 2553 by the 15th day or the third month of its tax year for the flow-through tax election to become effective. A limited liability company or limited partnership receives this treatment without the necessity of such a filing.

Another issue with the Subchapter S corporation is that flow-through taxation can be lost when one shareholder sells his stock to a nonpermitted owner, such as a foreign individual or trust. By so terminating the Subchapter S election, the business is then taxed as a C corporation and the company cannot reelect S status for a period of five years. The potential for this problem is eliminated by using a limited liability company.

Still, there are plenty of good reasons to use an S corporation, including the minimization of self-employment taxes, as we will explore in Chapter 3.

Both C and S corporations require that stock be issued to their shareholders. While limited liability companies may issue membership interests and limited partnerships may issue partnership interests, they do not feature the same ease of transferability and liquidity (or salability) of corporate shares. Neither limited liability companies nor limited partnerships have the ability to offer an ownership incentive akin to stock options. Neither entity should be considered a viable candidate for a public offering. If stock incentives and public tradability of shares are your objective, you must eventually become a C corporation.

——————————— **Rich Dad Tips** ———————————

- If you think you may want to go public at some point in the future but want initial losses to flow through, consider starting with an S corporation or a limited liability company.
- You can always convert to a C corporation at a later date, after you have taken advantage of flowing through losses.

Limited Liability Companies

The limited liability company is a good entity to use in certain situations. Because it provides the limited liability protection of a corporation and the flow-through taxation of a partnership, some have referred to the LLC as an incorporated partnership.

There are two more features that make the LLC unique:

- Flexible management structure
- Flexible allocation of profit and loss

These features will be illustrated in our next case.

Case No. 4—Thelma/Millennium Salsa

Thelma was looking to start a salsa business with two partners, Pepe and Hans. They had taken the beneficial step of preparing a business plan. They analyzed the market and their competition. They calculated their expenses, projected conservative revenues, and figured that Millennium Salsa could break even in two years.

The problem was that each partner had his or her own agenda that was difficult to reconcile. They had agreed that for their efforts each was to receive a one-third interest in Millennium Salsa. But beyond that it was looking doubtful that they could structure the business in such a way that it would work. Pepe was putting in $200,000 of start-up money to get the business going. He wanted no part of managing the business but wanted, first, to use any losses to offset other business/personal income; and, second, that all of the first profits be paid directly to him until he was paid back $300,000, or one and one half times what he had invested. Hans, on the other hand, was putting his salsa recipe into the company. It was a well-known and world-famous recipe renowned for its freshness and long shelf life, but beyond that, Hans's contribution to the company would be limited. He had offered to work for the company, but for Thelma and Pepe, who both knew of Hans's odd work habits and culinary eccentricities, that was more of a threat than a promise.

Thelma was going to work in the business. Her contribution was to spend the next two years—or however long it took—working for a very low wage to make a go of it. She had learned from her cousin Louise that a general partnership was a bad entity to use. The last thing Thelma wanted was for Hans to be out obligating their business to another bizarre food project like the banana-shaped onion fiasco.

The management of the business, and keeping Hans out of it, was one issue. But an even bigger issue was how to satisfy Pepe's demands for all the losses to flow through to him and the first $300,000 in profits to go to him.

Thelma knew that in a Subchapter S corporation when profits and losses flowed through the entity, they flowed rigidly according to the shareholder's ownership percentage. If you owned 50 percent, then 50 percent flowed through to you. In the case of Millennium Salsa, each person would have a one-third interest in whatever entity was to be used. But they needed to initially distribute more than one third to Pepe.

How could they satisfy Pepe's demands? Thelma knew she had to figure out some way to get it done or Pepe would not agree to the project.

Thelma went to her part-time bookkeeper, who told her she had to use an S corporation. Thelma was told that Pepe's demands could not be met and that the only way to handle the corporate structure was to allocate profits and losses on a one-third basis to each Millennium Salsa shareholder. The bookkeeper said she used an S corporation for every such situation and that most of her clients were satisfied.

Thelma then sought the advice of a local attorney who specialized in business formation and structure. It was during her initial consultation that Thelma became aware of the limited liability company. She learned that special allocations according to partnership formulas could be made to accommodate Pepe's conditions. She learned that a flexible LLC management structure could be implemented so that neither Pepe nor Hans would be involved as decision makers.

The attorney charted for her the difference between the rigidity of an S corporation and the flexibility of an LLC when it came to distributions:

Millennium Salsa, Inc., an S Corporation

Owner and Interest	Year One $60,000 Loss	Year Two $30,000 Loss	Year Three $300,000 Gain	Year Four $600,000 Gain
Pepe—33⅓%	<$20,000>	<$10,000>	$100,000	$200,000
Hans—33⅓%	<$20,000>	<$10,000>	$100,000	$200,000
Thelma—33⅓%	<$20,000>	<$10,000>	$100,000	$200,000

In Millennium Salsa, Inc. the flow-through distributions have to be made according to each shareholder's percentage ownership. Because Pepe owns one third there is no way to allocate him 100 percent of either profits or losses. He is stuck with what flows through to him strictly according to his ownership interest. However, Thelma liked what could be accomplished with an LLC:

Millennium Salsa, Limited Liability Company

Owner and Interest	Year One $60,000 Loss	Year Two $30,000 Loss	Year Three $300,000 Gain	Year Four $600,000 Gain
Pepe—33⅓%	<$60,000>	<$30,000>	$300,000	$200,000
Hans—33⅓%	0	0	0	$200,000
Thelma—33⅓%	0	0	0	$200,000

In the LLC scenario, Pepe's goals are achieved. He is able to take the first losses and receive the first $300,000 in profits. It should be noted that special allocations such as this must be based on legitimate economic circumstances as opposed to simply shifting tax obligations from one taxpayer to another. For more information, see Garrett Sutton's *How to Use Limited Liability Companies and Limited Partnerships* (SuccessDNA, 2008). The attorney informed Thelma she needed to work with a tax professional so that Millennium Salsa's objectives were properly documented and carried out.

The attorney also noted that money flowing through the LLC to Thelma, as an employee, was subject to self-employment taxes of 15.3 percent to the statutory salary maximum of now above $100,000 and 2.9 percent over that salary amount for the Medicare portion. Because Pepe and Hans were not employees but rather investors, their flow-through of monies, as of this writing, was not subject to self-employment tax. It was noted that an S corporation, where self-employment taxes were only paid on monies deemed to be salaries, and profits above that were not taxed as self-employment income, might be an option for Thelma's distributions. But again, the attorney noted the flexible distributions Pepe wanted could not be achieved in an S corporation. One entity did not fit all situations.

Thelma also learned that the management structure of an LLC was different, and much more flexible, than that of a corporation. A corporation had directors elected by shareholders, officers elected by directors, and employees hired by officers. By contrast, an LLC could be managed by all its members, which are akin to shareholders in a corporation, or be managed by just some of its members or by a nonmember. The first was called a member-managed LLC, the second a manager-managed LLC. Because Pepe wanted no management responsibility and neither Thelma nor Pepe wanted Hans anywhere near management authority, it was decided that Thelma would be the sole manager of a manager-managed LLC. As manager she had complete authority for the company's affairs. In corporate terms, she was the board of directors, the president, secretary, treasurer, and all vice presidents of Millennium Salsa. And all her business card had to say was "Manager, Millennium Salsa, LLC."

Pepe liked the plan that Thelma brought back from the attorney's office. He funded the project and they were in business.

The LLC was designed to overcome the problems corporations faced in attempting to avoid double taxation. In the process, as we have seen, some unique and useful features were created as additional benefits to the entity. The main features are as follows:

LIMITED LIABILITY PROTECTION

In an LLC, like a corporation, the owners do not face personal liability for business debts or for legal claims made against the company. In this day and age when litigation can unexpectedly wipe out a lifetime of savings, limited liability protection is of paramount importance.

The LLC, as well as the LP, offers even greater protections through the changing order procedure. This will be further discussed in Chapter 4.

It is important to note that in an LLC, as with a corporation, you may become personally liable for certain debts of the company if you sign a personal guarantee. As an example, most landlords will require the owners or officers of a new business to personally guarantee that the lease payments will be made. If the business goes under, the landlord has the right to seek monthly payments against the individual guarantors until the premises are leased to a new tenant. Likewise, loans backed by the Small Business Administration will require a personal guarantee. The SBA's representative will state that they will only loan to those persons committed enough to put their own assets at risk. In truth, as with any bank, they want as much security as they can get. Such personal guarantees are standard business requirements that will not change.

The important point to remember is that you are not going to sign a personal guarantee for each and every vendor agreement and customer transaction you enter. And in these matters, you will be protected through the proper use of an LLC. To obtain such protection it is important to sign any agreement as an officer of the LLC. By signing an agreement "Joe Doe" without adding "Manager, XYZ, LLC" you can become personally liable. The world must be put on notice that you are operating as an independent entity. To that end, it is important to include LLC—or Inc. if you use a corporation, or LP for a limited partnership—on all your stationery, checks, invoices, promotional literature, and especially written agreements.

UNLIMITED OWNERSHIP

One of the reasons people have a problem utilizing the S corporation is the limits on owners. An S corporation can only have one hundred or fewer shareholders. As well, some foreign citizens and certain entities are prohibited from becoming shareholders of an S corporation.

The LLC offers the flexibility of allowing for one member to an unlimited number of members, each of whom may be a foreign citizen, spendthrift trust, or corporate entity. And unlike an S corporation, you won't have to worry about losing your flow-through taxation in the event one shareholder sells their shares to a prohibited shareholder.

FLEXIBLE MANAGEMENT

LLCs offer two very flexible and workable means of management. First, they can be managed by all of their members, which is known as member-managed. Or they can be managed by just one or some of their members or by an outside nonmember, which is called manager-managed.

It is very easy to designate whether the LLC is to be member- or manager-managed. In some states, the articles of organization filed with the state must set out how the LLC is to be managed. In other jurisdictions, management is detailed in the operating agreement. If the members of an LLC want to change from manager-managed to member-managed, or vice versa, it can be accomplished by a vote of the members.

In most cases, the LLC will be managed by the members. In a small, growing company, each owner will want to have an active say in how the business is operated. Member management is a direct and simple way to accomplish this.

It should be noted that in a corporation there are several layers of management supervision. The officers—president, secretary, treasurer, and vice presidents—handle the day-to-day affairs. They are appointed by the board of directors, which oversees the larger, strategic issues of the corporation. The directors are elected by the shareholders. By contrast, in a member-managed LLC, the members are the shareholders, directors, and officers all at once.

In some cases, manager management is appropriate for conducting the business of the LLC. The following situations may call for manager management:

1. One or several LLC members are only interested in investing in the business and want no part of management decision making.

2. A family member has gifted membership interests to his children but does not want them or consider them ready to take part in management decisions.

3. A nonmember has lent money to the LLC and wants a say in how the funds are spent. The solution is to adopt manager management and make him a manager.

4. A group of members come together and invest in a business. They feel it is prudent to hire a professional outside manager to run the business and give him management authority.

As with a corporation, it is advisable to keep minutes of the meetings

held by those making management decisions. While some states do not require annual or other meetings of an LLC, the better practice is to document
such meetings on a consistent basis in order to avoid miscommunication,
claims of mismanagement, or attempts to assert personal liability. It should
be noted that in Germany, where the first LLC format was adopted over one
hundred years ago as the GmBH, a failure to prepare annual minutes can
lead to piercing of the LLC veil. One can assume that states throughout the
United States will adopt such a requirement in the future. The safer practice
is to prepare annual minutes for your LLC as you do for your corporation.

Rich Dad Tips

- While all fifty states have adopted LLCs, so far only two Canadian
  provinces—Alberta and Nova Scotia—have provided for them.
- Investors in Canada frequently use a limited partnership instead of a
  ULC (Unlimited Liability Company), as LLCs are known in Canada.

DISTRIBUTION OF LLC PROFITS AND LOSSES/SPECIAL ALLOCATIONS

One of the remarkable features of an LLC is that partnership rules provide
that members may divide the profits and losses in a flexible manner. This is
a significant departure from the corporate regime whereby dividends are allocated according to percentage ownership.

For example, an LLC can provide 40 percent of the profits to a member
who only contributed 20 percent of the initial capital. This is achieved by
making what is called a special allocation.

To be accepted by the IRS, special allocations must have a "substantial
economic effect." In IRS lingo this means that the allocation must be based
upon legitimate economic circumstances. An allocation cannot be used to
simply reduce one owner's tax obligations.

By including special language in your LLC's operating agreement you
may be able to create a safe harbor to insure that future special allocations
will have a substantial economic effect. (As with ships at sea, a safe harbor
for IRS purposes is a place of comfort and certainty.) The required language
deals with the following:

1. Capital accounts, which represent the investment of the owner plus

accumulated undistributed earnings, less accumulated losses, less any distribution of capital back to the owners. Each member's capital account must be carried on the books under special rules set forth in the IRS regulations. Consult with your tax advisor on these rules. They are not unusual or out of the ordinary.

2. Liquidation based upon capital accounts. Upon dissolution of the LLC, distributions are to be made according to positive capital account balances.

3. Negative capital account paybacks. Any members with a negative capital account balance must return their account to a zero balance upon the sale or liquidation of the LLC, or when the owner sells his interest.

It should be noted that complying with the special allocation rules and qualifying under the safe harbor provisions is a complicated area of the law. Be sure to consult with an advisor who is qualified to assist you in this arena.

FLOW-THROUGH TAXATION

As has been mentioned throughout, one of the most significant benefits of the LLC, and a key reason for its existence, is the fact that the IRS recognizes it as a pass-through tax entity. All of the profits and losses of the business flow through the LLC without tax. They flow through to the business owner's tax return and are dealt with at the individual level.

Again, a C corporation does not offer such a feature. In a C corporation, the profits are taxed at the corporate level and then taxed again when a dividend is paid to the shareholder. Thus, the issue of double taxation. Still, with proper planning, the specter of C corporation double taxation can be minimized.

In an S corporation, profits and losses flow through the corporation, thereby avoiding double taxation, but may only be allocated to the shareholders according to their percentage ownership interest. As described above, LLC profits and losses flow through the entity and may be freely allocated without regard to ownership percentages. As such, the LLC offers the combination of two significant financial benefits that other entities do not.

LACK OF PRECEDENT

One of the limits to the LLC is the fact that it is a new entity. As such, there are not many court decisions defining the various aspects of its use. With corporations and partnerships, on the other hand, you have several hundred years of court cases creating a precedent for their operation.

As the years pass this LLC drawback becomes less and less of an issue to many practitioners. But until a cohesive body of LLC law emerges, owners of an LLC must be cognizant that the courts may interpret a feature, a benefit, or even a wrinkle of LLC law in a way that does not suit them. If you are on the fence between selecting a limited partnership, a corporation, or an LLC and do not like the uncertainty associated with a lack of legal precedent, you may want to consider utilizing an entity other than an LLC.

Rich Dad Tips

- California residents must be cautious when considering the use of an LLC. The fees are onerous.
- In addition to the annual LLC tax of $800, the state of California hits LLCs with a fee based on their gross income. This fee has nothing to do with whether your company is profitable or not. It is only based on revenue generated, so you can lose money and still owe the fee.
- On gross income of $250,000 to $499,999 the fee is $900. The fee gradually rises to $11,000 on gross income of over $5 million. Be sure to consider this fee when analyzing which entity to use in California.

Limited Partnership

A limited partnership is similar to a general partnership with the exception that it has two types of partners. The first type is a general partner who is responsible for managing the partnership. As with a general partnership, the general partner of a limited partnership has broad powers to obligate the partnership and is also personally liable for the business's debts and claims. If there is more than one general partner involved they are all jointly and severally liable, meaning that a creditor can go after just one partner for the entire debt. However, a corporation or an LLC can be formed to serve as a general partner of a limited partnership, thus isolating unlimited liability in a good entity.

The second type of limited partnership partner is a limited partner. By definition, a limited partner is "limited" to his contribution of capital to the partnership and may not become actively involved in the business of the partnership. A limited partner may then be owner but have absolutely no say in how the entity operates. This was exactly what Jim wanted.

Case No. 5—Jim

Jim was the proud father of three boys in high school. Aaron, Bob, and Chris were coming of age. They were active, athletic, and creative boys almost ready to embark upon their own careers. The problem was that they were sometimes too active, too athletic, and too creative.

Aaron was seventeen years old and every one of the seemingly unlimited hormones he had was shouting for attention. He loved the girls, the girls loved him, and his social life was frenetic and chaotic. Jim knew his son was smart but worried whether he would ever settle down enough to complete one homework assignment, much less go to college.

Bob was sixteen years old and sports were all that mattered. He played sports, watched sports, and lived and breathed sports. Bob was hoping to get a college scholarship to play football and/or baseball. But Jim worried that if a scholarship wasn't offered whether Bob would ever get into or be interested in going to college.

Chris was fifteen years old and the lead guitarist in a heavy metal band known as Shrike. When Shrike practiced in Jim's garage the neighbors did not confuse them with the Beatles. The members of Shrike had pierced appendages, graphic tattoos, and girlfriends who looked like wild animals. Jim worried about the company that Chris kept. When you could make out the lyrics, Shrike's songs made frequent reference to school as a brainwashing tool of the elite. And while Jim may have also believed that to be true when he was fifteen, he worried that Chris would still embrace the idea at age twenty-five.

Compounding Jim's concerns was that he had five valuable real estate holdings that he wanted to go to the boys. His wife had passed on several years before and he needed to make some estate planning decisions. But given the boys' energy level and lack of direction he did not want them controlling or managing the real estate.

Jim knew that if he left the assets in his own name, when he died the IRS would take 55 percent of his estate, which was valued at over $10 million. And while estate taxes were supposed to be gradually eliminated, Jim knew that Congress played politics in this arena and no certainty was guaranteed. Jim had worked too hard, and had paid income taxes once already before buying the properties, to let the IRS's estate taxes take away half his assets. But again, he could not let his boys have any sort of control over the assets. While the government could squander 55 percent of his assets, he knew that his boys could easily top that with a 100 percent effort.

Jim asked his friends to refer him to a good attorney who could put together a plan to assist him. The attorney he met with suggested that Jim place the five real estate holdings into five separate limited partnerships.

It was explained to Jim that the beauty of a limited partnership was that all management control was in the hands of the general partner. The limiteds were not allowed to get involved in the business. Their activity was "limited" to being passive owners.

It was explained that the general partner can own as little as 2 percent of the limited partnership, with the limited partners owning the other 98 percent of it, and yet the general partner can have 100 percent control in how the entity was managed. The limited partners, even though they own 98 percent, cannot be involved. This was a major and unique difference between the limited partnership and the limited liability company or a corporation. If the boys owned 98 percent of an LLC or a corporation they could vote out their dad, sell the assets, and have a party for the ages. Not so with a limited partnership.

The limited partnership was perfect for Jim. He could not imagine his boys performing any sort of responsible management. At least not now. And at the same time he wanted to get the assets out of his name so he would not pay a huge estate tax. The limited partnership was the best entity for this. The IRS allowed discounts when you used a limited partnership for gifting. So instead of gifting $12,000 tax free to each boy he could gift $16,000 or more to each boy. Over a period of years, his limited partnership interest in each of the limited partnerships would be reduced and the boys' interest would be increased. When Jim passed on, his estate tax would be based only on the amount of interest he had left in each limited partnership. If he lived long enough he could gift away his entire interest in all five limited partnerships.

Except for his general partnership interest. By retaining his 2 percent general partnership interest, Jim could control the entities until the day he died. While he was hopeful his boys would straighten out, the limited partnership format allowed him total control in the event that did not happen.

Jim also liked the attorney's advice that each of the five properties be put into five separate limited partnerships. It was explained to him that the strategy today is to segregate assets. If someone gets injured at one property and sues, it is better to only have one property exposed. If all five properties were in the same limited partnership, the person suing could go after all five properties to satisfy his claim. By segregating assets into separate entities the person suing can only go after the one property where they were injured.

An added benefit to segregating assets in Jim's case was the boys were interested in different activities. One of the properties housed a batting cage business and another a Laundromat. He could see Bob being interested in the batting cage business and Aaron meeting girls while owning the Laundromat. (Jim owned nothing that would currently appeal to Chris.) As the boys got older he could gift more of one limited partnership to one boy and more of another to another.

Jim liked the control and protections afforded by the limited partnership entity and proceeded to immediately form five of them.

To organize a limited partnership you must file a certificate of limited partnership, otherwise known as an LP-1, with your state secretary of state's office. This document contains certain information about the general partner and, depending on the state, limited partners and is akin to the filing of articles of incorporation for a corporation or articles of organization for a LLC.

As with the LLC, the LP offers certain unique advantages not found in other entities. These features include:

LIMITED LIABILITY

Limited partners are not responsible for the partnership's debts beyond the amount of their capital contribution or contribution obligation. So, as discussed, unless they become actively involved, the limited partners are protected.

As a general rule, general partners are personally liable for all partnership debts. But as was mentioned above, there is a way to protect the general partner of a limited partnership. To reduce liability exposure, corporations or LLCs are formed to serve as general partners of the limited partnership. In this way, the liability of the general partner is encapsulated in a limited liability entity. Assume a creditor sues a limited partnership over a business debt and seeks to hold the general partner liable. If the general partner is a corporation or LLC, that is where the liability ends. No one's personal assets are at risk.

A chart helps to explain this concept:

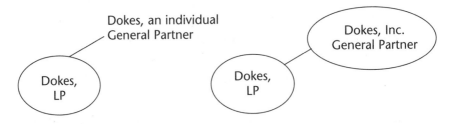

In the scenario on the left, with Joe as an individual general partner, he is personally responsible for all activities of Dokes, LP. All his personal assets are at risk. In the scenario on the right, Dokes, Inc. carries all of the liability. Joe's personal assets are not exposed.

As such, many, if not most, limited partnerships are organized using corporations or LLCs as general partners. In this way, both the limited and general partners achieve limited liability protection.

RETAINED MANAGEMENT

Because by definition limited partners may not participate in management, the general partner maintains complete control. In many cases, the general partner will hold only 2 percent of the partnership interest but will be able to assert 100 percent control over the partnership. This feature is valuable in estate planning situations where a parent is gifting or has gifted limited partnership interests to his children. Until such family members are old enough or trusted enough to act responsibly, the senior family members may continue to manage the LP even though only a very small general partnership interest is retained.

RESTRICTIONS ON TRANSFER

The ability to restrict the transfer of limited or general partnership interests to outside persons is a valuable feature of the limited partnership. Through a written limited partnership agreement, rights of first refusal, prohibited transfers, and conditions to permitted transfers are instituted to restrict the free transferability of partnership interests. It should be noted that LLCs can also afford beneficial restrictions on transfer. These restrictions are crucial for achieving the creditor protection and estate and gift tax advantages afforded by limited partnerships.

PROTECTION FROM CREDITORS

Creditors of a partnership can only reach the partnership assets and the assets of the general partner, which is limited by using a corporate general partner. Thus if, for example, you and your family owned three separate apartment buildings, it may be prudent to compartmentalize these assets into three separate limited partnerships, using three separate corporate general partners. If a litigious tenant sued over conditions at one of the properties, the other two buildings would not be exposed to satisfy any claims.

Creditors of the individual partners can only reach that person's partnership interest and not the partnership assets themselves. Assume you've gifted a 25 percent limited partnership interest in one of the apartment building partnerships to your son. He is young and forgets to obtain automobile insurance. Of course, in this example, he gets in a car accident and has a judgment creditor looking for assets. This creditor cannot reach the apartment building asset itself because it is in the limited partnership. He can only reach the limited partnership distribution interest through a charging order procedure. A charging order allows the creditor of a judgment debtor who is in a partnership with others to reach the debtor's partnership distributions without dissolving the partnership. Charging orders, which can result in phantom income to the creditor, are not favored by creditors. This is because phantom income is the allocation of a tax obligation to the creditor without the receipt of money to pay the taxes on such income. Not many creditors enjoy paying taxes on an uncollectable debt.

The state laws of Nevada and Wyoming offer the best charging order protections. California offers the weakest protection. A strategy then is to form your LP (or LLC) in Nevada or Wyoming and then qualify in California. (Qualifying is the process of registering your out-of-state entity to do business in your home state and includes paying the same annual fees as if you have started the entity in your home state to begin with.) By using a Nevada or Wyoming LLC or LP in your home state you can obtain the benefit of a better asset protection law. This strategy is discussed further in Chapter 3.

FAMILY WEALTH TRANSFERS

With proper planning, transfers of family assets from one generation to the next can occur at discounted rates. As a general rule, the IRS allows one individual to give another individual a gift of $12,000 per year (at this writing).

Any gifts valued at over $12,000 are subject to a gift tax starting at 18 percent. In the estate planning arena, senior family members may be advised to give assets away during their lifetimes so that estate taxes of up to 55 percent are minimized.

By using a limited partnership for the management and gifting of family assets, gifting can be accelerated with an IRS-approved discount. As discussed, because limited partnership interests do not entitle the holder to take part in management affairs and are frequently restricted as to their transferability, discounts on their value are permissible. In other words, even if the book value of 10 percent of a certain limited partnership is $16,000, a normal investor wouldn't pay that much for it because, as a limited partner, they would have no say in the partnership's management and would be restricted in their ability to transfer their interest at a later date. So, instead of valuing that limited partnership interest at $16,000, the IRS recognizes that it may be worth more like $12,000.

The advantage of this recognition comes into play when parents are ready to gift to their children. Assume a husband and wife have four children. Each spouse can gift $12,000 per year (at this writing) to each child without paying a gift tax. As such, a total of $96,000 can be gifted each year (two parents times four children times $12,000). With the valuation discount reflecting that the $16,000 interest is really only worth $12,000 to a normal investor, each parent gifts a 10 percent limited partnership interest to each child. Their combined gifts total an $96,000 valuation, thus incurring no gift tax. However, of the partnership valued at $160,000 they have gifted away 80 percent of the limited partnership with a book value of $128,000. Had they not used a limited partnership they would have had to pay a gift tax on the $32,000 difference between the $96,000 discounted gifted value and the $128,000 undiscounted value of eight $16,000 10 percent partnership interests that were gifted.

As the example illustrates, transfers of family wealth can be accelerated through the use of limited partnership discounts. Once this technique is appreciated, the question always becomes: How much of a discount will the IRS allow? Is it 25 percent, 35 percent, or can you go as high as 65 percent? While there is no bright-line test or number, the simple answer is found in this maxim: Pigs get fat, hogs get slaughtered. If you get greedy with your discounting, the IRS will call into question all of your planning. In my practice, I do not advise my clients to go over a 33 percent discount. The IRS has been questioning cases where the discounts are above that percentage. That said, the 33 percent limit may be conservative. I have dealt with some professionals who with certainty assert that higher discounts are easily justified. Again, there is no correct answer. You and your advisor should establish your own comfort level.

FLEXIBILITY

The limited partnership provides a great deal of flexibility. A written partnership agreement can be drafted to tailor the business and family planning requirements of any situation. And there are very few statutory requirements that cannot be changed or eliminated through a well-drafted partnership agreement.

TAXATION

Limited partnerships, like general partnerships, are flow-through tax entities. The limited partnership files an informational partnership tax return (IRS Form 1065, "U.S. Return of Partnership Income," the same as a general partnership), and each partner receives an IRS Schedule K-1 (1065), "Partner's Share of Income, Deductions, Credits, etc.," from the partnership. Each partner then files the K-1 with their individual IRS 1040 tax return.

FAMILY LIMITED PARTNERSHIPS

A word must be said here about the term "family limited partnerships." There are promoters crisscrossing the country selling an expensive version of supposedly bulletproof asset protection secrets known as the family limited partnership. It is important for you to know: There is no such thing as a family limited partnership! Yes, there are limited partnerships that are used to hold family assets. But, contrary to promoter claims, there is no such creature under any state law as a family limited partnership. They do not exist. So do not pay any money for a super-secret, special system that has been fabricated out of thin air. A limited partnership, properly structured, can protect you and be very useful for gifting. You don't need to pay extra for illusory entities.

Following is a table comparing the good and bad entities we have discussed. From there we will further explore the use of C and S corporations, LLCs and LPs.

Entity Comparison

	C Corporation	S Corporation	Limited Liability Company	Limited Partnership	General Partnership	Sole Proprietorship
Personal liability for business debts	No personal liability of shareholders	No personal liability of shareholders	No personal liability of members	General partner(s) personally liable; limited partners not personally liable	General partners personally liable	Sole proprietor personally liable
Who can legally obligate the business?	Officers and directors	Officers and directors	In member-managed, any member; in manager-managed, any manager	Any general partner, not limited partners	Any general partner	Sole proprietor
Responsibility for management decisions	Board of directors, officers	Board of directors, officers	Same as above	Same as above	General partners	Sole proprietor
Ownership restrictions	Most states allow one-shareholder corporations; some require at least two	No more than 100 shareholders allowed; no domestic or foreign entities or non-resident aliens allowed	Most all states allow one-member LLCs	At least one general partner and at least one limited partner required	At least two general partners	Only one sole proprietor and no more
Start-up and ongoing formalities	Articles filed with state; bylaws and annual meetings required	Articles filed with state; form 2553 filed with IRS; bylaws and annual meetings required	Articles filed with state; operating agreement and annual meetings not required, but strongly recommended	LP-1 filed with state; partnership agreement and annual meeting not required but recommended	No state filing; partnership agreement recommended; no meetings required	No state filing; no meetings required

	C Corporation	S Corporation	Limited Liability Company	Limited Partnership	General Partnership	Sole Proprietorship
Limits on transferability of interests	Transfers may be limited by agreement or by securities laws	Transfers may be limited by agreement or by securities laws; transfers to nonqualified persons may cause loss of S corporation status	Unanimous or super-majority consent may be required by nontransferring members	Consent of all partners may be required	Consent of all partners may be required	Can sell business to another
Business effect on death or departure of owner	Corporation continues	Corporation continues	In some states, dissolution unless members vote to continue	Automatic dissolution unless provided for in partnership agreement	Automatic dissolution unless provided for in partnership agreement	Automatic dissolution
Taxation of business profits	Corporate profits taxed at corporate rates; dividends taxed at individual rates of shareholders	Individual tax rates of shareholders	Individual tax rates of members unless LLC elects corporate taxation (Californians beware of additional state fees)	Individual tax rates of general and limited partners	Individual tax rates of general partners	Individual tax rate of sole proprietor

Chapter 2

Corporation or LLC?

S-C-L-L-C!

S-C-L-L-C!

It sounds like a college cheer, something you would hear at a football game. But for entrepreneurs and investors it is more often not a chant but a rant:

S Corporation?
C Corporation?
Limited Liability Company?
What should I do?

By the end of this chapter you will further appreciate certain key differences and will be much closer to making the right choice. Armed with the knowledge gained in this book, you and your advisors will carefully consider the options and select the right entity.

It shall be so.

In our last chapter we explored some of the differences between entities. In this section we will build upon that foundation to erect several structures for your consideration. Please note that we have not included limited partnerships in this discussion. The reason is not due to any unfavorable prejudices against LPs. As in Jim's case in the last chapter they have great utility. However, the LP requires a corporate or LLC general partner for complete asset protection and thus the filing and maintenance of two entities instead of just one as with an LLC. As well, aside from that difference, LLCs and LPs are similar and so for ease of discussion we will utilize the more popular of the two—the LLC.

Just as with personal ads, where you need to get to the liking of piña coladas on the beach and disliking of mean people very quickly, the following are key distilled likes and dislikes about corporations and LLCs:

C Corporations

Likes: No limits on shareholders and classes of stock. Lower tax rates on first earnings allowing for future expansion. The best entity for going public. Maximum fringe benefits allowed. Free transferability of stock.

Dislikes: Double taxation on profits, once at the corporate level, next at the shareholder level. Fixed allocation of profits and less flexible management structure (the same is true for S corps).

S Corporations

Likes: Efficient tax treatment. The best entity for minimizing payroll taxes.

Dislikes: Must apply for flow-through tax treatment. Can inadvertently lose flow-through tax treatment (see Case No. 6 ahead). Limits on shareholders and classes of stock. No flow-through of business debt. Fixed allocation of profits.

Limited Liability Companies

Likes: Excellent asset protection via charging order rules in Nevada and Wyoming. Flow-through of business debt. Flexible allocation of profits. Flexible management structure.

Dislikes: Difficulty of minimizing payroll taxes. Extra state taxes in California. Newer entity with less case law to interpret future events. Less free transferability of interests than corporate stock (some may see this as an advantage).

Using these guidelines, let's apply them to the two main reasons for forming an entity:

1. To operate a business
2. To hold assets

Operate a Business

When it comes to choosing the right entity for operating a business several factors must be considered.

While both corporations and LLCs offer limited liability protection, that issue will be fully discussed in the next section. For now, in the business context, the first issue is:

PAYROLL TAXES

Salaries paid to employees (including owner-employees) are subject to FICA and Medicare taxes, otherwise known as payroll taxes. (For the current taxable limits visit www.corporatedirect.com/accounting.) At 15.3 percent of payroll, these taxes will be one of the largest expenses a business will have. If you are savvy you have not bought into the argument that these taxes are "only" 7.65 percent of payroll. If you own the business you are paying both halves of that, or a whopping 15.3 percent on all of your payroll. Given that our Social Security system is near bankruptcy and that citizens under forty may never see any of the promised benefits, it becomes important to consider how to best minimize payroll taxes.

In a C corporation, which features a double tax on profits, it makes sense to pay as high a salary as possible in order to avoid the tax on dividend distributions. But with salaries come payroll taxes.

In an LLC, with its flow-through tax treatment, profits flow through to the owners. The problem is that at this writing, under IRS guidelines all such profits, whether taken as a salary or not, are subject to payroll taxes for those LLC members active in the business.

In an S corporation you can pay yourself a reasonable salary, on which you pay payroll taxes. Profits after salary can be flowed through to the owner without payroll taxes.

For example, Brendan makes $200,000 a year in his pool cleaning business. As a single-member LLC, he would pay over $18,000 in payroll taxes on the entire $200,000 profit. If Brendan used an S corporation and paid himself a $72,000 a year salary and flowed the rest through as profits without payroll taxes, his payroll taxes would be $11,000 per year. As such, Brendan could save $7,000 a year, year in and year out, by using an S corporation over an LLC. Who says choice of entity isn't important?

BUSINESS DEBTS

An S corporation's business debts cannot be utilized by the shareholders unless they have personally guaranteed the debt. Of course, a personal guarantee means that if the corporation can't pay the debt then you are obligated as an individual to repay the money. It is best to avoid personal guarantees if possible (see Chapter 13 on business credit). In an S corporation, when the company takes on debt without shareholder guarantees the shareholder's tax basis does not increase. As a result, more distributions are subject to tax.

In an LLC, the members get the benefits of business debt, whether guaranteed or not. An example helps to explain this advantage.

Melanie, Kelsey, and Alicia are equal owners in a children's clothing business. Their LLC has good credit and is able to borrow $600,000 without the need for personal guarantees. The loan has the effect of increasing each owner's tax basis by $200,000. Because distributions are taxed only when they exceed an owner's basis, this means that Melanie, Kelsey, and Alicia can each receive $200,000 in profit distributions tax free from the LLC. The company's borrowings have improved their tax situation.

By contrast, in an S corporation, unless a personal guarantee was signed, Melanie, Kelsey, and Alicia would not receive such a tax benefit. The $600,000 loan would not provide them with the tax benefits in an S corporation as it would through an LLC. Be sure to work with your advisors to maximize this benefit.

FRINGE BENEFITS

While in recent years certain benefits such as health insurance premiums have been granted as write-offs for all entities the best entity for fringe benefits is still the C corporation.

With a C corporation, the company can write off employees' health insurance premiums. The company can also provide group term life insurance and medical reimbursement plans for its employees at company expense. These benefits are tax-free to the employees. By contrast, with a S corporation, health insurance premiums are listed as a W-2 item on an employee's statement and deducted through the individual's personal return. While the insurance premium may be written off, it is a more cumbersome procedure for the S corporation than it is for the C corporation. Also, the S corporation cannot provide key fringe benefits such as medical reimbursement and group term life insurance plans.

The LLC offers lesser advantages than the S corporation. As with the S corporation, group term life insurance and medical reimbursement plans are not tax-free to employees. Unlike the S corporation, health insurance premiums are subject to self-employment taxes. So while you can write off the insurance premium in an LLC, you will pay those social security taxes on the benefits received.

OWNER FLEXIBILITY

In both a C corporation and an LLC there is flexibility of ownership. Shareholders in a C corporation and members of an LLC can be individuals, trusts, corporations, foreign citizens, aliens, Martians, whatever. There is no such flexibility in an S corporation, as our next case illustrates.

Case No. 6—Burnham's Baked Hams

Jeanne, Elizabeth, and Bernie were ready to enter the baked ham business. They had done their homework and felt they knew their niche and could succeed in it. Elizabeth had done quite a bit of studying. Being cautious by nature she knew they had to form a corporation to protect themselves. Jeanne was more concerned about how the money flowed. If they were going to form a corporation it had to be an S corporation. She did not want to pay a double tax on profits above salaries. Bernie was a sunny optimist. He just wanted to be in business making money selling his delicious baked hams. He left the details to Jeanne and Elizabeth.

After incorporating they obtained their EIN (Employer Identification Number—their taxpayer ID number) from the IRS. With that they filed Form 2553 within forty-five days of incorporating in order to qualify for S corporation status. They issued themselves each 100,000 shares and were one-third equal owners of Burnham's Baked Hams, Inc.

Right off the bat, in their first year of business, they were successful. Bernie baked a tasty ham. They each took a salary of $40,000 per year. Self-employment taxes were paid on those salaries. At the end of the year there was a profit of $120,000. They each received a dividend of another $40,000.

Because they were an S corporation, the $120,000 in profits was not taxed as a dividend as in a C corporation. Instead, it flowed through the corporation without tax to their individual returns. And, unlike an LLC, where the flow-through could be subject to self-employment taxes, the dividends came to them free of Social Security and Medicare taxes.

Their S corporation was a beautiful thing. Ordinary income and payroll taxes were paid on salaries and only ordinary income taxes were paid on profits. Bernie was happy, as always, Jeanne was pleased to be getting her money, and even ever cautious Elizabeth was content.

As always, an S corporation can work wonderfully until you break some arcane rule that, bingo, automatically terminates your tax status.

Burnham's Baked Hams, Inc., was expanding rapidly. Bernie had negotiated a very large and favorable deal for distribution throughout Canada. In order to get the deal done, Basil Lee, a Toronto-based distributor, wanted to receive 5 percent of the company. Bernie and, surprisingly, prudent Elizabeth were for this arrangement. But Jeanne did not want Basil in the company. She did not like him or trust him. Still, the deal would be huge for their company. So a compromise was reached whereby the corporation would authorize two classes of stock—one class of common voting shares that could elect the board of directors and a second class of nonvoting preferred that would not elect any directors and thus have no say in management. Basil was then issued preferred shares equal to 5 percent of the total authorized shares (common and preferred together) but he had no power to control the company, which is how Jeanne wanted things.

Elizabeth had her own issues. She did not like holding the company shares in her own name. There were too many unethical potential creditors, too many vexatious potential litigants, just too many questionable people out there for her liking. She knew her views were justified and wanted to have the shares held by an irrevocable spendthrift trust where they would be safe from the claims of others. She formed an irrevocable trust to hold the shares and transferred them from her name to that of the trust.

Sometime thereafter the company received a notice from the IRS. Their S corporation status was terminated.

Why?

Because Burnham's Baked Hams, Inc. had the following:

1. A non-U.S. shareholder (Basil the Canadian)
2. More than one class of stock (preferred for Basil and common for the others)
3. A trust as a shareholder (Elizabeth's trust)

Any one of those three is enough to terminate S status. And that is how Jeanne, Elizabeth, and Bernie learned the problem with an S corporation. Things can be going along just fine when through some unforeseen transaction (a shareholder unwittingly sells to a nonresident alien, for example) you lose your tax status. And when that happens you become a C corporation and cannot be taxed as an S corporation for five years.

As it turned out, Burnham's Baked Hams, Inc., was better off as a C corporation. Basil's deal took the company into a much higher realm of revenue. It probably would not have happened if he was not a shareholder. As well, with more money coming in, the company needed to accumulate monies for even greater expansion. That would be tough to do with an S corporation, for one needs to allocate profits to flow through and at least pay taxes on that income. With corporate tax rates being lower in a C coporation, profits may be better used for growth. Further, with an S corporation, fringe benefits for shareholders owning greater than 2 percent of the company's stock must be included as income to the shareholder. A comprehensive and generous fringe benefits package had been developed for Jeanne, Elizabeth, Bernie, and now Basil. With a C corporation it could be deducted, as opposed to each of them paying tax on the value received in an S corporation.

Fortunately, the S corporation tax status termination did not hurt Burnham's Baked Hams, Inc.

As discussed, for certain businesses an S corporation is the right choice. You just need to be careful not to lose your tax status through inadvertence or a less than complete understanding of the rules. What follows is a more detailed and technical discussion of S corporations.

S Corporation Eligibility Requirements

- The corporation must be a corporation organized in any U.S. state but not one from outside the U.S.
- It must not be an ineligible corporation (certain types of businesses are not eligible).

- It must not have more than one hundred shareholders.
- Only individuals, decedents' estates, estates of individuals in bankruptcy, and certain trusts may be shareholders. Corporations and many types of trusts may not be shareholders.
- No shareholder may be a nonresident alien. Only U.S. individuals or resident aliens paying U.S. taxes may be shareholders.
- The corporation may have only one class of stock, but different voting rights are allowed.

Corporate Form

The primary advantage of S corporation status is that it allows businesses to operate in corporate form without paying income tax at the corporate level. The S corporation is a flow-through entity; it allows losses and other deductions to be taken at the shareholder level.

The primary disadvantage to S corporation status is its complexity. There are many technical rules that can serve as pitfalls for the unwary. S corporations have ownership and class-of-stock restrictions that are more burdensome than those of other entities. For instance, shareholder loans can create a second class of stock causing termination of S status.

As such, in terms of owner flexibility a C corporation or LLC may be the best choice. But then again, many of my clients use S corporations for the payroll tax minimization benefit. Work with your advisors and weigh which attributes of each entity are most important for you.

Hold Assets

Just as limited liability entities are necessary when operating a business so are they important for holding assets. For just as you can get sued in the everyday course of business you can be sued when holding real estate. Tenants and vendors sue real estate owners all the time. And because there are so many lawsuits associated with business and real estate, we want to protect our other valuable assets, such as our intellectual property and brokerage accounts, in separate entities as well. The key element when using an entity to hold assets is then: asset protection.

When holding an asset, as a general rule you will be better protected using an LLC instead of a corporation. Our next case illustrates why.

Case No. 7—Teo and Mitch

Teo owns a fourplex in an LLC. Mitch owns his in a corporation. A tenant suing over an accident on the property can, if insurance fails to cover the claim, reach inside either entity and get the property. The difference in protection arises when an outside claimant, for example, a victim of a car wreck, tries to satisfy his claim by reaching the judgment debtor's assets. Suppose Teo and Mitch are in a car wreck with Chalmer. The wreck had nothing to do with the real estate, but now Chalmer wants to collect against Teo's and Mitch's personal assets. The result is as follows:

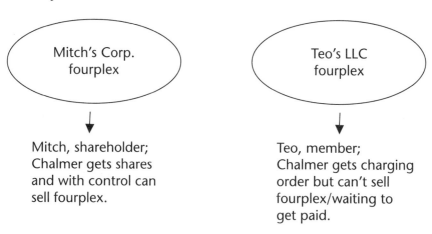

Mitch's Corp.
fourplex

Teo's LLC
fourplex

Mitch, shareholder;
Chalmer gets shares
and with control can
sell fourplex.

Teo, member;
Chalmer gets charging
order but can't sell
fourplex/waiting to
get paid.

In Mitch's case, Chalmer can utilize his court-sanctioned judgment to get control of Mitch's shares. With 100 percent ownership in the shares, Chalmer can sell the fourplex to satisfy his judgment. And remember, the result is the same for a C or S corporation. While the C or S designation applies to taxation, they are both corporations with the same less than stellar asset protection outcome when holding assets.

It should be noted that Nevada recently changed its state law to allow for charging order protection for corporations with between two and seventy-five shareholders. This is a dramatic development that will further the use of Nevada corporations for asset protection. However, in Mitch's case, because he is the sole corporate shareholder, the asset protection benefits of this new Nevada law would not apply. Again, there must be at least two shareholders of a Nevada corporation to gain charging order protection.

In Teo's case, the LLC provides significantly better protection, especially using LLCs formed in Nevada or Wyoming. In those two states, the charging order is a creditor's sole remedy. The charging order allows Chalmer the creditor to stand in Teo's shoes and receive money distributions. But that is it. Chalmer can't take possession of Teo's membership interests and force a sale of the fourplex as he did with Mitch's corporation. (It should be noted that under California law Chalmer could force a sale of Teo's fourplex, which is why you want to use Nevada and Wyoming LLCs in California. For more information on this see Chapter 3.)

Merely standing in Teo's shoes waiting for distributions is not the best option for Chalmer. This is because under current tax law, Chalmer, being charged with Teo's interest, is now responsible for paying any taxes on Teo's profits. But what if there are no monies distributed to pay the taxes? Too bad for Chalmer. He has phantom income and must pay taxes on money he has not received. Not many creditors want to be in this situation.

It should be noted that two states, California and Colorado, do not afford charging order protection to single-member LLCs. If you are in those states, or are concerned that such a concept may spread to other states (as is evidenced by Nevada only granting protections in corporations with more than one shareholder), you may want to have your LLC owned by more than one person. Even if one tenth of one percent is owned by another individual or entity you will have created a multi-member LLC and thus be better protected.

A second major concern arises when holding assets. We want to separate them from each other. For example, you wouldn't put two free and clear $5 million apartment buildings in the same LLC. If a tenant fell at one property he or she could reach both properties.

For the same reasons, you will not put a brokerage account or an intellectual property portfolio in the same entity that operates a business or holds real estate. You want your assets segregated into separate compartments.

Let's review another case on how to structure things.

Case No. 8—Armon

Armon has a trucking business, expensive tractor-trailers and equipment, a valuable trademark, a ten-unit apartment building, and a million-dollar brokerage account. How should he structure his affairs? One strategy is as follows:

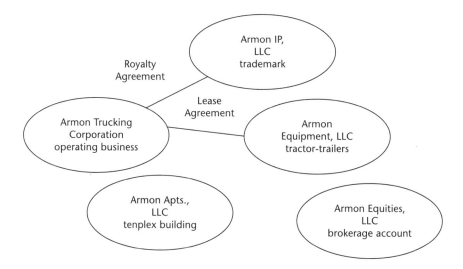

As we have discussed, the LLC offers much better asset protection than a corporation. And we are better protected segregating assets from each other. For example, if Armon were sued over his ten-plex we wouldn't want the brokerage account or the valuable trademark to be in the same entity. It is far better to have them in separate entities, protected and apart.

Likewise, because a creditor could sue Armon personally and reach his shares of Armon Trucking Corporation, we don't want a lot of valuable assets in the corporation. As such, the equipment is in a separate entity and then leased to the corporation. Someone suing the corporation or Armon as an individual is not going to reach the valuable equipment. If they do gain control of the corporation, what do they get? Not much. A typewriter. Some computers. A number of bills.

Sophisticated entrepreneurs know you don't want a lot of assets in a corporation that deals with the public and is subject to being sued. Better to have it relatively empty, with valuable assets in separate protected entities. As with Armon's structure, the good assets are best protected when segregated with separate entities away and apart from the operational entities.

As well, you don't want a lot of assets in one LLC (or LP). An LLC that holds ten properties is a much bigger target than ten LLCs each holding one property. In the first case, a fall at one property exposes the other nine properties to a judgment creditor. In the second scenario, an action arising from an injury on one property means the claim is brought against the one LLC holding the one property. The other nine LLCs holding the remaining nine properties are not exposed to the claim.

But maintaining ten separate LLCs is expensive some will claim. There must be a better way, and so certain promoters went to work and came up with . . .

The Series LLC

The series LLC is supposedly designed so that by setting up (and paying the fees on) one asset-protected LLC you can protect a number of properties in separate series within the one LLC. A graphic example follows:

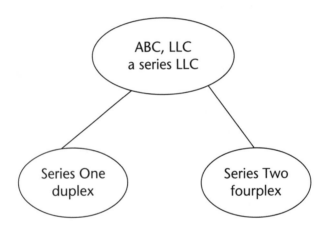

The supposed benefit is that if there is a claim against the duplex in Series One a creditor could not reach the fourplex in Series Two. It is in a separate asset-protected series the promoters will claim, and therefore can't be reached.

There are several problems with the series LLC. The first is, conceptually it doesn't make sense. If you form one entity and it is sued, all of the assets within that entity are exposed—whether they are in a separate series (or buckets or whatever else the promoters use to describe them) or not. Significantly, there is not one court case extending asset protection to assets held in a separate series. I personally do not want to put my assets into an entity and hope for the best in a future court ruling. By using separate LLCs we have the certainty that assets in a remote LLC will not be exposed to claims brought against a target LLC. The series LLC does not offer such certainty.

As mentioned, the series LLC has been sold as a state-fee-savings device. By using a series LLC holding, for example, four assets, it is claimed that you only have to pay one filing fee instead of the four fees for the four separate LLCs. That argument worked until the state of California decided that each series would be taxed as a separate LLC. So instead of paying just $800 for one series LLC in California you would pay, in our four-asset example, $3,200 for the series—the same as if you'd used four separate LLCs with greater certainty of protection. While not every state is as aggressive a tax collector as California, you can be certain that some will follow suit and charge a filing fee per series.

There are other issues surrounding the various unknowns posed by the series LLC. Will the supposed "internal liability shield" of the series LLC be respected in states that do not have series provisions? No one knows. In a bankruptcy of one series would the court consolidate all of the various series into the parent? No one knows. But you can be certain that by forming separate LLCs you will not face such sleep-losing unknowns.

It is interesting to note that the American Bar Association committee on uniform state laws looked into the series LLC. After reviewing all of the uncertainties and record keeping complexities of the series LLC, the ABA declined to endorse them. When some of the nation's smartest lawyers take a pass on the series LLC, maybe you should too.

Taxation

A second issue when using entities to hold real assets has to do with taxes. And here we are not talking about payroll taxes. Typically, in an asset-holding entity payroll taxes are not an issue. The asset generally offers a passive income stream for which no salary, and thus no payroll taxes, are involved. Be sure to check with your advisor to make certain this is your situation.

The key taxation element with asset-holding entities has to do with transferring the asset in and out of the entity. Suppose, for example, you want to convert a single family home you own in an entity to personal use. If that home were owned in a corporation, distributing it out to yourself would be a taxable event. In other words, the corporation would have distributed a valuable corporate asset, the house, to you, the shareholder. When shareholders receive distributions from a corporation the transaction is taxed.

On the other hand, transferring the house out of an LLC is not a taxable event. The house comes out at its basis, the amount it was transferred in at. For example, if you bought a house for $100,000 three years ago in the name of the LLC and wanted to convert it from the LLC property to your personal property it would come out at the same $100,000 value, your basis or cost of the property. Of course, if you later sold it for $150,000 you would pay tax on the $50,000 gain. But importantly, unlike a corporation, real estate, intellectual property, stocks, and bonds in a brokerage account can be transferred in and out of an LLC at their basis, thus incurring no taxation.

As you might imagine, this beneficial LLC treatment of asset transfers is another significant reason why LLCs are favored for asset-holding entities.

Conclusion

You now have a better understanding of when to use certain entities for specific uses. And remember, there is no one right answer in all of this. Be sure to work with your advisors to come up with the right entity mix. Also know that setting up entities is not very expensive. Our firm charges a flat fee of just $695 (plus filing fees, which vary by state) for a complete package. And you can save $50 per entity by looking on the pages at the end of this book. So do not worry about asset protection being unaffordable.

Now let's consider using the best states for asset protection . . .

Chapter 3

Using Nevada and Wyoming Entities to Your Maximum Advantage

If you are an entrepreneur or investor the chances are good you have read or heard the brazen ads touting the amazing benefits of Nevada and Wyoming corporations. Some of these claims are so over the top we have included a cautionary chapter on it all (see Chapter 17).

That noted, there really are legitimate benefits to utilizing Nevada and Wyoming corporations, LLCs, and LPs. On the issue of the taxes it is important to know that Nevada and Wyoming have no state income or corporate taxes. Nevada, of course, derives much of its state budget from gaming taxes, as well as mining royalties. Wyoming also relies on mining royalties to fund their budget. Plus, there are only 600,000 or so self-reliant citizens in Wyoming so the state does not have that much to fund.

Of importance to you is that by organizing your corporation, LLC, or LP in Nevada or Wyoming for their legal benefits you will not be incurring any additional state taxes. You will pay an annual fee of $225 in Nevada and $50 in Wyoming but that's all.

So knowing that the extra cost is not significant, the question becomes: "How can I use a Nevada or Wyoming corporation to my benefit?"

Let's look at several ways.

Strategy One: Doing Business in Your State

For purposes of this discussion "Your State" refers to the state where you do business. From Your State we will consider using Wyoming and Nevada entities. As we shall learn, both states work well. But for ease of discussions in Strategies One and Three we will use Nevada and in Strategy Two we will use Wyoming. In all of this remember that in situations where a number of entities are needed you will use some in Nevada and some in Wyoming to make it even more difficult for predators to try to seize your assets. The idea is to force a predator to have to fight it out, and retain attorneys in two states, both Nevada and Wyoming, instead of just one. The more roadblocks the better.

A key to Strategy One is understanding where you must pay taxes: Whether you have a dry cleaning business in California or a consulting business in New York, if you are doing business in and generating revenues in Your State you need to pay the applicable taxes there. Remember, it's legal and acceptable to avoid taxes. However, evading taxes is not something you want to do. The difference between tax avoidance and tax evasion is twenty years. So you pay the state taxes on money earned in your state.

How can a Nevada corporation help if you are only doing business in Your State?

First of all, by incorporating in Nevada you can take advantage of Nevada protections and flexibility. For example, suppose an Arizona consulting firm only does business in Arizona. They incorporate in Nevada and qualify to do business in Arizona. This means they go to the Arizona secretary of state with their Nevada corporate papers and pay the same fee a new business incorporating in Arizona would pay. In this way they are "qualified" as a Nevada corporation to operate as an Arizona corporation would.

The cost is minimal. On an annual basis you are essentially paying the extra cost of maintaining a Nevada corporation—$225 to the Nevada secretary of state and $125 (or so) for a resident agent in Nevada. You have to pay the same Arizona fees whether you are a Nevada or Arizona corporate entity.

So for a small extra amount every year you get the benefits of Nevada's corporate laws:

- No sharing of corporate information with the IRS
- Greater protections for officers and directors

- Flexibility in corporate management
- Flexibility in capitalization and corporate structuring
- Privacy (subject to new rules discussed below)

Because you have incorporated in Nevada, not in Your State, Nevada's corporate laws govern. And better yet, someday you may choose to use Strategy Two below or you may just move your entire business to Nevada for the taxation, ease of doing business, and quality-of-life benefits. In those situations, you will not have to pay more money to reincorporate in Nevada and merge your state corporation into the new entity. You will already be "home" as it were.

It is important to know that Nevada has new laws regarding ownership privacy. Whereas the owners of a Nevada entity used to be completely confidential, the number of scam artists using this law to their improper advantage led to law enforcement agencies demanding a change from the Nevada legislature.

The new rules provide that law enforcement agencies engaged in a criminal investigation can request that the Nevada secretary of state contact the entity's resident agent for information. Within three days of this request, the resident agent must turn over a current list of the owners or a statement indicating where such a list is maintained.

While privacy of ownership is somewhat compromised by this new law (which applies equally to corporations, LLCs, LPs, and business trusts) there are two key points to note:

First, the Nevada secretary of state still does not ask for ownership information up front. The requirement is that the registered agent keep a list of owners or the name of a contact who has the list of owners. Ownership remains confidential until there is trouble.

Second, the trouble has to be big. The investigation must be criminal in nature. The new law does not apply to civil investigations. As well, absent litigation, private parties are still not entitled to ownership information.

Which means that if your asset protection plans are on the up-and-up, if you are not out there scamming people and ripping them off, your privacy will be maintained.

One can expect that such rules will spread to other states. Until they do, people greatly concerned about privacy may want to use Wyoming entities.

Strategy Two: Doing Business in Your State and in Wyoming

Case No. 9—Ken and Cindy

Ken and Cindy have a furniture business in Your State. It is an S corporation known as KC Homes, Inc. With four stores in the region they do a lot of advertising on local TV stations, spending over $200,000 per year. They needed to spend that much to keep a steady stream of customers coming in the doors for various blowout sales.

Ken realized that if he had his own ad agency he could take the 15 percent agency commission as his own. Cindy realized that if they created a Wyoming corporation to be the ad agency they could minimize their state taxes. They consulted with their accountant, who being open-minded, agreed that several thousand dollars a year in taxes could be saved.

So Ken and Cindy formed K&C Advertising, Inc., a Wyoming corporation. They continued to promote their mega-blowout furniture sales. But they had K&C, not themselves or a local agency, place the advertising. For very little money they had a Wyoming office set up. K&C did the ad placement and billing through a service from Wyoming and all the banking and accounting was located and performed in Wyoming.

As a result, when their furniture store chain did $200,000 in local advertising, $30,000 went to their ad agency, K&C Advertising in Wyoming. They did not want to use an S corporation because all profits would flow back to them in Your State and be taxed on their individual returns. So they had K&C Advertising, Inc., be a C corporation. They paid the small expenses to operate the company each year and paid low federal corporate taxes of 15 percent on the first $50,000 of profits. After expenses and taxes they had $23,000 left over, which they allowed to accumulate in the Wyoming corporation as their private piggy bank.

After four years Ken and Cindy had a fund of $100,000 in their Wyoming corporate account. As they were interested in real estate investing they formed a Nevada LLC to purchase a fourplex. They had their Wyoming corporation loan the Nevada LLC the $100,000 for the down payment. Through Ken and Cindy, the LLC then arranged bank financing through a first deed of trust to complete the purchase. The Wyoming corporation secured its loan with a second deed of trust, thus fully encumbering the property against would-be predators. The strategy was an excellent financial move for Ken and Cindy.

What kind of arrangements can be used to achieve this strategy? They are numerous:

- Research and development
- Marketing services
- Consulting services
- Sales agencies
- Equipment leasing
- Receivables factoring

By entering these arrangements you can legitimately "upstream" income from Your State to Nevada and/or Wyoming.

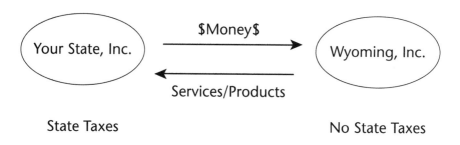

What are the advantages of upstreaming? They are several and we'll use Wyoming, Inc. to explain:

EXPENSES IN YOUR STATE—INCOME IN WYOMING.

By having Wyoming, Inc., perform a legitimate service for Your State, Inc., Your State, Inc., has an expense to write off against its income, thus reducing taxable revenues. Wyoming, Inc., on the other hand, has income. After all deductions are taken and a profit remains, taxes are paid to the IRS (at only 15 percent on the first $50,000 if it is a C corporation). Remember, there are no state taxes in Nevada or Wyoming. So just by shifting income from a taxable state to a no tax state you are saving money.

What does the IRS think of this? They are okay with it. They get their money in corporate taxes in either event. (But see the discussion on controlled group status ahead.)

ASSET PROTECTION

By using Wyoming, Inc., to hold and lease assets to Your State, Inc., you can protect valuable corporate assets. Assume Your State, Inc., is involved in a day-to-day business where it could be sued. By having all the good assets in Wyoming, Inc., and leasing them to Your State, Inc., you have removed these assets from risk. If someone sues Your State, Inc., there is not much to get. All the valuable assets are in Wyoming, Inc. Remember, segregating assets in separate entities away from risk is a cornerstone business strategy. As well, remember that Nevada has given charging protections to corporations with two or more shareholders. If asset protection is greatly important, Ken and Cindy may want to use a Nevada corporation with the two of them as shareholders. Or, for the time being, if privacy of ownership is of greater importance, they may want to utilize a Wyoming entity. Once again, there is no one right answer. It all depends on what is important to you.

LOWER CORPORATE TAXES

Subject to the controlled group rules, two or more corporations may pay less in federal corporate taxes. First let's look at the corporate tax rates:

Taxable Income Over	But Less Than	Tax Rate*
$0	$50,000	15%
50,000	75,000	25%
75,000	100,000	34%
100,000	335,000	39%
335,000	10,000,000	34%

*As of this writing. For the most recent tax rates, visit www.corporatedirect.com/accounting.

Assume Your State, Inc., a corporation, makes a $150,000 annual profit. Your federal corporate income tax is $58,250. What if you used two Nevada corporations in addition to Your State, Inc., and by upstreaming income each has a profit of one cent less than $50,000 each. The tax on each corporation is 15%, or $7,500 each. Instead of Your State, Inc., paying $58,250, the three corporations together only pay $22,500, a savings of $35,750.

The problem is, for all you may think or say about the IRS, they are not stupid people. They are not going to let you get out of paying that much in taxes that easily. Which is why in the cat-and-mouse game of finding loopholes and then closing them, the IRS came up with controlled group status.

WHAT IS CONTROLLED GROUP STATUS?

If you are found to be a controlled group you can lose your dual and multiple corporation benefits. And note, this is a complicated area so be sure to consult with your tax advisor for specific advice.

That said, the following applies:

A Controlled Group Exists when:

1. Two people own 50 percent of each of two corporations. For Ken and Cindy, half ownership of KC Homes, Inc., and K&C Advertising, Inc., would result in controlled group status if both were C corporations. But KC Home, Inc., is an S corporation so there is not an issue. Controlled group status applies to two or more C corporations.

2. One corporation owns at least 80 percent of another corporation; this is called a parent subsidiary controlled group.

3. Five or fewer persons (including individuals, trusts, etc.) own at least 80 percent of the shares of both corporations; this is called a brother-sister controlled group.

A controlled group does not exist when:

1. One spouse owns 100 percent of one corporation and the other spouse owns 100 percent of a second corporation. Each spouse maintains separate control of corporate assets and separate management control.

2. You own less than 50 percent of one corporation and your child over twenty-one years old owns the rest. You then own 100 percent of the second corporation.

3. You own less than 80 percent of the first corporation and an unrelated person owns the rest. You then own 100 percent of the second corporation.

It should be noted that controlled group status relates to the payment of taxes. If you want to own 100 percent of two corporations for asset protection purposes and are willing to pay any higher taxes the IRS will assess you will be fine. In that case, even the IRS will approve of your asset protection strategies.

But it should also be noted that if two or more corporations are not controlled group entities you can take advantage of reduced corporate taxes. Again, please be sure to consult with your tax advisor before venturing into this arena.

Strategy Three—Doing Business in Your State
Borrowing Money from Nevada, Inc.

Case No. 10—John and Denise

John and Denise owned a crafts store in a busy local mall. They were incorporated as a C corporation in Your State under the name Neesette Crafts, Inc. While they had not yet learned how to establish and use business credit (as we will learn in Chapter 10) they found that they needed credit at times to purchase inventory. They had their own personal monies to lend the company but wanted it protected. John was also aware that it was best to minimize their exposure by protecting and segregating whatever Neesette assets they could.

After consulting with their advisors they decided that the best thing to do was to combine both needs (credit and protection) into one strategy. Their plan was as follows:

Neesette Crafts, Inc.   ◄—$50,000 Loan   John's Nevada, Inc.

Denise owns 100%   Promissory Note/UCC-1 —►   John owns 100%

To avoid controlled group status, Denise owned and managed 100 percent of Neesette, Inc., and John owned and managed 100 percent of John's Nevada, Inc., a newly formed Nevada C corporation.

Neesette, Inc., borrowed $50,000 from John's Nevada, Inc., and signed a promissory note to pay the money back with interest. The note was due on demand so that if trouble arose, John's Nevada, Inc., could demand payment at any time. A security agreement was signed whereby all the assets of Neesette were used as collateral for the loan. To reflect this collateralization, a UCC-1 form detailing the secured assets was filed with the secretary of state in Your State and in Nevada and with any county recorder's offices, if appropriate.

As long as no one else filed first, John's Nevada, Inc., had a priority over the assets of Neesette, Inc. The assets were encumbered, or subject to the claims of others. If a lawsuit was filed and judgment was rendered, the creditor could not collect until the debt to John's Nevada, Inc., was first paid. This priority is true as against all creditors—except, of course, the IRS.

This was the perfect solution for John and Denise. They were able to lend money to Neesette, Inc., without tying it up. It could be demanded back at any time. And they had encumbered all of the assets of Neesette, Inc., thus removing them from creditor claims. They felt much more secure about their business situation.

Concerns When Transferring Assets

There are three major issues that arise when you transfer or encumber property and assets:

FRAUDULENT CONVEYANCE

When property is transferred or encumbered it is effectively put out of the reach of a creditor. A problem arises when the transfer is accomplished with an identified creditor in mind. That is, if someone has a judgment against you, is in the process of suing you, or is even threatening to sue you, you cannot just start transferring assets to others to avoid the payment of a claim. Think about it: It would be too easy to avoid your debts if you could just give your assets away. So the courts and legislatures have come up with the concept of a "fraudulent conveyance" and they have given the courts the power to undo a transfer of property that is fraudulent and unjust.

Most states have passed the Uniform Fraudulent Transfer Act. Under the UFTA, the term "creditor" means simply "a person who has a claim," even if that claim is disputed and is not yet reduced to judgment. If the court determines that a "transfer" was made with the actual intent to hinder, delay, or defraud a creditor, the transfer is subject to a variety of legal challenges. The law requires the court to consider a variety of "factors," some of which indicate the absence of fraudulent intent. These factors include whether:

- The transfer was to an "insider" (which includes a relative, a corporation in which the debtor is an officer, director, or a person in control, a partnership in which the debtor is a general partner, or an "affiliate");

- The debtor retained possession or control over the property transferred;
- The transfer was disclosed or concealed;
- Before the transfer was made, the debtor had been sued or threatened with suit;
- The transfer was of substantially all the debtor's assets;
- The debtor absconded;
- The debtor removed or concealed assets;
- The debtor received reasonably equivalent value as consideration for the transfer;
- The transfer rendered the debtor insolvent;
- The transfer occurred shortly before or shortly after a substantial debt was incurred; or
- The debtor transferred the essential asset of a business to a lienor, who then transferred the assets to an "insider."

A creditor who proves that a transfer was made with the requisite intent to hinder, delay, or defraud the creditor can request the court to void the transfer, enjoin future transfers, appoint a receiver, and/or satisfy the claim out of the transferred property.

How do you avoid a fraudulent conveyance issue?

By setting up your asset protection structures long before you ever get sued. For example, if John and Denise set up and implement their Nevada corporation, promissory note, and UCC-1 when they first get into business, a creditor who they start doing business with a year later cannot say their structure was somehow fraudulent. There was no intent to defraud the creditor—they did not even *know* the creditor when it was implemented.

The rule of thumb is to set up your asset protection when the seas are calm. When there is clear sailing and no troubles ahead you are perfectly within your rights to structure your affairs to your advantage. When the seas get rough, either your assets have been previously protected or they have not. At that point it is too late for transfers.

BEARER SHARES

Bearer shares have been used by some to engage in fraudulent conveyances. As a result, Nevada and Wyoming recently outlawed the use of bearer shares.

Bearer shares are stock certificates that, instead of listing the owner by name, list the owner only as "The Bearer." The supposed advantage of this was to maintain privacy of ownership. The bearer was whoever held the certificate, so shares could be transferred from one person to the next without notice to anyone or recordation anywhere.

But bearer shares bore problems. If someone comes to you with a bearer certificate, how do you know the certificate wasn't stolen or forged? The idea of simply handing a certificate from one person to the next may sound nice and easy (if a bit crafty) but such a transfer can create all sorts of tax problems. If you hand a certificate representing a million-dollar business over to your friend you've made a significant gift, for which gift taxes are due. And when by prearrangement he hands the certificate back to you there's another taxable event. Worse yet, what if your "friend" won't give you the certificate back?

The reason bearer shares were outlawed in Nevada and Wyoming had to do with fraud. Less than ethical corporate promoters would sell their less than ethical corporate clients on the idea that by simply handing the bearer certificate over to a friend they could deny a judgment creditor (one with a court-awarded judgment) access to the business or other asset. Of course, such a transfer is a fraudulent conveyance, meaning that a court could overturn the transfer if anyone ever found out about it. The problem was that it could be very difficult to find out about it. Look for bearer shares to be outlawed everywhere.

MONEY LAUNDERING

A third concern when transferring assets involves the Money Laundering Control Act.

The Money Laundering Act makes it criminal for anyone to conduct or attempt to conduct certain financial activities that involve the proceeds of unlawful activities. The transfer of assets into a corporation, limited partnership, trust, or other entity can constitute a financial activity within the scope of the act. The specified unlawful activities under the act consist primarily of drug-trafficking offenses, financial misconduct, and environmental crimes.

Drug trafficking offenses include the manufacture, importation, sale, or distribution of controlled substances; the commission of acts constituting a continuing criminal enterprise; and transportation of drug paraphernalia.

Covered financial misconduct includes the concealment of assets from a receiver, custodian, trustee, marshal, or other officer of the court, from creditors in a bankruptcy proceeding, or from the Federal Deposit Insurance Corporation, the Resolution Trust Corporation, or a similar agency or person; the making of a fraudulent conveyance in contemplation of a bankruptcy proceeding; bribery; the giving of commissions or gifts for the procurement of loans; theft, embezzlement, or misapplication of bank funds or funds of fraudulent bank or credit institution entries or loan or credit applications; and mail, wire, or bank fraud, or bank or postal robbery or theft.

Environmental crimes include violations of the Federal Water Pollution Control Act, the Ocean Dumping Ban Act, the Safe Drinking Water Act, the Resource Conservation and Recovery Act, and similar federal statutes.

Other specified crimes include counterfeiting, espionage, kidnapping or hostage taking, copyright infringement, entry of goods by means of false statements, smuggling goods into the United States, removing goods from the custody of Customs, illegally exporting arms, and trading with United States enemies.

So by engaging in those activities, and then transferring the proceeds into another entity, you have compounded the claims against you.

How do you avoid a money laundering issue? Do not do it. There is too much money to be made in this world by engaging in legal activities. You really do not need the sleepless nights of criminal enterprise.

One Final Point on Maximizing Corporate Benefits

In putting together strategies to benefit you and your family the courts allow flexibility in your arrangements. A classic example of this involves the payment of taxes.

> Anyone may so arrange his affairs that his taxes shall be as low as possible: he is not bound to choose that pattern which will best pay the Treasury; there is not even a patriotic duty to increase one's taxes. —Federal Judge Learned Hand, *Helvering v. Gregory*, 69 F.2d 809 (2d Circ. 1934)

This ruling was in turn confirmed by the U.S. Supreme Court:

The legal right of the taxpayer to decrease the amount of what otherwise would be his taxes, or altogether avoid them, by means which the law permits, cannot be doubted. —*Gregory v. Helvering*, 293 U.S. 454 (1935)

And, as we have learned, the best states for legally reducing your tax obligation are Nevada and Wyoming.

Chapter 4

How a Charging Order Works to Your Advantage

We have already mentioned the charging order several times in the previous three chapters. Now it is time to delve into how charging orders can protect you. The charging order procedure is a unique part of the asset protection offered by limited partnerships and limited liability companies. The concept has been extended to Nevada corporations with between two and seventy-five shareholders. In certain states, a judgment creditor—one who has sued and obtained a court judgment—may only obtain a charging order against an LP, LLC, or Nevada corporation. This means that a creditor does not get title to the property owned by the LP, LLC, or Nevada corporation, but rather only the right to receive the interest holders' distributions.

The state laws of Nevada and Wyoming provide that the only remedy a creditor may pursue is the charging order. Combined with their tax free status, Nevada and Wyoming are popular states for asset protection strategies.

An example helps explain the charging order concept. Please note that we will use an LP for our case, but that an LLC or Nevada corporation would apply as well.

Case No. 11—Joe and Family

Joe had a thriving forklift sales and repair business. He had started as a sole proprietorship and had grown it over the last seven years. His accountant said it was definitely time to protect his now considerable assets, especially since he was thinking of investing in an unrelated and far riskier venture. Joe liked the idea of using a limited partnership. He wanted to maintain control as general partner and yet gift limited partnership interests to his children.

With the help of his accountant Joe understood that he did not want the liability as a general partner. So Joe's Management, Inc., was formed to be the general partner of Joe's Forklift, LP. Joe's Management, Inc., had a 4 percent interest in the limited partnership. Because Joe might get sued in the new, unrelated venture, he could not be the majority owner of Joe's Management, Inc. If he was a majority owner, a creditor could get at Joe's shares, assert control over Joe's Management, Inc., and, as general partner of Joe's Forklift, LP, thwart the whole plan by making distributions from the LP as the creditor saw fit to satisfy his debt. It was best that he not give his spouse control of Joe's Management, Inc., since she may be found jointly liable with Joe for any debts if he is sued. So Joe gives 60 percent of Joe's Management, Inc., to his trusted adult son, Paul. Joe is still the chairman, CEO, president, and all other officers of Joe's Management, Inc. He has overall authority for both Joe's Management, Inc., and as corporate general partner, over Joe's Forklift, LP. (Please note that the use of Nevada's charging order protections for the corporate shareholders would modify some of the strategies just mentioned.)

Once the forklift business was contributed to Joe's Forklift, LP, Joe began a gifting program of limited partnership interests. After two years, Joe, his sons, Paul, Scott, and Dave, each owned limited partnership interests of 24 percent of Joe's Forklift, LP. The remaining 4 percent was held by the general partner, Joe's Management, Inc. All was in place.

Joe had always wanted to own a sports bar. And against his wife's, his accountant's, and everyone else's advice, he and two others put $100,000 each into a business that was by any standard high-risk. Their town already had three sports bars and Joe's location was not prime. But Joe and the other investors wanted to do it and that was that. The three had used a corporation for the sports bar business but they needed a bank loan for another $500,000 to get the bar open. The bank, quite prudently, demanded and received personal guarantees for the loan. The three new owners obtained the loan, made the improvements, and opened in June.

Two weeks after the bar opened the baseball players and owners started feuding again. A week later the players went on strike before the owners locked them out. The owners cried that they had locked the players out first. And the players whined that they went on strike first. No one expected a World Series, and for the immediate future no games were to be played or televised. Needless to say, this was bad for business. The fans were once again disgusted. "Take me out to the . . ."—nah, forget it. Joe's Sports Bar closed within three months.

Because he was the most solvent of the three bar owners, the bank immediately proceeded against Joe. His only asset was his 24 percent limited partnership in Joe's Forklift, LP.

The bank's exclusive recourse was to obtain a charging order against Joe's interest, which meant that they could not just march into Joe's Forklift, LP, and take 24 percent of the equipment, furniture, and receivables. They had to wait until the corporate general partner decided, in its sole discretion, to make a distribution to the limited partners. The bank then gets to stand in Joe's shoes and receive whatever is distributed.

Now remember, Joe is the CEO of Joe's Management, Inc. He does not own a majority of the shares because the bank, as creditor, could get ahold of the shares, vote themselves into control of Joe's Management, Inc., and decide, as corporate general partner, to make favorable distributions to Joe's Forklift, LP, limited partners. With their charging order the bank would receive Joe's 24 percent of those distributions.

But as CEO of Joe's Management, Inc., without fear of being voted out, thanks to Paul's ownership, Joe can decide to not make any distributions. So the bank, as well as his other children, get nothing. And, because profits are required to flow through a partnership, Joe can allocate profits on a Form K-1 filing with the IRS but not provide any money to pay the taxes on the gain. This is what is known as phantom income, and it is frustrating for creditors.

Say each 24 percent limited partner receives a taxable gain of $100,000 and the taxes on such a gain are $20,000. Joe decides to hire each of his boys in the business and pays them enough in salary to cover their tax obligation. The only one without money to pay the taxes is the bank. Oh sure, they can pay the taxes—they're a bank. But for the privilege of trying to collect from Joe it is going to cost them $20,000 this year. And maybe $40,000 next year. And after the money flows out without any hope of coming in, the bank is ready to settle their claim for 10 cents (or less) on the dollar.

And that is what happened. Joe settled the bank's claim for $50,000 and listened to his wife and accountant from then on.

While each state is different, there are a number of procedural hoops that a judgment creditor must jump through to collect on a charging order. Some include:

- Litigating the case and securing a judgment against a limited partner
- Going back to court to obtain a charging order
- Applying to foreclose on the limited partners' limited partnership interest
- Appointing a receiver to receive limited partnership distributions

As discussed, the steps that a creditor must take are a very large incentive for settlement.

Some readers may question whether the charging order is really fair to the bank. They loaned the money, they have a judgment, and they should be able to collect. There are three issues that arise in a discussion of that point:

1. The California Court of Appeal in similar-fact situations agreed that the creditor should collect. See *Crocker National Bank v. Perroton*, 208 Cal. App.3d 1 (1989) and *Hellman v. Anderson*, 233 Cal. App.3d 840 (1991). The court noted that the original purpose of the charging order was to protect limited partners who were not debtors and to prevent the interruption of partnership business. They noted its intent was not to allow partners to avoid debts. As remedies, the court in one case ordered the partnership interest sold with the other partners' consent. In the second, where it was found the sale would not interrupt the partnership business, the sale was ordered without the other partners' consent.

This remedy is limited to California and Colorado at this writing but could be adopted by other states in the future. While it is important to know and recognize this possibility, as discussed below in point three, it should not deter one from using an LP or LLC. (It should be noted that Nevada and Wyoming hold that the charging order is the exclusive remedy for LLC and LP creditors, a useful and significant asset protection benefit. As well, once again, Nevada extends charging order protections to corporate shareholders.)

2. In the case above, the bank conducted (or should have conducted) a due diligence investigation into Joe's financial condition. As long as Joe did not lie on his loan application—a Money Laundering Act violation—the bank should have known that his sole asset was a limited partnership interest that would be difficult to get at. If the bank had a problem with it the solution was simple: Do not lend Joe the money.

3. The advantage of the charging order is not that it hurts legitimate creditors but that it deters frivolous litigation. Although many attorneys are honorable people, as in any profession there are some unscrupulous lawyers out there. The notions of justice, civility, and fair play are lost on these people. They do not care about you or your family or the fact that you do good things in the community. They just want to win and they like to win by aggressively pursuing you and making your life miserable. These people are despised by their mothers. That's not enough for them to lose their law license. And with a system that rewards lawyers quite well for taking on larger net worth individuals, you need to take every step you can to protect your assets as best you can. Be assured, lawyers and their staff have ways of finding out what assets you own. (It is incredible what you can learn about someone on the Internet.) So it is important to take steps to keep your name off public records, use entities that are not legally tied to you, and take ownership in a form that is difficult to reach.

The limited partnership or LLC interest is one of the best ways to hold ownership for the protection of assets. When the ambulance-chasing or Mercedes-chasing attorney sees that your assets are in LP or LLC form — or better yet sees no assets—he will think hard about pursuing a case against you. Any step taken to deter frivolous litigation can bring peace of mind. Again, assets held by an LP or LLC are an excellent step in the direction of asset protection. As well, the use of Nevada corporations featuring asset protection benefits is another prudent way to conduct your affairs.

Rich Dad Tips

- The strategy in today's litigious environment is to segregate assets.
- Keep the operating entities—the ones that deal with the public—away from the asset-owning entities.
- Consider having the operating entities hold fewer assets and lease expensive assets from the asset-owning entities.
- Consult with your accountant to ensure that controlled group status issues are addressed.

Now let's address how you take Nevada and Wyoming benefits home . . .

Chapter 5

Crossing State Lines

Whether you use a Nevada or Wyoming entity in your home state, or form an entity in your home state and expand your business into a neighboring state, you must be aware of the issues associated with crossing state lines.

Two cases help provide an overview of the issues involved. For purposes of this discussion instead of "Your State" we will use the term "Business State" to refer to the state where you are conducting business.

Case No. 12—Curtis and Diana

Curtis and Diana are California real estate investors and own a fourplex in Truckee, California, and a sixplex in Rocklin, California. They are aware that California's asset protection laws, as enforced by the courts in California, are among the weakest in the nation. On the advice of their attorney, they decide to form a Wyoming LLC and a Nevada LLC to take advantage of those states' superior asset protection laws. They then take title to the fourplex in the Wyoming LLC, and the Nevada LLC is used for the sixplex.

Their lawyer advises them that one additional step must be taken. Because Curtis and Diana are collecting rents from their two buildings in California, they are doing business in California. And when you do business in California you must "qualify" with the California secretary of state, meaning that the Wyoming and Nevada LLCs must each get permission to operate as an out-of-state entity in California. The lawyer noted that this requirement to qualify with the local secretary of state's office:

1. Applies to any entity, be it a corporation, nonprofit corporation, limited liability company, or limited partnership;
2. Applies in all fifty states; and
3. If properly submitted, is always granted.

So Curtis and Diana engaged their attorney's firm at a minimal cost to qualify the Wyoming and Nevada LLCs in California. The process of qualifying entails submitting the out-of-state articles of organization, a certificate of good standing from the state of formation, and a fee to the Business State's secretary of state's office. Typically, you pay the same fee for qualifying that you would have paid if you had set up the entity in the Business State to begin with. (Texas, however, is one state that charges out-of-state entities more in fees than it does in-state or Texas-formed entities.)

Of course, the consequence of qualifying is that now the Business State has a way to tax you on activities occurring within their borders—which is why states assess some pretty hefty fees if you fail to qualify. In California, for example, the penalty is $250 plus $20 per day, or over $7,000 per year. As well, many states will not allow the filing of a lawsuit in their courts unless you have properly qualified the business in their state. These are referred to as "closed-door statutes" and, like the significant financial penalties, can be quite an inducement for compliance.

But with Curtis and Diana's out-of-state LLCs qualified to do business in California, they are covered. But there is one more important point to consider. In the event of a lawsuit, which state's law will apply? Will it be the Business State (in our example, California) or the outside formation state, in this case Wyoming and Nevada?

Like so many legal questions, the answer is: It depends.

A chart on page 71 helps to explain why.

In Attack #1, a lawsuit is filed by one of the tenants in the Truckee fourplex. The tenant claims to have fallen down a flight of steps that are alleged to have been improperly maintained. Because the attack involves California real estate, the courts in California have held that California law applies. If the tenant is successful in court and Curtis and Diana's insurance company finds a reason not to cover the claim (always a very real concern), the tenant

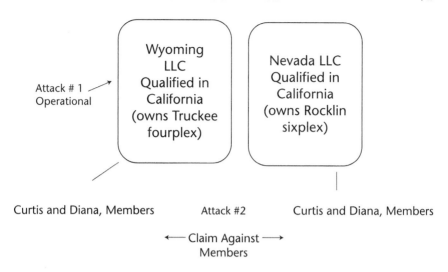

could force a sale of the fourplex to satisfy the claim. This outcome is the case in most states.

With such dramatic consequences you might ask: Why even use an LLC at all? A key to remember is that if an LLC had not been used the result would have been much worse. With the fourplex, the sixplex, and their other significant assets (including their home and brokerage accounts) all held in their own name, the tenant could reach all of Curtis and Diana's assets. Even under California law, the LLC shields the other assets from attack.

The bigger issue involving state law comes with Attack #2. In the second attack, a lawsuit is brought against Curtis and Diana by an individual or company over a matter wholly unrelated to their real estate. In America, the land of the free and the home of frivolous litigation, it may be a baseless case completely without merit, and yet the party bringing the suit may prevail. The attacker now has a judgment against Curtis and Diana and wants to satisfy it by getting at their real estate holdings.

In such a case, you want the strongest asset protection law available. California's law, as we have discussed, is very weak. If the LLC was formed under California law, the attacker would have the ability to pierce through both LLCs and force a sale of the buildings.

But by forming the entities in Nevada and Wyoming, the laws of those states apply. As we have discussed, both states feature outstanding charging order protection. Better yet, under current interpretations, the attacker may have to seek redress in the state where the entities were organized. By using the two best states available, the attacker will have to fight it out in both Nevada and Wyoming. This alone may be a suitable deterrent to litigation. When it comes to collecting, attorneys prefer the path of least resistance. Having to fight the very steep uphill battle against charging order protections in Nevada and Wyoming, as well as paying attorneys licensed in both states to assist, may be too much trouble.

That is what you want. And that is why, as Curtis and Diana continued to acquire real estate, they used a mix of Nevada and Wyoming entities, and then qualified them into the state where the property was located.

Now let's look at a case wherein a business expands from their home state into a neighboring state. What are the tax and legal consequences of such growth?

Case No. 13—Paul

Paul owned a retail store in his home state of Idaho and did a profitable Internet business selling to customers around the country,

Paul's attorney and CPA both suggested that Paul use an S corporation for his Coeur d'Alene retail store. He had people coming into his place of business, any one of whom could sue for a trip and fall, or some other real or imagined event. Using a corporation, it was suggested by his advisors, was an excellent way to protect his other personal assets, including his house and bank accounts, from attack. So Paul's Idaho, Inc., an Idaho S corporation, was formed.

Paul ran his Internet business through Paul's Idaho, Inc., as well. He could have run it through a separate corporation or LLC in order to segregate assets. By using two entities, an attack by someone falling at the retail store would not expose the inventory and assets of the Internet business to such a claim. But Paul did not want the extra expense (primarily, the extra annual filing fees and another tax return) associated with two entities. And since it was Paul's decision, only one entity was used.

Paul paid all the taxes that were required in his home state of Idaho: corporate and personal income taxes, state employment taxes, and sales taxes. When he sold his products over the Internet he had to collect sales tax only on those Internet sales that occurred in his home state of Idaho. If the product was shipped from his home state to South Carolina, for example, he did not have to collect any South Carolina sales tax because he wasn't doing business there. He had no presence in South Carolina: no store, no employees, no warehouse. In the field, these connectors are called nexus. And because he was from Idaho, Paul had no nexus with South Carolina.

In terms of future flexibility, his advisors suggested that when the Internet business got big enough, a second company could be later formed to segregate the two activities and assets from each other, thus improving his asset protection prospects.

Eventually, as his business grew, Paul decided it was time to expand to a second location. From Coeur d'Alene he saw an excellent opportunity to expand west into Spokane, Washington. Because Paul would have a physical presence in the state of Washington, the Spokane store, and Washington employees working in the Spokane store, his advisors informed Paul he would have to qualify to do business in Washington.

At this point, Paul had one of two choices on how to proceed. First, he could qualify Paul's Idaho, Inc., the Idaho S corporation, into the state of Washington. This was the process described above whereby the Idaho articles of incorporation, a certificate of good standing from the Idaho secretary of state, and related documents and fees are submitted to the Washington secretary of state's office.

By completing this process the Idaho corporation obtains permission to do business in Washington. This meant that Paul now had to pay taxes in both states.

It is relatively easy to determine how much state unemployment tax to pay on each employee. Paul would pay Idaho taxes on the Idaho employees and Washington taxes on the Washington employees.

But what about corporate income taxes? Since both stores contributed to the profits of one company, did Paul have to pay state taxes on all profits in both states?

The answer is no. It would not be fair for both Idaho and Washington to collect state taxes on profits earned outside their borders. So state laws look to apportion profits between the states based on the property, sales, and payroll in each state. Many states have adopted UDITPA, which stands for the Uniform Division of Income for Tax Purposes Act. UDITPA apportions business income for state taxation by the property, sales, and payroll factors. For more information, visit, www.mtc.gov, the Web site for the Multistate Tax Commission. And be sure to work with your tax advisor on how to apportion income to arrive at the right amount of taxation.

But what about the second option?

Paul could also have the Spokane store be run by a separate Washington corporation. There are several reasons why this is a viable option.

First, after the Washington corporation is set up, the annual cost for two entities is the same as one. Either, as in option one, Paul pays the corporate fees for the Idaho corporation to do business both in Idaho and Washington, or option two, he pays the fees for an Idaho company and a Washington company. The same amount of money for corporate fees is spent. But the asset protection is better with two entities. By using two corporations we are segregating assets (the Coeur d'Alene store from the Spokane store) at no extra additional annual cost. When crossing state lines one should always consider the merits of using two separate corporations instead of one.

But the key for Paul was Washington's unique business and occupation (B&O) tax, a state tax that is assessed on both the retail and wholesale transactions of tangible personal property and services. Paul didn't want Washington possibly assessing that tax against his Idaho activities. So it was an easy choice to use two separate entities to segregate Idaho revenues from the threat of Washington taxes.

The use of two separate entities is an excellent strategy when dealing with aggressive taxation states. It is a fact of life that certain states are very difficult to deal with when it comes to fairly apportioning taxes. California is a notable example of this. Until recently, California levied a significant excess fee on LLC revenues, regardless of whether this income was generated in California or not. Finally, a court declared California's tax scheme unconstitutional, but not before tens of thousands of tax-paying businesses paid tens of millions in tax dollars they shouldn't have. A better strategy is to use only a California entity for California activities, and keep all other income out of California and beyond the reach of their very zealous, and often abusive, Franchise Tax Board. (It will be interesting to see when the citizens of California finally wake up to how many productive people are being driven from their state by California's Franchise Tax Board.) The two-entity strategy is suggested as an option for other states with very aggressive tax collection departments, including New York.

Paul followed his advisor's advice when he expanded. He used two separate corporations for the Idaho and Washington activities. He also kept in touch with his advisor as to changes in the taxation of Internet sales. He knew it was an evolving area of the law to keep up with.

What are the typical situations in which a company must qualify to do business in a new state? The following tend to trigger qualification requirements:

1. A physical presence in the state. If you rent or own property used in business in the state you will have to qualify there.
2. Employees in the state. Employing someone in the new state is a sure sign that your business must qualify in the new state.
3. Construction in the state. When an out-of-state construction company operates in a new state for several months, qualification will be required.

That noted, there are certain activities that are defined by most states as not requiring qualification. These include:

1. Mail, telephone, or Internet sales originating from a separate state
2. Isolated transactions within the state usually completed within thirty days and not involving a pattern of repeated dealings
3. Holding board of directors/manager meetings
4. Holding bank or securities accounts
5. Appearing in court, mediations, or arbitrations on your company's behalf
6. Selling into the state through independent contractors

Nevertheless, certain states take aggressive positions when it comes to the use of independent contractors in their state. For example, Michigan, Missouri, Ohio, Pennsylvania, and Texas assert that direct selling companies, or network marketers, with independent sellers in their state must pay the applicable income or business activity taxes, even though the companies have no office or employees in the state. There is pending federal legislation that would prohibit states from taxing entities without a physical presence in the state.

As is apparent, the issue of state taxation is a dynamic and ever changing area. Be sure to check with your advisor when contemplating any serious repeated activities in a new state. State (and even local) rules can vary and it is best to know the necessary requirements, up front.

Chapter 6

Professional Corporations

Case No. 14—Denny

Denny was a well-liked dentist with a thriving practice. It had taken him several years to reach his now lucrative status as a professional earning well over six figures per year. During all those years of building up to his current level—dental school, a new start-up practice, equipment loans, buying his own building and other real estate assets, and constant networking—Denny had failed to spend the time to properly structure his practice. Not knowing any better, he conducted all of his business in his own name. As such, Denny was a sole proprietor.

Denny learned the hard way the consequences of being a sole proprietor. A hefty patient who was a professional wine taster came onto his premises and fell when a creaky hand railing gave way under his weight. The patient was severely injured (or was he really? wondered Denny) and filed a claim. Fortunately, Denny's insurance company covered the claim. Of course, Denny's premiums were promptly doubled the next year.

The whole incident was a wake-up call for Denny. In speaking with some of his colleagues Denny learned that if his insurance company hadn't covered him then all of his personal assets would have been exposed to satisfy the claim. In the wrong circumstances he could have lost everything. Denny learned that many of his dentist friends had incorporated their practices to avoid such a consequence. One of his friends suggested Denny speak to an asset protection attorney about his situation. But Denny didn't like attorneys or their fees and felt he could set things up by himself for a lot less money.

So Denny found a discount paralegal firm on the Internet to set up his professional corporation. For just $199 he received the articles of incorporation for his new corporation, Denny's Dental, Inc. The paralegal firm had worked with him to get his professional certificate from his state's dental board over to the secretary of state's office (a prerequisite in most states) where the corporation was formed. With his certificate from the state Denny felt protected.

Then Denny experienced how much protection a professional corporation really provided. The hefty professional wine tasting patient who had filed a claim for falling on the property now claimed that Denny had committed dental malpractice. A root canal job had become infected and it appeared the patient might lose part of his jaw as a result.

Initially, Denny felt protected. His malpractice insurance policy was in place and his professional corporation was there to back him up against any excess claims.

But when he sat down with the insurance company's attorney he learned the truth. First, his malpractice policy was only for $1 million and the patient's attorney was seeking damages in excess of $5 million. The patient claimed he could no longer taste wine and thus couldn't work. Denny told the attorney that this frivolous claim would be covered by insurance and if a claim ever did go beyond the $1 million his professional corporation would protect him against the excess $4 million. The attorney promptly corrected Denny's misinterpretation of the law. A professional could not hide behind a professional corporation when it came to malpractice claims. The professional—be it a doctor, lawyer, dentist, or whatever—was personally liable for all claims over their insurance coverage.

Denny was incredulous. All of his assets were exposed?

The lawyer calmly replied that it depended. Certainly, he inquired, Denny had met with an asset protection attorney as he was growing his practice and acquiring real estate?

Denny replied that he had not and that all his assets, his office complex, apartment buildings, and brokerage accounts, were held in his individual name. The lawyer informed Denny of the bad news: If a judgment exceeded the insurance coverage, all his assets could be reached by the patient and his attorney.

Denny then asked if he could set up LLCs right now to protect his assets. The lawyer replied it was too late. Once the claim was filed, or even threatened to be filed, it was too late for asset protection.

A year later, a jury believed the patient's claim and awarded a $5 million judgment. After his insurance company paid their $1 million, the remaining amount was Denny's obligation. With $4 million in liability, Denny lost everything. As he picked himself up to start all over again, he bought plenty of malpractice insurance and consulted with an attorney for solid protection strategies. Denny now understood the limits of a professional corporation.

In many states, professionals who want to incorporate their business can do so only as a "professional corporation." In other states, professionals have a choice of incorporating as either a professional corporation or a standard corporation. What services constitute professional services are defined by state law, and vary from state to state. However, it is typically professions requiring a license, such as doctors, engineers, chiropractors, lawyers, and accountants, among others.

Professional corporations provide a limit on the owner's personal liability for the regular commercial debts and other business liabilities of the corporation. However, incorporating does not protect a professional against liability for negligence or malpractice. Generally, licensed shareholder-employees of professional corporations remain personally liable for their own negligent or wrongful acts, or acts of those under the professional's direct supervision or control, if performing professional services on behalf of the corporation. Thus, asset protection planning for the professional's other personal assets must be implemented. The limited liability shield of the corporation may, however, protect professionals from personal liability for the negligent acts of other professionals in the incorporated professional practice.

The formation requirements for a professional corporation are similar to those of a standard corporation, with a few exceptions. The articles of incorporation for a professional corporation resemble those of a standard corporation; however, approval by the state licensing body and signature of a licensed professional as the incorporator, as well as their license number, may also be required prior to filing the formation documents with the secretary of state.

Depending on your state of incorporation, there are some other key differences between a professional corporation and a standard corporation. For example, some states restrict who may own stock in a professional corporation. Certain states require that the shareholders and the board of directors must all be licensed practitioners of the specific service the corporation provides. Other states require that at least half of the shareholders and directors be licensed professionals.

Furthermore, most state laws dictate that an indicator showing that the company is a professional corporation must be listed in the name, such as "Professional Corporation," or "PC," and must meet any further business name requirements imposed by the state, such as requiring that the profession be listed as part of the company name (e.g., Jones Architects, PC).

Generally, the corporation must be formed to render only one professional service, but some professions are allowed to form a corporation to render more than one service in related fields. For example, a licensed physician may be allowed to incorporate a professional corporation together with a licensed surgeon. It is important to note that the corporation must render professional services only through licensed members, managers, officers, agents, and employees and each licensed professional must carry the amount of liability insurance specified under the rules that apply to the profession.

Some states allow professionals to operate through an LLC, while others do not. For example, Nevada allows professional LLCs, while California does not.

If you are a licensed professional be sure to speak with your professional advisors about the advantages and limits of a professional corporation (or LLC, if allowed), and about related asset protection strategies *before* there is a problem.

Chapter 7

Organizational Steps for Forming a Corporation, Limited Liability Company, and Limited Partnership

Once you have decided to form a good entity you need to take certain organizational steps. Even if your professional advisor is going to prepare these documents for you the following is good to review and know.

Corporations

The first step in organizing a corporation is to prepare the articles of incorporation for filing with the secretary of state. While each state has its own rules and requirements, there are common requirements:

ARTICLES OF INCORPORATION

Corporate Name

Select a name that you can grow with and then check with the secretary of state (and trademark office, if appropriate—see Chapter 12) on name availability.

Purposes and Powers

Nevada, Wyoming, and certain other jurisdictions allow the articles to state that the purpose of the corporation is to engage in any lawful activity for which a corporation may be organized. Others, such as Massachusetts, require that at least one specific purpose be stated in the articles of incorporation.

Board of Directors

Some states require that the names and addresses of the initial board of directors be listed.

Authorized Capital

The total number of shares the corporation is authorized to issue, the rights and preferences of each class, and the par value of the shares need to be included. Some states, such as Virginia, charge you more money if large numbers of shares are authorized. Be aware of this going in.

Duration

Because most states allow a corporation to continue indefinitely, the articles of incorporation will permit a perpetual duration.

BYLAWS

The bylaws of a corporation are the rules for the conduct of business affairs. While each version is different, they generally contain the following common provisions:

Meetings of Directors

The bylaws will set out what kind of notice requirements are needed to call meetings and the minimum number of annual meetings that are required.

Meetings of Shareholders

The date for the annual meeting will be fixed, along with requirements for calling special meetings.

Officers and Directors

The responsibilities of each officer and the director(s) will be set out in the bylaws, as will be the procedures for removing them.

Records and Reports

Procedures for inspection of the books by shareholders as may be required shall be set out in the bylaws.

Name and Address of Resident Agent

States require that a resident agent be designated. The purpose of the resident agent is to receive the service of a summons and complaint (a lawsuit) in the state. So do not have someone serve as your resident agent who will not fully appreciate the importance of being sued and the need to answer a complaint promptly.

Rich Dad Tips

- The fact that each state requires that a corporation, LLC, or LP have a resident agent in that state underlines the importance of choosing a reliable agent.
- Do not have some mom-and-pop resident agent service perform this function. They may not be around a year from now. In such a case, you could be sued, never receive a notice to defend yourself, and have a default judgment entered against your company.

Limited Liability Companies

The first step in organizing an LLC is to prepare and file the articles of organization. Again, there are common requirements:

ARTICLES OF ORGANIZATION

LLC Name

Check for name availability and consider separately protecting the name.

Purposes and Powers

As with corporations, many states allow a broad unlimited power to be stated.

Name and Address of Resident Agent

For the same purposes as a corporation, the resident agent and address are listed. Note that, as with LPs and corporations, if you live in your state of organization you can serve as your own resident agent.

Manager- or Member-Managed

Unlike a corporation, either all of the members or just a manager(s) may run the LLC. Usually, this decision must be stated in the articles of organization.

OPERATING AGREEMENT

Like the bylaws of a corporation, the operating agreement provides the rules for operation of the LLC. Common provisions likely to be found are:

Managers

The number of managers and the term, election, and removal of managers will all be set out.

Restrictions on Transfer of Interests

Unlike shares of a corporation, the transfer of LLC membership interests is more complicated. The rules are set out in the operating agreement.

Distributions to Members; Profits and Losses

Distributions are governed by partnership law, unlike dividends in a corporation. The rules are more complex and are set out in the operating agreement.

Meetings

Many states leave the whole need for meetings up to the members. Any requirements should be set out in the operating agreement.

Charging Order

Although many states require creditors to follow the charging order procedure as a matter of state law, it may be a good idea to include it in the operating agreement.

Limited Partnerships

To organize an LP most states require that a certificate of limited partnership be filed with the secretary of state. The following are common requirements:

CERTIFICATE OF LIMITED PARTNERSHIP

Limited Partnership Name

As with the other corporate entities, check on availability with the secretary of state and remember that there are separate trademark requirements (see Chapter 12).

General Character of Business

You need not be too specific in most states.

Name and Address of Resident Agent

Again, for the same reasons as with an LLC and corporation, choose a resident agent that will be in business next year.

Name and Address of General Partner

Some states also require the names and addresses of all limited partners.

Amounts of Contributions

Not all states require this and for good reason. Not many investors want it on the public record that they put $1 million into XYZ, LP.

Duration

Many states limit a limited partnership to only thirty years' duration. You must specify a termination date.

Events of Termination/Dissolution

Some states require the certificate of limited partnership to state what triggers dissolution or termination.

LIMITED PARTNERSHIP AGREEMENT

The limited partnership agreement, like the LLC's operating agreement and a corporation's bylaws, sets out the roadmap for operations. Common provisions include:

Management by General Partner

The agreement will set out the duties, authority, and compensation of the general partner.

Limited Partners' Role

The rights, powers, and voting rights of the limited partners will be set out.

Restrictions on Transfers/Distributions to Partners

Like an LLC, partnerships can be fairly complex with regard to these issues. They should be set out in detail.

Events of Termination/Dissolution

Because limited partnerships generally have a fixed duration (e.g., thirty years), the provisions for termination and dissolution will be detailed.

Charging Order

As with LLCs, you may want to provide that a charging order is a creditor's exclusive remedy.

And with these formalities completed, we will want to review the onging importance of corporate formalities . . .

Chapter 8

The Importance of Corporate Formalities

The benefits of a corporation, as you have learned, are significant. From the English Crown in the 1500s to the legislatures of all U.S. states and territories, all Canadian provinces, and all other states and countries based on English common law, the historical means for encouraging risk taking while personally protecting the risk taker has been the corporation.

But with every right comes a responsibility. In the corporate realm that means following certain very basic but necessary rules. These rules are generally known as "corporate formalities." By abusing or ignoring these formalities you can lose corporate protection and become personally liable for your business's debts and claims.

And keep in mind that these rules may apply to LLCs as well. As mentioned, while the LLC is a new entity and a body of law has not developed, one can easily foresee without squinting that an LLC's veil of limited liability will be allowed to be pierced. Already, Colorado statutorily allows for this with a law that states:

> In any case in which a party seeks to hold the members of a limited liability company personally responsible for the alleged improper actions of the limited liability company, the court shall apply the case law which interprets the conditions and circumstances under which

the corporate veil of a corporation may be pierced under Colorado law. (Colorado Revised Statutes Annotated, Section 7-80-107(1)).

For an LLC, a corporation—for any business no matter what form—it is prudent to follow the basic formalities.

Here are the simple rules:

1. *Annual Filings.* After filing your initial articles of incorporation you will need to file an annual report and pay an annual fee to your state. It is not difficult. In Wyoming, for example, you send in a one-page list of officers and directors along with a check for $50 each year.

2. *Minutes of Meetings.* Most states require a corporation's shareholders and directors to meet once a year. It is good protection and proper corporate form to prepare minutes of these meetings. Our firm charges $150 per year to perform this service. Others may charge less. Or you can quite easily do it yourself.

3. *Corporate Notice.* It is very important that you let the world know you are operating as a corporation as opposed to as an individual, sole proprietorship, or other format. On your business cards, letterhead, invoices, company checks, brochures, and the like you must identify yourself as doing business as a corporation. Do not just use "XYZ" when you are "XYZ, Inc." You want the world to know you are a corporation. Likewise, all contracts should be signed by you as president of XYZ, Inc. Signing your name without your corporate officer designation can lead to personal liability.

4. *Separate Bank Account.* You cannot run a corporation's banking out of your own personal bank account. A corporation is a separate tax entity with its own tax identification number. You must maintain a separate and independent bank account at all times.

5. *Separate Tax Returns.* Because the corporation is a separate tax entity it is necessary to file a separate corporate tax return. Listing revenue and/or expenses on your personal tax return that properly belong on the corporate tax return is not a good idea.

Failure to follow these five simple rules can allow a creditor to pierce the corporate veil and seek personal liability. What does it take to pierce the corporate veil?

Case No. 15—Roger and Donny

Roger Morton and Donny Brooks were excited about their new business venture. This was going to be their dream, their business home run. They had been working for eighteen months to get it to this point. They were about to acquire the local territorial franchise rights to Burger Bell, the hottest new food franchise since Taco King. Roger was going to handle the construction of the first location through his own construction company and Donny was going to handle the business details.

In preparation for doing this business, eighteen months ago Donny had filed the articles of incorporation with his local secretary of state. He did not use an attorney for this or consult with an accountant. They were a start-up and they needed to save money. He had recalled that an organizational meeting was needed but forgot to get it done.

Donny did not know that a corporation, as a separate legal entity, needed to file a tax ID number (EIN—Employer Identification Number) request with the IRS. If he had gone to a bank to open a corporate bank account he would have learned this, as banks will not open corporate accounts without an EIN for the corporation. Instead, Donny just assumed that you could use your own personal bank account and sort out what was what later. Monies that he and Roger advanced to the company were deposited to his personal account. As things progressed he tried to keep up by putting the checks he wrote for the business and some of the receipts in a specially marked shoebox.

About six months ago Donny had received a letter from his secretary of state's office requesting the payment of the upcoming year's annual fees. The letter also said he needed to return the check with his list of officers and directors for the upcoming year. Donny did not really understand what was needed, and was too busy with other tasks he felt were more important to deal with the request.

Donny recalled hearing that when you received the request from the state it meant that it was time to hold the corporation's annual meeting of shareholders and directors. Again, he was too busy to deal with some archaic requirement. And besides, it was just he and Roger. They spoke every day. What did they possibly have to meet about?

Recently, Roger had sent over a contract for Donny to review. It was for hiring a telephone answering service to handle their overflow calls. Donny reviewed it, signed "Donny Brooks" on the signature line, and sent it back to the answering service.

All was proceeding well. Until a woman fell on the construction site. While Roger had some insurance through his construction company it was not enough. It was an unfortunate accident and the young woman's injuries were serious. Two weeks later Roger and Donny learned the meaning of piercing the corporate veil.

The corporate veil of limited liability as to individual shareholders can be pierced, or set aside, in cases where the shareholders fail to follow corporate formalities. When a shareholder conducts his business as though the corporation does not exist or is so careless in his dealings that the proper recognition of a separate corporate identity is ignored, personal liability to each shareholder may attach.

A piercing of the corporate veil can be devastating, as it was for Roger and Donny. The attorney for the young woman had absolutely no problem proving a complete lack of corporate formality. The evidence was:

- A corporation EIN was never obtained;
- No corporate bank account was ever opened;
- The corporate charter was revoked for failure to file the annual report and pay the annual fee;
- No organization or annual meetings of shareholders and directors were ever held;
- No corporate tax return was ever filed; and
- In at least one contract Donny signed as an individual, not as an officer.

Roger and Donny were held personally liable for the young woman's injuries. Their franchise rights were withdrawn due to their financial condition, which was the filing of bankruptcy. All their work, efforts, and dreams were lost for the failure to take some very simple protective steps.

To avoid your corporation (or LLC) ever being pierced you need to develop a mind-set of separateness. You are not the corporation. The corporation is not you. You will help the corporation by serving as an officer and/or director and holding its shares. In return, the corporation will help you with limited liability and other protections. This beneficial symbiotic relationship cannot last if separateness is not respected.

To maintain separateness, consider the following rules as guidance:

1. Never see corporate assets as your own. They are not. They belong to the corporation. Title is (or should be) held in the corporate name and you as an officer have a duty to administer these assets in the best interests of the corporation. The fact that you own 20 percent, 70 percent, or 100 percent of the corporation is of no consequence. You only own shares, not corporate assets. You are one step removed from ownership of the assets.

2. Never commingle corporate and personal assets or monies. Deposit all corporate monies into the corporate account. Putting corporate money into your personal account and later paying the corporation back is a bad idea. Using corporate funds to cover a personal obligation, even though you pay it back, is another bad idea.

3. Never divert corporate funds to noncorporate uses. Protestations of honest mistakes are useless. You have a duty to know what is right and wrong. If you have the slightest suspicion or twinge of guilt, do not do it. It is not worth the trouble, and it is not worth the consequences.

4. Never sell company stock without board authorization. You cannot be issuing stock without corporate management discussing it and approving it. To do otherwise is a clear securities law violation.

5. Never start out undercapitalized. In some states, including California, failure to properly capitalize the company can lead to a piercing of the corporate veil. If it is going to cost $50,000 to open your business, do not start signing corporate contracts and making obligations with vendors with only $500 in the bank.

6. Never go a year without holding an annual meeting. Minutes of annual meetings—documents proving you understand the difference between you and the corporation on a continuing basis—are an absolute must. The annual and consistent preparation of meeting minutes is worthy of greater discussion.

Minutes of Meetings

An excellent way to prevent having your corporate veil pierced is to type up and keep minutes of your board of directors and shareholder meetings. Besides that, in most states, it is a matter of state law that you hold these meetings anyway. And while the LP and LLC laws in most states do not require annual meetings, it is not a bad idea to hold them as well, if only to avoid future miscommunications and misunderstandings.

People frequently state how difficult it is to prepare annual meeting minutes. For some it is like going to the dentist.

Fear not! It is not that difficult.

What follows are samples of the minutes of the first meeting of shareholders, the minutes of the board of directors' organizational meeting, as well as samples of the minutes of the annual meetings of shareholders and directors. You can use them to tailor meeting minutes to suit your needs. Or, if you still feel like you are about to sit in the dentist's chair, our firm or another service provider can do it for you. Our fee is $150 per year. (I guess that's better than going to the dentist.) The important thing is that they are prepared by someone on an annual basis to preserve your entity's limited liability protection.

Minutes of the First Meeting of Shareholders of XYZ, Inc.

Upon proper notice, the first meeting of XYZ, Inc. was held on _____,
20__. The meeting was called to order by Jack Smith, the incorporator, and the
following shareholders, being a majority of the shareholders of the Corporation,
were present:

Jack Smith
Jill Jones

Jack Smith acted as Secretary of the meeting.
There was presented to the meeting the following:

1. Copy of Certificate of Incorporation;
2. Copy of the Bylaws of the Corporation;
3. Resignation of the Incorporator;
4. Corporate certificate book; and
5. Corporate certificate ledger.

The Chairman noted that it was in order to consider electing a Board of Directors for the ensuing year. Upon nominations duly made, seconded, and unanimously carried, the following persons were elected as Directors of the Corporation, to serve for a period of one year and until such time as their successors are elected and qualify:

Jack Smith
Jill Jones

Upon motion duly made, seconded, and unanimously carried, it was

RESOLVED, that the items listed above have been examined by all shareholders, and are all approved and adopted, and that all acts taken and decisions reached as set forth in such documents be, and they hereby are, ratified and approved by the shareholders of the Corporation.

There being no further business to come before the meeting, upon motion duly made, seconded, and unanimously carried, it was adjourned.

_____
Jack Smith, Secretary

Organizational Minutes of the Board of Directors of XYZ, Inc.

The organization meeting of the Board of Directors of XYZ, Inc. was held on _____, 20__.

Jack Smith and Jill Jones constituting the total members of the initial Board of Directors of the Corporation, and a quorum, were present.

Jill Jones acted as Secretary of the meeting and Jack Smith acted as Chairman of the meeting.

The Chairman reported that the Articles of Incorporation had been filed with the Secretary of State of the State of _____. The Secretary was directed to insert a certified copy of the Articles in the minute books as part of these minutes.

The Secretary then presented the resignation of the incorporator. After reviewing the resignation of the incorporator, and upon motion duly made, seconded, and unanimously carried, it was:

RESOLVED, that the Board accept the resignation of the incorporator.

The Secretary submitted to the meeting a seal proposed for use as the corporate seal of the Corporation, along with a form of the stock certificate. After reviewing the seal and the stock certificate, and upon motion duly made, seconded, and unanimously carried, it was:

RESOLVED, that the form of the seal and the stock certificate submitted to this meeting are adopted and approved as the corporate seal and stock certificate of the Corporation. The Secretary of the Corporation is hereby authorized and directed to insert a copy of the stock certificate with these minutes, and to affix an impression of the seal on the margin of these minutes.

The Secretary then presented the proposed Code of Bylaws relating to the regulation of the business and affairs of the Corporation, its shareholders, Directors, and officers. After reviewing the proposed Code of Bylaws and upon motion duly made, seconded, and unanimously carried, it was:

RESOLVED, that the Bylaws presented to this meeting are adopted as the Bylaws of the Corporation, and the Secretary is directed to certify and insert the Bylaws into the minute book (containing the minutes of the proceedings of the Board of Directors and other relevant corporate documents).

The Chairman stated that the next order of business was the election of the officers as specified in the Bylaws. The Chairman called for nominations for officers to serve for one year or until their successors are elected or qualified. After discussion, the following persons were nominated and seconded to the following positions:

Jack Smith	President
Jill Jones	Secretary/Treasurer

The Chairman called for further nominations, but none were made. A voice vote was taken and since there was no opposition, the Chairman declared that the nominees are the duly elected officers of the Corporation to serve until the next annual Board meeting, or until their successors are elected and shall qualify.

The Chairman stated that the next order of business was to determine the compensation of the officers. After discussion and upon motion duly made, seconded, and unanimously carried, it was:

> **RESOLVED,** that the salary of the corporate officers shall be (_____) or (determined at a later date).

The Chairman stated that the next order of business was to consider paying all expenses and reimbursing all persons for expenses paid or incurred in connection with the formation and organization of the Corporation. After discussion, upon motion duly made, seconded, and unanimously carried, it was:

> **RESOLVED,** that the Treasurer of the Corporation be authorized and directed to pay all charges and expenses incident to the formation and organization of this Corporation and to reimburse all persons who have made any disbursements for such charges and expenses.

The Chairman stated the next order of business was to consider reimbursement to officers and Directors of the Corporation of travel and other expenses which such employees expend on behalf of the Corporation. After discussion and upon motion duly made, seconded, and unanimously carried, it was:

> **RESOLVED,** that the Corporation shall reimburse each officer and Director for any reasonable necessary expenses which they incur in connection with the purposes of the Corporation and in furtherance of its business.
>
> **RESOLVED FURTHER,** that it shall be the policy of this Corporation to reimburse each officer and Director or to pay directly on behalf of each officer or Director necessary and ordinary out-of-pocket expenses incidental to travel for all business activities of the Corporation requiring travel.

The Chairman stated that the next order of business was to consider an election under Section 248 of the Internal Revenue Code to amortize the organizational expense of the Corporation over a period of sixty (60) months, beginning with the first month of business of the Corporation. The Chairman explained that if the election was not made, the organizational expenses would constitute a nondeductible capital expenditure. After discussion, upon motion duly made, seconded, and unanimously carried, it was:

> **RESOLVED,** that beginning with the month in which the Corporation begins business, the Corporation commence amortizing its organizational expense over a period of sixty (60) months in accordance with Section 248 of the Internal Revenue Code.

The Chairman stated that the next order of business was the designation of a depository for the funds of the Corporation. After discussion, upon motion duly made, seconded, and unanimously carried, it was:

RESOLVED, that _____ is designated as the depository for the general account of the Corporation, and all checks, drafts, and orders on any of the accounts with the depository may be signed by the following: Jack Smith or Jill Jones. The President, Secretary, and Treasurer are authorized and directed to execute any documents necessary to open and continue any accounts with the depository.

FURTHER RESOLVED, that the Secretary of this Corporation be, and hereby is, instructed to annex a copy of such documents to the minutes of this meeting.

The Chairman stated that the next order of business was to consider the designation of a Registered Agent and registered office of the Corporation in the State of _____. The Chairman stated that the Articles of Incorporation stated that _____ is the Registered Agent of the Corporation and the principal place of business is _____. Upon motion duly made, seconded, and unanimously adopted, it was:

RESOLVED, that _____ be, and hereby is, appointed Registered Agent for the Corporation in the State of _____. The office of the Registered Agent is to be located at _____.

After a discussion and upon motion duly made, seconded, and unanimously carried, it was:

RESOLVED, that _____ be retained as the Corporation's legal counsel.

The Chairman stated that the next order of business was to consider the issuance of capital stock of the Corporation pursuant to Section 1244 of the Internal Revenue Code. The Chairman stated that Section 1244 permits ordinary loss treatment, as opposed to capital loss treatment when the holder of Section 1244 stock either sells or exchanges such stock at a loss or when such stock becomes worthless. After discussion, upon motion duly made, seconded, and unanimously carried, it was:

RESOLVED, that the capital stock of the Corporation shall be issued pursuant to Section 1244 of the Internal Revenue Code. The Corporation is authorized to offer and issue its authorized common stock. Said stock shall be issued only for money and other property (other than stock or securities). The officers of the Corporation are authorized and empowered, and directed to perform, any and all acts necessary to carry out this plan and to qualify the stock offered and issued under it as Section 1244 stock as that term is defined in Section 1244 of the Internal Revenue Code and the Regulations thereunder.

The Chairman stated that the next order of business was to consider the issuance of shares of the capital stock of the Corporation. The Chairman stated that the following individuals offered to acquire a total of _____ shares of common stock of the Corporation, $_____ par value, in exchange for a total of $_____.

Name	No. of Shares
Jack Smith	_____
Jill Jones	_____

The Chairman further explained that the stock, upon issuance, is to be fully paid and nonassessable. After discussion, upon motion duly made, seconded, and unanimously carried, it was:

RESOLVED, that in consideration for the payment of _____ Dollars ($_____), the Corporation shall issue to Jack Smith _____ shares of the Corporation's fully paid, nonassessable common stock having $_____ par value per share.

RESOLVED, that in consideration for the payment of _____ Dollars ($_____), the Corporation shall issue to Jill Jones _____ shares of the Corporation's fully paid, nonassessable common stock having $_____ par value per share.

RESOLVED FURTHER, that the President or Secretary of this Corporation be, and they hereby are, authorized and empowered to execute any and all other instruments and certificates, and to do and perform all other acts and things necessary, or by them deemed desirable, to effectuate the purposes of the foregoing resolutions.

The Chairman stated that the next order of business was to consider the adoption of a fiscal year for the Corporation. The Chairman explained that the Corporation could elect to end its fiscal year during any calendar month. Upon motion duly made, seconded, and unanimously carried, the following resolution was adopted:

RESOLVED, That any one of the President, Secretary, or Treasurer of this Corporation is hereby authorized to select _____ fiscal year for the Corporation by filing of a tax return, other appropriate tax form, or by any other proper action.

The Chairman stated that the next order of business was to authorize certain corporate officers to execute and deliver deeds, conveyances, promissory notes, deeds of trust, mortgages, and other instruments necessary to accomplish the aims and purposes of this Corporation. After discussion, and upon motion duly made, seconded, and unanimously carried, it was:

RESOLVED, that the Officers of the Corporation, and only the Officers of this Corporation, be and they hereby are, authorized and empowered, for and on behalf of this Corporation, and as its corporate act and deed, at any time, or from time to time, to negotiate for and/or to enter into any lease, leases, mortgages, promissory notes, other agreement, or other agreements with any party or parties, containing such terms and conditions as said Officers may deem necessary or desirable in order to promote and fully effectuate the conduct, by this Corporation, of its business and/or businesses.

The Chairman stated that the next order of business was to establish a time for the regular meetings of the Board.

RESOLVED, that the meetings of the Board of Directors of this Corporation be held at the principal office of the Corporation, or at such other location as a majority of the Board may determine, from time to time, as may be called by the President, and that no further notice of such regular meetings need be given.

There being no further business to come before the meeting, upon motion duly made, seconded, and unanimously carried, the Chairman declared the meeting adjourned.

_____
Jill Jones, Secretary

APPROVED:

_____
Jack Smith, Chairman

Minutes of Annual Meeting of Shareholders of XYZ, Inc.

The Meeting of Shareholders of the above-named Corporation was held upon proper notice on _____, 20__, at _____, __:__. The meeting was called to order by the President, heretofore elected by the Board of Directors, and the following shareholders, being a majority of the shareholders of the Corporation, were present:

Jack Smith
Jill Jones

Jill Jones was elected temporary Secretary of the meeting and took Minutes of it for the corporate records.

A discussion was then held regarding the election of the Board of Directors for the coming year. As the current board had performed well in the previous year and wished to continue, upon motion duly made, seconded, and unanimously carried, it was:

RESOLVED, that the following persons are elected Directors for the forthcoming year:

Jack Smith
Jill Jones

Further discussion was held regarding the services rendered by the previous year's Board of Directors, up to and including today's date. Services had been well performed. As a result, upon motion duly made, seconded, and unanimously carried, it was:

RESOLVED, that the shareholders ratify the actions of the Board of Directors for the previous year.

There being no further business to come before the meeting, upon motion duly made, seconded, and unanimously carried, it was adjourned.

_____
Secretary

Minutes of Annual Meeting of Board of Directors of XYZ, Inc.

The annual meeting of the Board of Directors of XYZ, Inc., a Nevada corporation, was held upon proper notice on _____, 20__, immediately following the conclusion of the annual meeting of shareholders of the corporation.

Present in person or telephonically were the following directors:

Jack Smith
Jill Jones

The President called the meeting to order. The meeting then proceeded to elect officers to serve until the next annual directors meeting. The following nominations were made and seconded:

NAME	OFFICE
Jack Smith	President
Jill Jones	Secretary/Treasurer

There being no further nominations the foregoing persons were unanimously elected to the offices set forth opposite their respective names. Each of the officers so elected thereupon accepted the office to which he was elected as aforestated.

[Insert any specific corporate issues here.]

A discussion was then had regarding the actions taken in the preceding year on behalf of the company.

After further discussion it was:

RESOLVED, that the actions taken by the officers in the preceding year on behalf of the company were approved and ratified.

There being no further business, the meeting was adjourned.

_____
Secretary

Wasn't that easy. You just saved your home and your car and your bank account. Now your spouse won't leave you for screwing up and allowing the corporate veil to be pierced. Prepare the minutes. Follow the formalities.

Rich Dad Tips

- It is important to keep your minutes in a safe place. Obviously, losing or misplacing them does not fit into your protection strategy.
- Corporate minute books are binders for holding your meeting minutes as well as articles, bylaws, and other corporate documents. They generally cost about $75, and if they force you to be organized it will be money well spent.

Again, remember that minutes are your friends. By illustrating an appropriate level of duty to the corporation, they will protect officers and directors from litigation. The following list contains some of the items to be reviewed by the officers and directors and reflected in the minutes:

- Electing officers of the company
- Amending the articles of incorporation
- Amending the bylaws
- Adopting a stock option plan
- Approving the issuance of securities and granting warrants and options
- Declaring stock splits or dividends
- Entering into a buy-sell agreement (see Chapter 16)
- Entering into employment contracts with key employees
- Approving contracts, leases, and other obligations
- Borrowing significant sums and the granting of security in connection therewith
- Acquiring other businesses
- Buying or selling significant assets
- Forming subsidiaries
- Merging or reorganizing the company
- Responses to tender offers
- Resistance to proxy contests

- Approval of proxy statements
- Taking other actions material to the business

The formalities are not that difficult. And it is certainly worth the protection. And since you are following the formalities, now you can take advantage of all the deductions . . .

Chapter 9

Business Tax Deductions

Are tax deductions available to the average employee?

No.

Once the required income and employment taxes are withheld from the wage earner's paycheck are there any useful deductions for an employee to take?

Not really.

What about business owners? Do they get to take advantage of tax deductions?

Absolutely.

Read on to understand the reasons why...

As a business owner, a whole range of useful and beneficial tax deductions are available to you that are not available to employees.

While this may not seem fair to some at first, it is important to understand a key difference between business owners and employees, a difference savvy business owners keenly appreciate:

Employees are paid first.

Business owners risk their money (as well as time and energy) to make more money. But when they hire people to work for them, state and federal laws essentially require that employees be paid first, even if the business owner is losing money. Failure to pay employees (and especially their payroll taxes) can lead to big problems for the entrepreneur, including civil and criminal penalties.

But in exchange for this regimen the tax code acknowledges the risks that entrepreneurs take every day.

Business owners spend their own money, other people's money, and even borrowed money to make even more money. And they don't make a profit until all the various expenses are taken into account. So taxes are based on net profits, the money left over after all the employees, vendors, landlords, advisors, and various other service and product providers are paid first.

The difference in how businesses are taxed (last—after everyone else is paid) versus how employees are taxed (first and forever—on the very first and the very last dollar of income) is a crucial one to understand. For in the ability to take business tax deductions comes one of the finest, most beneficial, and thoroughly legitimate ways to reduce your taxes.

By paying attention to your deductions and by working with your tax advisor and bookkeeper to legally maximize your write-offs, you can save thousands to tens of thousands of dollars a year or more in taxes. These savings are money in your pocket. Business owners can also improve the quality of their lives with a proper deduction strategy.

Entrepreneurs can deduct four types of business expenses:

- Start-up expenses
- Operating expenses
- Inventory costs
- Capital expenses

Let's briefly understand each category.

Start-up Expenses

The various costs involved in getting your business up and running such as attorney and CPA fees, office and printing expenses, license fees, and the like are deductible. Some fees can be deducted in the first year. Others are deductible over a period of sixty months. Work with your advisor on maximizing these rules.

Operating Expenses

The day-to-day expenses of keeping the business open are deductible in the year the expense is incurred. Salaries, rent, utilities, travel and auto expenses, supplies, and repairs are examples of operating expenses. It is in this category that business owners may find the most beneficial deductions.

Inventory

If you make or buy products to resell to others you have inventory. The costs of inventory are dealt with separately from other expenses and are deducted as you sell your inventory. Be sure to work with your CPA to properly track your inventory expenses.

Capital Expenses

Cars, equipment, office furniture, and other assets that have a useful life of over one year are considered capital assets. The costs associated with these assets are called capital expenses and are treated differently from operating expenses. Capital expenses must be depreciated, which means deductions are pro-rated over the capital asset's useful life. A car may have a five-year useful life whereas a desk may have a twelve-year life. You will work with your advisor to establish the appropriate depreciation schedules.

A great option for small business owners involves Section 179 deductions. Instead of depreciating capital assets over a period of years, Section 179 allows annual deductions of up to $128,000 as of this writing. For the current Section 179 deduction, visit www.corporatedirect.com/accounting. Using Section 179 at the end of your accounting year, for example, can provide your business with the necessary equipment, vehicles, and the like, while also providing a welcome business deduction to reduce your yearly tax obligation.

Now let's review a case where business deductions make a big difference in one couple's life.

Case No. 16—Tony and Theresa

Tony and Theresa were happily married with two young children, a dog, and a monthly mortgage. Tony worked as a lab technician at a local hospital. Theresa took care of the children and did part-time floral arranging for a local florist while they were in school. While Tony made a decent salary they never seemed to have enough money at the end of the month. They had not started to save for their children's college tuition, nor had they started to save for their own retirement.

Tony and Theresa knew a number of other couples who faced the same situation. In many cases both spouses were working at full-time jobs and still not getting ahead. Many were resigned to the hope that somehow things would work out. Their children would get college scholarships and student loans. Social Security would provide comfort in retirement.

But Theresa could not rely on such fuzzy hopes. She did not want her children starting out with huge student loans to pay back. And she certainly did not believe that Social Security would be there for her. Not with millions upon millions of baby boomers set to retire.

So Tony and Theresa talked about how they could improve their financial situation. They reviewed their current needs. Tony was a full-time employee at the hospital. He received medical insurance but had to pay for the rest of the family's coverage with after-tax dollars. He also received a small retirement benefit. The two of them liked to travel and tried to take one or two decent trips per year. In terms of cars, Tony had a newer Ford Escape that served them well. But Theresa had a beat-up Honda Civic that she did not like taking the children around in. And the children were getting older and needed to start using a computer at home in order to keep up in school. The family did not own a computer.

Tony and Theresa listed these and many other factors on a piece of paper. Upon review, it seemed that Tony was in a good position to provide for the family. What was needed was a way for Theresa to be able to work and provide some additional benefits for the family.

Theresa had learned that a friend of hers recently went into a network marketing business. In network marketing, one can benefit from the sale of a product that is personally distributed, as well as from sales of a product sold by persons he or she brought into the program. In some cases these outside salespeople can be quite lucrative for the person at the top of the network. While she knew network marketing was not for everyone, Theresa's friend said she had formed a corporation so that she could take pretax deductions for expenses that benefited the family.

Theresa was personable and confident and felt she could do well in network marketing. And she liked the idea of using the corporate tax laws to benefit her family.

With the help of a professional Theresa formed T&T, Inc., to pursue her network marketing business. She investigated a number of network businesses carefully and found a good opportunity for growth and income. After several hard months Theresa started making headway. Soon she was bringing money into the corporation. And, as importantly, she was benefiting her family as follows:

Office Rent Expense

Theresa set up a spare bedroom in her house as her office. She learned that to rent 140 square feet (the size of the bedroom) in her town would cost $1.75 per square foot, or $245 per month. T&T, Inc., then paid this amount to her and Tony for the use of the office. This payment to them was rental income against which they wrote off a pro rata portion of the property taxes, mortgage interest, insurance, and utilities.

Start-up Expenses

The cost of printing up business cards, incorporating, joining the network marketing program, and the like were all expenses that T&T, Inc., could and did deduct.

Meals

Theresa, along with Tony and their children, could have meals at T&T, Inc.'s expense as long as they were furnished on the premises of the business. That was easy: On occasion they went into the spare bedroom for a tax-free business meal.

It should be noted that caution is required in this realm. Remember, pigs get fat and hogs get slaughtered. You are not going to eat every possible meal in the spare bedroom and hope to get a year's deduction on meals. Be prudent. Also note that only 50 percent of your meal costs can be deducted while traveling.

Computer Expense

Theresa needed a computer for her business. She learned that she could deduct $128,000 a year (the law at this edition) for the purchase of equipment and business assets. Amounts over $128,000 in purchases needed to be depreciated (written off) over a five-year period. So Theresa spent $1,500 on a new computer and printer and wrote the whole amount off against income. If she had purchased the computer outside the business she would have had to use after-tax dollars, monies already reduced by Tony and Theresa's 28 percent tax bracket. In essence the computer equipment would have cost her another $420.

The family had needed a computer. While its actual main use was for T&T, Inc.'s business, the fact that the children used it now and then to explore the Internet and play computer games was de minimis, meaning not enough for T&T, Inc., to charge Theresa for its personal use. And now there was a way for Theresa to keep upgrading her computer with pretax dollars.

Telephone Expense

The IRS does not allow a family's main telephone line to be a business deduction. That was fine with Theresa. The company needed its own line listed in its own name anyway. And the second line was useful when people were on the Internet or the fax machine was being used. The business line was a fully deductible expense.

Employee Expense

As Theresa began to succeed in her network marketing business and money flowed into T&T, Inc., it came time to draw an employee paycheck. This meant calculating payroll taxes and making mandatory tax deposits with the IRS.

It is not that hard to do. On a salary up to $102,000 (as of this edition), the employee and the corporation split the 15.3 percent tax that goes for Social Security and Medicare. On a salary above $102,000 (again, as of this writing), the Medicare tax of 2.9 percent is split between employee and employer (T&T, Inc.). Your accountant can easily calculate these numbers for you. It is important to note that if Theresa did not use a corporation but rather was self-employed, she would have to pay the 15.3 percent herself, without half of it being a deduction to the corporation.

Now that she was an employee, Theresa had even more benefits available to her.

Auto Allowance

The Honda Civic was on its final lap. It was time to get another car. Theresa had a choice of buying or leasing a car herself and charging T&T, Inc., for its use, or having T&T, Inc., buy or lease the car itself. For Theresa the deciding factors were that she could use the Civic personally as a trade-in and that T&T, Inc., was a new corporation and not likely to get financing.

Theresa traded in the Honda Civic for a three-year-old Ford Windstar minivan coming off a lease. It was a good vehicle for transporting her network marketing products. And it was safe and roomy for the children. She and Tony worked out the deal and arranged to purchase it over a five-year period. She estimated her miles at 1,000 per month and had T&T, Inc., pay her an auto allowance of $505.00 per month (1,000 miles x 50.5¢ [at this writing] per mile IRS car allowance). It was her responsibility to pay for the gas, maintenance, and car insurance. But the $505.00 was enough to pay for all that and the monthly car payment. The money T&T, Inc., paid to her for the car allowance was not reportable on her personal tax return but she was responsible for keeping good records and reporting her mileage to the corporation on a consistent basis.

Achievement Awards

A corporation can give up to $400 a year for a nonqualified achievement award or up to $1,600 under a defined qualified plan. While the qualified plan requires a written plan that does not favor the top paid employees, the nonqualified plan has no specific guidelines. So Theresa gave herself a $400 award for being T&T, Inc.'s best employee. It did not matter that she was the only employee. This was a tax free gift to her and a deduction for the corporation.

Travel Expenses

Theresa's network marketing group had fantastic annual meetings in desirable destinations. She could deduct her travel, lodging, transportation, and half her meals. Tony would have to pay his own travel and meals, but the rest was paid for by the business. One year the group held their meeting in Paris. Tony and Theresa had never been to Europe. Theresa had learned from her accountant that there were special rules for writing off foreign travel. But as long as there was a business purpose to the travel, it was for one week or less (not counting travel days), and Theresa spent 75 percent or more of the time involved in business, she could write off her foreign travel. The trip to Paris was a memorable deduction for them.

Health Insurance

The corporation paid for Theresa's health, dental, and eye insurance, and for her dependents as well. In this way Tony could stop paying extra for dependent health coverage at work, saving the family $175 a month. T&T, Inc.'s health insurance plan also paid for disability insurance in case something happened to Theresa.

Group Term Life Insurance

T&T, Inc., provided each employee (Theresa) with $50,000 worth of term life insurance. This was a valuable benefit to Theresa and a deduction for the corporation.

Dependent Care

T&T, Inc., could pay up to $5,000 in dependent care services per employee. (The amount is $2,500 if you are married and filing separately.) This deduction is only available for dependents under the age of thirteen. (If you have children over age thirteen, a cafeteria plan, described below, can be used.) This deduction of $5,000 was valuable to Theresa because with all her work she needed help covering the children after school.

Cafeteria Plan

In order to maximize deductions for day care and term life insurance, Theresa looked into instituting a cafeteria plan. This is a benefits package that allows employees the choice of receiving cash or qualified benefits. A set amount is withheld from the employee's check, before payroll taxes. This amount is set aside for the employee to later use in the benefits cafeteria. Some can be used for day care, even for children over thirteen, some can be used for additional term life insurance, medical insurance, or medical expenses. Like a cafeteria, you get to select what you want.

It was also favorably noted by Theresa, as the employer and owner of T&T, Inc., that the monies put into a cafeteria plan were not subject to payroll taxes. Neither T&T, Inc., nor Theresa individually had to pay their half of the 15.3 percent in payroll taxes to receive the significant benefits of the cafeteria plan.

Education/Dues/Subscriptions

Theresa had always wanted to finish her college degree. She only had ten units to go. With T&T, Inc., now able to deduct day care, she had time to go to her local college again. And the beauty was, because her degree would improve her skills needed for her trade and business, her education expenses, including tuition and books, were deductible for T&T, Inc. By later hiring her children as employees, T&T, Inc., could set up an educational assistance plan and pay up to $5,000 per year of their education.

Theresa had also joined a Women in Business organization. She found it valuable to meet with other entrepreneurs and share ideas. As long as the organization's principal purpose was not simply to hold entertainment activities for its guests (like a country club), the dues and related expenses could be deducted. In this case, the group conducted professional seminars and workshops and so Theresa was justified in writing off the dues.

Theresa also loved reading magazines like *Inc.* and *Entrepreneur.* These were expenses that T&T, Inc., could write off.

Retirement Plans

Theresa learned that there were two types of retirement plans she could utilize that were available to corporations, LLCs, and sole proprietorships. But with a sole proprietorship there were significant disadvantages. The sole proprietorship is a bad entity when it comes to retirement because:

(1) All retirement contributions are subject to self-employment taxes; and

(2) There is no ERISA (Employee Retirement Income Security Act) protection, and therefore no asset protection, in a sole proprietorship retirement plan.

A defined contribution plan allows for 15 percent of eligible compensation up to $35,000 (or more in later years) per year to be set aside for retirement. This is a deduction to the corporation and a benefit to Theresa.

A defined benefit plan allows contributions in excess of $140,000 based upon your salary. It is important to note that a defined benefit plan is a yearly requirement—your corporation, whether it had a good year or not, must put in a fixed amount of money in order to meet a defined benefit in the future. As a start-up Theresa did not favor such a requirement.

Because the defined contribution plan was more flexible and contributions could be based upon how well the corporation did in a given year, Theresa chose to set up an adjustable 401(k). If the corporation did well and her salary was $100,000 she could have T&T, Inc., set aside $15,000 for her retirement.

As well, if her defined contribution plan or defined benefit plan was qualified (meaning approved by the IRS under ERISA rules), she had tremendous asset protection. A creditor cannot touch an ERISA. Your retirement monies are safe.

Conclusion

Both Theresa and Tony were pleased with the way T&T, Inc., worked for them. They used the tax code to their advantage, freeing up Tony's salary for greater retirement and college savings and quality-of-life improvements.

Rich Dad Tips

- To fully maximize your corporation (or LLC or LP) and the available deductions it offers, consider adding a good accountant to your team.
- You may want to also consider going to the IRS Web site and obtaining Publication 334, "Tax Guide for Small Businesses," to learn more about the deductions you can take.

Chapter 10

Building Corporate Credit

Another advantage of owning a corporation is the ability to build a corporate credit rating separate from your personal credit. Properly established, a corporate credit rating will:

- Allow you to borrow in the business's name rather than your own name.
- Protect your personal credit score, which can be easily damaged if you carry a lot of debt for your business on your own personal credit cards and lines of credit.
- Maximize business tax deductions.
- Write off certain losses, including in many cases, loans you make to your business.
- Avoid personal guarantees on certain loans, leases, and lines of credit.
- Grow your business!

Statistics show that most small businesses will borrow at some point or another. If you really want a successful business, you will want to leverage other people's money using corporate credit.

To do this, though, you will have to navigate the complex world of business credit reporting. There are many agencies collecting and selling business credit reports, although there are several major players:

- D&B (formerly known as Dun & Bradstreet)
- Experian
- Small Business Financial Exchange (SBFE)/Equifax

In addition there are many smaller and specialized business credit reporting agencies. These include agencies that focus on certain industries, such as eCredit (transportation, industrial supply, manufacturing, office supply, equipment leasing, and other industries) and the National Telecommunications Data Exchange, Inc. (telecommunications account history). There are also credit groups that meet in person to share information and trends, as well as companies that focus on selling public information.

Most businesses move through a series of three levels in building business credit. It is important to know these three levels, and where you fit among them.

Level One: Whatever It Takes

Many entrepreneurial businesses have not built business credit. They use whatever method of financing they can get. At Level One, they have "bootstrapped it" and used personal credit cards, loans from friends and family, equity from their home, and the like. They've often done this with no formal loan agreements between themselves and their business. And they've taken some serious risks:

- They are mixing business and personal credit, which can create major headaches at tax time.
- There is no asset protection whatsoever, as they are personally liable for personal debt.
- Their personal credit score will likely sink due to the level of debt they are carrying to fund their business. This can trigger higher interest rates on their personal credit cards, even if the bills are paid on time.

Level Two: Wising Up

At Level Two the business owner begins to separate business credit from personal credit. Most owners who move to this level have incorporated their business, since it is difficult to get separate business credit cards or loans in the name of a sole proprietorship. At Level Two, business owners will apply for credit cards, lines of credit, or trade accounts in their business name. You may still have to personally guarantee that credit at this stage, but those accounts usually will not be reported on your personal credit report unless you default.

While most business owners would like to avoid personal credit checks and personal guarantees (which generally happen at Level Three), Level Two business credit is still valuable, because it helps protect your own credit rating.

Using your personal credit for business can definitely have a negative impact on your credit score. We've talked to business owners with $50,000 to $100,000 in personal credit card debt for their businesses. Even if you pay your bills on time, having too many accounts with high balances, or balances too close to the limits on your individual accounts, can hurt your personal credit score—probably more than you realize. As a result of these high balances, it is not unusual for your interest rates on your credit cards to go up—sometimes to as high as 29 percent.

If, instead, you use business credit cards for business debt, in most cases that will not be reported on your personal credit and you will avoid hurting your personal credit. Even in cases where lenders check your personal credit report before extending business credit, the only impact on your credit will be that inquiry, which should be minor unless you are creating numerous inquiries in a short period of time.

Rich Dad Tip

- Whenever possible, use business credit cards or loans rather than personal credit, even if you have to give a personal guarantee.

A small business can chug along at Level Two for quite a while as long as the bills get paid on time. But if you are serious about your business you will want to move to Level Three.

Level Three: Established Business Credit

Level Three is where your corporation establishes its own business credit rating completely separate from your personal credit rating. At Level Three, you will have:

- Obtained credit with vendors and financial institutions that report to major commercial reporting agencies and paid those accounts on time.
- Followed steps to ensure that your business appears stable and solid.
- Established strong credit profiles with the major business credit reporting agencies.
- Implemented accounting systems that allow you to generate financial statements as needed.

At Level Three you will find yourself with opportunities to borrow or lease without having to rely on your personal credit or provide personal guarantees. This, of course, is the level most business owners want to reach as quickly as possible. There is no magical formula or guaranteed shortcut for reaching Level Three, and some businesses will get there faster than others.

Like personal credit reports, business credit is established when your bills are paid on time. There are some significant differences between business and personal credit reports however:

- No federal law covers business credit reports. That means there are no specific requirements regarding accuracy, disputes, or disclosure. If there is a mistake it can be difficult to correct!
- Income does matter. The best credit ratings go to companies with large revenues and large numbers of employees. However, do *not* provide financials to credit agencies that request it unless they are prepared by a tax professional, and you are willing to reveal that data on an annual basis.
- Business credit cards may *not* be a major factor in building business credit. Some may not even be reported.
- It can be much more difficult to find lenders and vendors that report to commercial reporting agencies, and also to identify the agencies to which they report.

The biggest difference, though, is that with corporate credit you must start building credit before you get your first credit reference. The process starts when you set up your corporation. You must make it appear as solid and stable as possible to the reporting agencies. This isn't all for show, though, because the same steps you take to establish your business for credit purposes will help your business in an overall sense anyway. Some of the steps you should take here include making sure your corporation is properly registered in your state and that your corporate filings stay up to date. You should get a business license from your state and/or local licensing agencies. You should have a phone number that is listed with 411 directory assistance. And you will definitely want a business bank account.

It's also important to keep in mind that as a business owner, you should diligently monitor your personal credit, and keep it in the best shape possible. You may have heard that small business and personal credit are completely separate, and often they can be. Some of the business credit bureaus, such as D&B, for example, do not collect information on individuals' personal credit histories, so that information will not become part of the business's credit score. But agencies such as Experian and Equifax also collect and maintain consumer's personal credit ratings, and they may blend that information with the business's credit score to produce a combined score for a small business, or a score for the business owner.

You may have also seen marketing hype about how a business credit profile can overcome a bad personal credit file. In most cases, however, it's important that small businesses have *both* good business credit, as well as solid personal credit on the part of the owners. Even established businesses at Level Three business credit will find it necessary in some cases to provide the business owner's personal guarantees on loans or credit cards.

Watch Out for Scams

As a small business owner, you wear many hats and you certainly do not have the time or money to waste on programs that don't work. There are many expensive business credit-building programs out there that make exaggerated promises. Watch out!

- Don't try to "buy" good credit. Some companies will offer to "sell" trade references for a large sum of money. This is a rip-off and if the credit reporting agencies find out, they will purge those references.
- Don't spend large sums of money on a shelf corporation—an entity formed several years ago that has sat inactive on the shelf. Some companies will "guarantee" you will be able to use it to get loans. More often than not, the company may not have the kind of credit rating you'll need to be successful. (That said, some properly aged

companies, ones which have built their business credit profiles, can be of benefit.)

- Don't try to get business credit as a substitute for bad personal credit. If you have damaged personal credit, work on rebuilding it at the same time that you are building business credit.

Get Started Now

Now is always the time to start building business credit. With legitimate trade references and by following the steps above you can reach Level Three.

Entrepreneurs are hardworking, creative, and willing to get the job done. Fortunately, those are the same qualities that will help you through the process of building strong business credit. For more information on these valuable strategies visit www.BusinessCreditSuccess.com.

Chapter 11

Insurance

Your business, your assets, your money, your reputation. You want to protect all of them. As a business owner today, you're working in a litigious world. You're also working in a business world that gives you the tools to protect yourself, your business, and your assets. But just as you need to know how to run your business, knowing how to protect your assets means understanding the ins and outs of insuring every aspect of it. Asset protection strategies (corporations, LLCs, and the like) are one line of defense. The first line of defense is insurance.

Insurance is a double-edged sword. The right policy can protect your property and your business. But assembled the wrong way, the premiums can eat up your profits. That said, going without insurance may put your asset protection strategies to the test. And let us be clear about the protection involved. If your business operates as a corporation and is sued, the corporation will protect your outside assets (your house and other nonbusiness assets) from attack. But your inside assets, the ones held by the business, may be reached in a lawsuit against the business. So in that case business insurance will assist in protecting business assets.

Before deciding whether or not to forgo insurance, weigh the pros and cons of having protection or going it on your own. What—and how much—do you have to lose? You might also determine whether a compromise would work for you—insure your business, but with very high deductibles so that if something happens, you're shouldering a considerable part of the burden of putting things back to normal. But if nothing ever happens, you're not losing all your profits to paying insurance premiums.

For many entrepreneurs, the safest route in the long run is to insure your business. Once you've determined to do so, you need to take a look at the types of protection and policies out there.

Real Property and Personal Property Insurance

If you own the building you're working out of, it is in your best interest to insure it. If you're a tenant renting space, you may be listed on your landlord's insurance agreement. Even so, it's probably a good idea to have your own renter's insurance policy rather than worrying about whether your landlord is keeping his or hers up to date, and how much of your property it protects.

If you're working out of your home, make sure your insurance agent knows it, because if it's not noted in the policy that some of your personal property is part of your business, the policy may exclude it, either intentionally or unintentionally.

You'll need to work with your insurance agent to determine what policy is going to work best for you. Ideally, when it comes to real property you should have enough coverage to handle replacing the building to meet your current needs. This may be easier said than done.

Putting together a policy where you're paying the lowest possible premiums may not be in your best interest. If you value your building and personal property at less than their replacement cost in order to pay lower premiums, the insurance company will reimburse you based on the lower valuation, leaving you to make up the difference while trying to pull your business back together after a disaster.

Valuation of real property will increase over the years, so work with your agent to make sure you understand how the insurance company determines increased valuation and what that means to your premiums. Some companies use actual value adjustment, and others calculate value based on the inflation factor. The language of insurance coverage can be confusing. Work with your agent to know exactly how your assets are being valued.

Replacement Cost vs. Current Value

For once, insurance-speak means exactly what it says. If you insure your property for replacement costs, it means the insurance company is going to reimburse you for the property you've lost, regardless of what wear and tear or depreciation that property has been subject to. If you insure for current value, the insurance company can reduce payments on lost property based on its age, perceived value, and depreciation. Replacement cost may be a better option for many.

When you're insuring the equipment and personal property that makes up your business, make a complete inventory, including all of the items the business is using that belong to you. This list, and even a video of your business operations, can be used to certify what was used in the business prior to a loss.

Liability Insurance

Remember, there's more to running a business than the equipment you use and the place you use it. If you're producing a product that goes out into the world to be used or consumed by others, there's a chance you could be sued by users or consumers of your product. Product liability insurance protects you by covering injuries caused by the products you manufacture or supply. In the event of a product liability lawsuit, there's apt to be multiple injured parties suing. Injuries can be extensive, and costs can be high. Work carefully with your insurance agent to determine the amount of product liability insurance your company needs.

If you're working in a professional capacity, such as a doctor, lawyer, or engineer, you'll want to look into professional liability insurance, which is essentially malpractice insurance. Such coverage is available but expensive, which leads some business owners to consider going it alone. There is certainly a risk in going without this type of insurance if you're working in a professional capacity. As we discussed in Chapter 6, professionals are personally liable for their professional acts. So even if you've set up a corporation or limited liability company for your business, you can still be vulnerable. In a malpractice action, without any additional planning, your personal assets can be at risk alongside your business assets. Professionals and business owners need to work with their advisors to minimize this exposure.

Many liability protection policies not only protect you and your personal assets in the event of a suit for injury, libel, or slander, they also afford you the additional benefit of having the insurance company's legal team on your side if you are sued. Of course when you are sued, the insurance company is at risk of having to pay up if the suit is lost. That's not their favorite part of the business, so they'll bring in their legal resources to support you from the beginning. With the costs of legal proceedings today, it is a valuable benefit.

And what if you can't work? If a natural disaster strikes or there's a fire, business interruption insurance will protect against lost income during the time it takes for you to get back on your feet again. Obviously your policy will determine the limits on how long the insurance agency will make payments and how much they will pay—the protection is just to see you up and running again. In determining whether to agree to a policy that includes business interruption insurance, take inventory of the equipment you would stand to lose if a natural disaster or fire occurred, what you would need to get started again, how long you think it would take, and how much you'd lose in profits while you were down. The right level of coverage could make a big difference.

Director and Officer Liability Coverage

In addition to protecting the real and personal property of your business and to having professional liability coverage, if your business is a corporation the directors and officers may also need coverage.

Insurance coverage for directors and officers (known as D&O policies) come in several types. The first, A-side coverage, covers directors and officers for wrongful acts committed in their capacity as officers or directors of the corporation that the company doesn't indemnify them against. An additional protection of A-side coverage is A-side DIC (difference in coverage), which covers directors and officers for acts for which they are not permitted or required to be indemnified.

B-side coverage covers the corporation itself for wrongful acts committed by directors and officers for which the company *has* indemnified them. C-side coverage covers losses suffered by the corporation due to such wrongful acts, regardless of whether the directors or officers suffer losses.

All of the coverages available to a corporation's directors and officers are expensive but may be worthwhile—the trick is trying to keep premiums low. We will make a few more points about D&O policies in Chapter 14, but for now consider that many outside directors (those not directly involved with the business) will not serve on a board of directors without such insurance. Know this before you ask someone with savvy to serve.

Reading the Fine Print

Just as with other types of insurance for your business, you need to make sure the policy covering directors and officers covers everything you intended. Carefully read the policy with your insurance agent and ask for explanations of anything that doesn't make sense. Coverage is determined by the terminology of an insurance policy. Make sure what sorts of claims are covered, and what determines the type of claims excluded. Understand such things as hammer clauses, which state the insurer may settle a claim for whatever it considers reasonable as long as it has consent of the insured, and that if the bullheaded insured (i.e., you) withholds consent, that the insurer may refuse to cover any part of the loss that exceeds what the settlement would have been. Can you feel that hammer?

When agreeing to any insurance policy, understand that the application process with the insurer is exacting and important to your business. Insurers will use any misinterpretation made in the application as a basis for denying a claim or rescinding the policy. If they find any evidence that the business knew of impending claims against the directors or officers, or knew of any act or omission that could result in a claim, you will be fighting not only the claimant but your insurance company as well.

For any type of policy you need to understand the amount and extent of deductibles required by the policy, and whether the insurer demands co-payments, which require the insured to pay a portion of any claim. Insurance policies may be basic, broad, or special, and while each policy has its advantages, special is the only one that covers everything that isn't specifically excluded in the policy. Basic and broad policies only cover items stated in the contract, so if you choose either, make sure you've done a complete, exacting inventory. Special form policies cost more in the form of premiums but may well be worth it.

When you're setting up your insurance policy, pay specific attention to the verbiage and terminology utilized. Again, insurers frequently try to limit their liability. If you don't understand something in the contract or if you're unsure what is being covered, contact your insurance agent in writing and keep a copy of the correspondence. If anything happens and you end up in court against the insurance agency, you'll have a paper trail.

The following is a useful Insurance Coverage Checklist:

1. What insurance policies do you currently have in place for your business?

   ____ Real property (real estate)   ____ Personal property
   ____ Liability insurance
   ____ Professional liability insurance   ____ Business interruption
   ____ Director/Officer liability

2. What is your deductible on your policies?
3. If you had a higher deductible, what would happen to your premiums?
4. Do you have a co-payment, and if so, how much?
5. Are you covered for replacement cost or current value?
6. Is your real property (real estate) covered 100 percent?
7. Is your personal property and equipment covered?
8. If you rent space, do you have your own insurance policy or are you depending on your landlord's policy?
9. If you have a home office, does your insurance company know about it?
10. What changes can you put in place to protect your business and lower your premiums?
11. What is the limit on your professional liability protection? What does it cover?
12. What protections does your insurance policy offer if a lawsuit against your company ends up in court?
13. Does the insurance company pay costs to defend the lawsuit?
14. Do you need the directors and officers liability protection?
15. Are you satisfied with your current insurance agent? Do they assist with risk management and planning, or do they just send you premium notices?

——————————— **Rich Dad Tips** ———————————

- Never let an insurance agent advise you that you don't need a corporation or LLC. They are commissioned salespeople, not asset protection attorneys.
- Insurance companies find reasons to deny coverage. Your properly formed corporation or LLC will never do that to you.
- Work only with an insurance professional you have enough confidence in to be on the same team with your attorney, CPA, and banker.

Chapter 12

Protect Your Entity Name

A very important and often overlooked element in forming a corporation, LLC, or LP is choosing the right name.

What's in a name? A lot of headaches if you are not careful.

Case No. 17—Cathy and Peter

Cathy and Peter had decided to form a computer leasing business to be called CompuCo. When they called their southeastern state's secretary of state to see if the name was available it was. They incorporated under the name CompuCo and started doing business. They thought the name issue was resolved by incorporating with the name they wanted.

But the name issue was far from over. Cathy and Peter were good businesspeople and their enterprise flourished. So much so that they started to attract the attention of other similar businesses. One was a large, well-financed company out of California's Silicon Valley. They were very interested in CompuCo's business because, of all things, their name was also CompuCo and they held the federal trademark registration on the name.

CompuCo of California sent Cathy and Peter a cease-and-desist letter demanding that they stop using the name CompuCo. It was asserted, correctly, that with their federal trademark registration they owned all rights to the mark throughout the entire United States.

And because they were from Silicon Valley, where everything regarding intellectual property is important and litigated, CompuCo demanded that

Cathy and Peter pay them $500,000 for their infringement of the CompuCo name.

Cathy and Peter were devastated. They did not have that kind of money. They had only been using the name locally for sixteen months. How much damage could there be?

They promptly went to an attorney. After reviewing the case, the attorney explained that they had to immediately stop using the CompuCo name. He explained that a corporate name is just that—the ability to use the name without confusion in the secretary of state's office. Your entity name has nothing to do with marketing a business. For that you need a trademark.

A trademark is any word, phrase, slogan, symbol, or design that is used to distinguish a product or service. Trademarks are usually a name or logo but they can be other distinguishing characteristics such as the shape of a container or the design and color of a label. You can now trademark a scent or sound. Marks that designate services are sometimes called service marks but their legal function is the same.

The attorney explained that if you do not do a search to see if a trademark is available for your name, and someone else is using that name, you can run into big problems.

Still, he saw CompuCo of California's letter for what it was: protection of the mark. If a trademark owner learns of someone else using their mark they must take all steps to protect it—or lose their own rights to the mark. CompuCo had to send such a letter to protect themselves.

The lawyer called CompuCo and worked things out. Cathy and Peter promptly stopped using the name without the payment of additional monies and the matter was resolved.

But it cost them over $25,000 to create a new logo and change their name on all their brochures and advertising, as well as pay their attorney's fees. This money would not have been lost if they had done a proper trademark search and trademark filing in the first place.

In a competitive marketplace, few things are as valuable as instant customer recognition of your product or service. Businesses in the United States invest billions of dollars each year to establish their products or services in the minds of their customers. Trademarks are the primary means of establishing instant customer recognition.

Trademarks can be stolen, lost, and weakened if they are not protected properly. Federal trademark registration is the strongest tool available for protecting trademarks. The benefits of federal trademark registration include:

- Protect customer recognition and goodwill developed in your mark
- Protect your investment in advertising and promotions
- Prevent conflicts with other companies that may use your name in the future
- Reserve names that you intend to use in the future
- Gain income from licensing the mark to others
- Give constructive notice of ownership to all later users of the mark
- Have the right to display the federal registration symbol: ®
- Gain the right to make the mark "incontestable" after five years of continuous use
- Have a presumption of ownership if the mark ends up in litigation
- Allow registrants to use the federal courts in a dispute

Mark Searches

Before choosing a name for your business, product, or service, you must do a mark search. As with the CompuCo example, a comprehensive search before you have developed a market presence with an unacceptable name prevents costly and frustrating name changes later. If you choose a name that is being used by another company, you may be drawn into litigation and forced to change your mark. A mark search can help determine if the name you choose conflicts with any other company's mark.

Searches are also recommended before applying for trademark registration. A search can save a lot of time and money by detecting possible conflicts early.

A common mistake made by small companies is relying upon a state business name search performed by a state government. This is inadequate as a mark search because it is limited to that state's list of registered business names. You must do a search on a powerful computerized database that is much more comprehensive and can detect names used in all fifty states.

The Registration Process

The federal registration process begins with an application to the United States Patent and Trademark Office. Once filed, the application is examined by a trademark examiner. The examination process may include one or two written exchanges with the examiner. The examiner may reject the application or it may be approved immediately.

You need to consider which classes to file under. For example, if you sell bath salts you may need to file under the two separate classes of "bath salts" and "medicated bath salts" in order to be fully protected. Analyzing which classes to file under is where a trademark attorney can be of service to you.

Once approved, the application is published for opposition. This allows another party to object to your application. However, most applications do not receive objections. If the mark is not opposed, the mark will be placed on the federal register.

The Patent and Trademark Office's registration process generally takes one to two years.

Types of Applications

There are two kinds of applications: in-use and intent-to-use. If the mark is currently being used with a product or service in interstate commerce, an in-use application may be filed. If the mark is not currently being used in interstate commerce but the applicant has a bona fide intention to use it, an intent-to-use application may be filed.

An intent-to-use application allows the applicant to establish an early priority date. Even though the applicant is not using the mark, the applicant can claim priority over all those who were not using the mark before the date the application was filed. Once the application is approved you must then file a statement of use. The period to file may be extended every six months up to a maximum of three years.

Getting Started

In order to start the application process, the following information and specimens must be assembled:

• The name, address, and telephone number of the applicant. If the applicant is a corporation, you must include the state of incorporation.

• The exact spelling of the mark as it is used in your business. If the mark includes a logo, you will need a clear drawing of the logo that can be placed on a drawing page. The drawing must be clear enough to photocopy and it must be no larger than 3.5 inches by 3.5 inches. If the logo is not available in this form, trademark artists can make the proper drawings. If you file online the mark sample must be in a jpg image file. (But check ahead since as the technology changes so do the Patent and Trademark Office requirements.)

• A complete list of the goods or services the mark is or will be associated with. The list should be as comprehensive as possible.

• How the mark is used on the goods. For example, printed on the goods, printed on the labels attached to the goods, printed on packaging material, and so on.

• The first date of use of the mark anywhere and the first date of use of the mark in interstate commerce. Interstate commerce means selling the goods across state lines or in another country. No dates are needed for an intent-to-use application.

• One specimen of the mark as it is used with the goods. (If you are filing in three separate classes, you will need to include three samples.) Specimens of marks used on goods may be labels, boxes, pictures of the goods, or the goods themselves if they are flat. Specimens of service marks may be promotional materials such as brochures or advertisements. No specimens are needed for intent-to-use applications.

Costs

The United States Patent and Trademark Office currently charges a fee of between $275 to $375 for each trademark application. Our firm charges $795 for a complete name and trademark search and $275 for preparing the application. Subsequent prosecution of the application, if necessary, is billed at an hourly rate. Other law firms or trademark services may charge more or less than the amounts quoted above.

Rich Dad Tips

- Consider registering your trademark, company name, and slogans as you would an improvement to your house.
- Just as a newly remodeled kitchen can increase the value of your house by two times the amount spent on the remodeling, trademarks can also increase your company's value in a similar way.
- A free eBook entitled "Winning with Trademarks" is available at www.sutlaw.com.

Licensing

A trademark owner has the right to sell or license his trademark. This may be an attractive option to trademark owners who have an underutilized mark with special appeal. Be sure to seek specialized assistance in negotiating and drafting license and assignment agreements.

And so, you have a great company name. It is trademarked and now you need help . . .

Chapter 13

Raising Money

You have prepared your business plan, you have assembled your business team, you have decided on your business entity—now you need money.

What do you do?

You can sell an ownership interest in your company. In a corporation you sell stock, in a limited partnership you sell limited partnership interests, in a limited liability company you sell membership interests. But you must be careful. Raising money for your business can be tricky. In fact, if you do it the wrong way you can land in jail. That is why it is important to read and understand this section. It is not rocket science. Look at all the businesses around you. A goodly number of them sold stock or limited partnership interests or membership interests to get into business. It can be done and it is done every day.

You can do it too. We'll show you how in our next case.

First, some background information.

Securities rules and regulations involve both federal and state law. The United States Securities and Exchange Commission—the SEC—was founded in the wake of an extraordinary number of false or misleading projects to separate naive investors from their money (think of the classic stories of people buying ownership interests in the Brooklyn Bridge, retirement paradises that proved to be Florida swamps, or interests in stage shows that, as in Mel Brooks's movie *The Producers*, amounted to an aggregate of 500 percent ownership). The SEC's approach to these problems was to require a company to provide:

(1) "Adequate full disclosure" to potential investors about the business history;
(2) Reasonable projections that are clearly noted as being speculative or "forward-looking"; and
(3) Serious discussion and warnings about the risks of investment.

That may sound hefty, but it is really not when you compare it to the seriously debated alternative, which was for the government to actually review the investment to determine if it was a good deal. How would they know? The last thing anyone wants in a free marketplace is for the government to decide what we can invest in. Not when they keep telling us that with a 2 percent annual return Social Security is a really good deal. So, instead, although you have to give investors a good bit of information, the SEC has prudently said, once you've done so, it's the investor's own choice and risk. They protect widows and orphans, not idiots.

Although many states follow the federal government's disclosure method, many others have gone with the alternative approach: You not only have to prove to the state government that you have provided full disclosure, but you must also give the government good reason to think it's a good investment for its citizens. This is called the merit review approach, and it creates tremendous burdens of time and effort to meet such high standards. And again, how can these states even begin to judge what is a good investment or not? No one is sure, but they define it as their duty to do so.

Merit Review States

If your company is making an offering of securities under a rule other than Regulation D, Rule 506 (as explained ahead, the most commonly used rule), then the transaction and required disclosure materials prepared in connection with your offering will likely become subject to a merit review by several (perhaps even all) states into which you are intending to sell securities. Under a merit review, your transaction and disclosure materials are not only scrutinized by each state securities agency for accuracy, level of disclosure, and compliance with state legislation, but also as to whether the transaction(s) your company is proposing to undertake with the monies raised from the private placement offering has merit as a viable business proposition. In practical fact, this can be a lengthy and extraordinarily expensive endeavor.

Currently, states that conduct a full, or substantial, merit review of private placement offerings not made under Regulation D, Rule 506, of the Securities Act of 1933, as amended, are as follows:

Alabama	Kentucky	New Mexico
Alaska	Maine	New York
Arizona	Massachusetts	Ohio
Arkansas	Michigan	Oklahoma
California	Minnesota	Oregon
Florida	Mississippi	Tennessee
Hawaii	Missouri	Washington
Indiana	Nebraska	West Virginia
Kansas	New Hampshire	

It is important, therefore, to consider how best to deal with potential subscribers from these states, and whether conducting a private placement offering under a rule or regulation other than Rule 506 is desirable. It may be that the cost of having a merit review conducted on your company's private placement memorandum outweighs the subscription funds to be received.

Keep this in mind as we go along, for you may want to consider the burdens of an offering to investors within a state based on the standard of review. When you start looking for serious outside financing, the time and costs of a merit review offering are going to become important for you to consider.

To begin with, however, let's just look at getting off the ground with something called founders' shares. There are two reasons for issuing these:

First, to get shares in the hands of the founders for a very low price, sometimes at the par value or founders' price of $0.001 (one tenth of one cent per share). If you are going to receive shares early on as a founder, if you are going to take a start-up risk, you want to pay as little as possible for your reward. The cost of one million shares at a founders' price of $0.001 is only $1,000. Even at one cent a share that rises to $10,000 for a million shares. Not everyone wants to—or should—pay that amount. You are much better off only putting in $1,000 and seeing where the company goes.

Please note, you cannot sell stock for less than the par value amount.

You have to pay at least $0.001 per share. Also note that when you take stock for services (organizing, managing, or promoting the company at the outset), you must pay taxes on the value received. So if you take one million shares at $0.001 for your services, you have an income tax obligation based on $1,000 of income; that is far better than having to pay taxes on the receipt of one million shares at one cent per share, or $10,000.

The second reason for using founders' shares is to create a stable group of interests that will hold enough control to prevent later investors from easily upsetting the ownership, management, and future of the business.

How do founders' interests sit in each of our good entities?

Limited Partnership

In a limited partnership, actual control of the operations of the business will be in the hands of the general partner; and, as discussed earlier, the very nature of an LP is that it limits liability for limited partners so long as they have no actual role in running the business. Thus, here you need mainly be concerned that if there will be more than one general partner, you'll want to have firm agreements as to who manages what, how voting control works, and how profit distribution is to be allocated among general partners in addition to allocation of profits among limited partners. Generally speaking, think of a good friendship where you still memorialize the important things in writing. Because limited partners are not "in control" but only entitled to their allotted profits and rights upon dissolution, the founders' interest issue is not a crucial one.

Limited Liability Company

It's different with a limited liability company. The articles of organization and operating agreement create an entity that is more democratic. Membership has its privileges. Whatever the capital contribution, you'll need to separately establish the value of the membership interest received in exchange for it. Because LLCs typically involve a small group of investors with a common mission, the founders' interest issue relates to essentially all original membership interests. Members are entitled to vote and approve major decisions not delegated to a managing member, so in terms of control consider the number and percentage of weight that multiple members will be able to swing in spite of the fact that you may be the managing member.

Sometimes LLCs organize so that a group of members with a controlling percentage for voting purposes operate collectively as managing members. You can also create mandatory buy-back provisions or rights of first refusal by the LLC or its members when a member wants to sell their interest so that you can increase your control and prevent unwanted investors from getting into the group. Thus, for an LLC, the most important founders' considerations are making sure you have the right group of individuals and providing that management and membership interests are well protected. This must be balanced against being so possessive that you deter any future investors from wanting to join in.

Corporations

For corporations, the concept of founders' shares is well established. These shares are created partly as a block of shares that will retain a fair level of voting control over the corporation, especially in its early and nonpublic years. The last thing a founders' group may want is for the first-round money guys to have immediate control. That can happen after a few rounds of funding; but not at the start.

Founders' shares are also a reward for investing what is often far more valuable at the inception of a corporation than money—the blood, sweat, and tears that will create a great business because of the founders' skills and dedication, in spite of a significant uncertainty of later reward.

As such, both reasons for issuing founders' shares are satisfied by issuing a substantial percentage of what will be the corporation's expected total number of outstanding shares after several rounds of funding.

However, although you'll be tempted to keep a tight grip on voting control, know that you'll eventually have to surrender some of it, especially if you want to become a public corporation. Both underwriters and general investors tend to steer away from public companies with highly concentrated control. On the other hand, at this stage it is best to keep a tight grip on things. It's a common tactic for early-round venture capitalists to offer what (to a fledgling business) seems like a staggering sum of money but require a huge percentage of stock. Often little further money follows, fault is found with existing management, and directors and the block of shares in the hands of the venture capitalists may be enough to grab your company right out from under your feet before it's six months old. Hence the term "vulture capitalists." Early-round private offering investors may be up to the same thing, so keep an eye on the percentage of control you'll need and how much other stock you can sell to well-trusted initial investors and later in private offerings without putting your company's future in unknown hands.

Next, you'll almost certainly need start-up capital—seed money—with which to get the business off and running and making money of its own, and that's way more than you've likely got in the bank. Most commonly, before incurring the great expense of (and finding the right kinds of investors for) a full-blown offering of stock, the initial round of raising capital is from so-called angel investors: friends, family, old business acquaintances, your college roommate, and others. These are not quite the same as your founders. These people are risking a lot of cold hard cash. Accordingly, they are often rewarded by getting their shares at a price much lower than you'll be asking for in a regular offering.

Let's look at a case involving a company that may someday go public.

Case No. 18—Z Tech

Robert, Sam, and Tom had a phenomenal idea that they had patented. Because they had a patent they now had a technology. And by owning a technology they absolutely had to use some derivation of the word "technology" in their corporate name.

Thus, Z Tech, Inc., was born and formed as a corporation.

The next step was to issue stock to founders and to raise money to commercially exploit their technology.

The three agreed that they did not want to lose control initially. They knew their business and their technology. If done properly it would be a once-in-a-lifetime opportunity. A huge and satisfying score for all of them. If handled poorly, they would have to keep working for the rest of their lives.

Z Tech, Inc., was incorporated in Nevada with a total of 20 million common shares and 5 million preferred shares authorized.

The total of 25 million shares each at a par value of $.001 per share, or a par value capitalization of $25,000, was a suitable amount of shares to be authorized for the company's future growth. The par value of shares is an antiquated concept not worth discussing. All you need to know at a cocktail party is that:

1. You cannot sell stock or grant founders' shares for less than par value, and
2. Par value is an antiquated concept not worth discussing.

Robert, Sam, and Tom agreed that they would each take 20 percent of the common shares, or 4 million shares each. Their contribution was valued at $4,000 each. While they could have received shares for services rendered (and paid tax on it), the three decided that the company needed the money and each paid $4,000 for their 4 million shares, which equaled $0.001 per share.

By each taking 20 percent of the authorized common shares they would have 60 percent control when all 20 million common shares were issued. As it was, with only 12 million shares issued, they each owned 33⅓ percent of all issued shares. Their current one-third ownership would be diluted or reduced as more shares were sold, which, of course, they needed to do to get the business going. But again, with 12 million shares between them, they would still maintain control of the company once all 20 million common shares were sold and until the 5 million nonvoting preferred shares were converted to voting common shares.

They had authorized the preferred shares for future flexibility. They were nonvoting so the three could issue them without worrying about losing control. If they were later converted to voting common shares and all shares were issued they could lose control. By holding only 12 million shares out of 25 million issued they could be voted out. But remember, their angel investors would have some shares and presumably they would side with them in a shareholder dispute. However, you can never know.

Once Robert, Sam, and Tom issued themselves their founders' shares they were ready to issue shares to their angels. Robert's mom, Ethel, was willing to invest $10,000 at the right price. Sam's brother, Lenny, was willing to invest $10,000 if he could get options, and Tom's best friend, Mason, was willing to invest whatever Tom needed just because. The three founders figured that they needed a total of $50,000 to get Z Tech, Inc., going. They had already together put in $12,000, so $38,000 more was needed fairly soon.

The $50,000 would take care of initial expenses and cover reduced monthly expenses for six months. They would not take salaries in order to conserve money. After they had proven their concept they would need $1 million to really pursue their business.

So the task was to figure out what to charge per share in the angel round and what to charge per share in the first round of funding. They wanted to benefit their angels with a low share price but also provide an attractive incentive for the $1 million investors.

Robert, Sam, and Tom figured it was fair to set the angel round at 5 cents per share and the first round at 25 cents per share. Once these rounds were completed their shareholders would be as follows:

Approximate Time	Round	Name	Shares	Price per share	Amount Raised
Day one	Founder	Robert	4,000,000	$.001	$4,000
	Founder	Sam	4,000,000	.001	4,000
	Founder	Tom	4,000,000	.001	4,000
Day ten	Angel	Ethel	200,000	.05	10,000
	Angel	Lenny	200,000	.05	10,000
	Angel	Mason	360,000	.05	18,000
Six months after angel round	1st Round	Investor	4,000,000	.25	1,000,000
Total			16,760,000		$1,050,000

It should be noted that if Lenny was granted stock options to purchase, for example, 100,000 more shares for 10 cents a share within two years, the same exact options would have been granted to the other angel investors. You must give all the investors in one round the exact same deal. You cannot change prices or any other terms within any round. If one gets options, they all get options. Everyone gets the same deal. Not only is this the law but as a very practical matter it keeps your shareholders happy. No one wants to find out he paid the same price as the next guy but did not get the options.

Also, in terms of prices, you should try not to go down in share price between offerings as a nonpublic company. When you are a public company and trading on an exchange the price will freely go up and down every day. But when the company is not public the share price is set by the founders or management. Unless there is a legitimate economic reason to do so, it is bad practice, and unfair to the shareholders, to set the price high in one round and low in the next. Put yourself in the shoes of your shareholders and ask yourself if you think it is fair. Not when your are the one who paid $1.00 a share for stock now selling for 5 cents a share.

Likewise, under the securities laws you cannot conduct multiple offerings of the same stock at the same time. And you should not conduct offerings of stock one right after the other. The SEC prefers to see a six-month quiet, nonselling period between offerings, although it may be reduced to a ninety-day wait. Consult your legal advisor as to the importance of these and other securities rules.

Robert, Sam, and Tom wanted to follow the securities laws. So when they granted Lenny his stock options they gave the same deal to Ethel and Mason. As well, when they stopped selling the angel round, they waited six months to go after their first round of funding.

They hired securities counsel to guide them through this complicated process. Z Tech, Inc., impressed its early investors, kept its promises and its books in order, and without too much delay was given permission by the SEC to do an initial public offering. Robert, Sam, and Tom became very wealthy.

LP and LLC Investor Rounds

LPs and LLCs are not usually associated with the funding of numerous rounds of investors. Because corporations are vehicles for going public, rounds of increasing share prices are more common. As well, LPs and LLCs do not offer the complete free transferability of interests, making a public market difficult.

Likewise, later contributors to LPs and LLCs are treated much the same as earlier partners or members. As a flow-through entity you are buying, for example, 10 percent of the LP or LLC for the flow-through of money, not for the appreciation of your interest. Investors in both need to think in terms of long-term investment and the attraction of consistent returns once the business begins realizing profits. The drill in an LP or LLC investment is not to bring in more investors at higher prices but to increase the profits on your percentage ownership of the entity.

How to Bring Investors In

The first step for bringing in investors is, no matter how thin it may be as yet, provide each one with a copy of your business plan. (For a useful book on preparing such plans see my book *The ABCs of Writing Winning Business*

Plans.) Also, give each potential investor copies of the required documents verifying the appropriate business and legal organization of the entity (articles of incorporation, bylaws, certification of the secretary of state, as applicable).

Included should be a realistic financial statement of the business, showing the costs to get it going, the minimum and maximum amounts you are expecting to raise, and fair projections showing where the business will be, both at its low-end and high-end estimates, in the next six months, a year, and so on. Remember, the further out you project, the less reliable these forward-looking statements will be. Make sure to state just that: (1) These projections are not verifiable or reliable; (2) These projections are provided with the warning that they may not be reached; and (3) The whole business may not even succeed.

You may not like the sound of that, but think back to the Brooklyn Bridge and Florida swamp examples. Potential investors have a right to know these significant material things, to be reminded of the risks that go along with faith, and to be warned about putting too much faith in dreams of the future. They could actually lose their whole investment!

Earlier, the full disclosure and merit review requirements that governments impose on those who sell interests to investors were discussed. At the very least, under either standard, you have to tell them all the risks you can think of. Try to trust that people will appreciate your candor about this; they may even be more inclined to invest if they know you have your feet on the ground and are studying all possibilities with a clear head. Thus, not only are such disclosures required, but they could actually help you get prudent investors. And to be sure, a sophisticated investor who has read an investment prospectus or two will just gloss over the risks and warnings. They're in every one.

Finally, create a subscription agreement. This is a formal document listing the materials given to the potential investor. It states that the investor has reviewed them and has had an opportunity to ask questions and review any other requested materials that you could reasonably furnish them. It affirms that they are aware of the risks of the investment, but states they have chosen to make the investment based on their own informed decision. Include a place to state the amount of the investment and what they are to receive in return, such as common or preferred stock.

Make sure the investor manually signs and dates the subscription agreement and gives the document to you along with payment. Finally, place a statement at the end by which the business accepts the subscription, and sign and date that in the capacity of your official corporate position. Make a photocopy of the fully executed subscription agreement and a copy of their check for them to keep with their other important documents. Now, and only now, can you take the check to the bank and deposit it in the business's account. As soon as possible, a certificate should be issued to each partner or member, indicating the business's name, the investor's name, the date of the issuance, and the type and amount of shares now owned by the investor. The stock certificate should be treated like handling a bar of gold. Be careful. Fill out and spell everything exactly as it should be, and sign and date it just before delivering it to the new owner. Don't skimp on the postage if sending it through the mail either. Pay a bit extra and send it certified, return receipt requested. Take the same care with each certificate and number them consecutively. Finally, keep a careful ledger recording the consecutive certificate numbers, investor names, issuance dates, payments for investment, and the type and amount of stock interest for each investor.

Your state may require that you file this information, fill out additional forms, perhaps receive advance approval by the state regarding the form and perhaps the content of investment documentation, and you'll quite likely be required to pay a fee. Check with your state and/or securities attorney for the most recent approval and filing requirements in advance of any offering, as such requirements frequently change in a number of states.

If you have investors from more than one state, include in your documents, especially the subscription agreement, that the offering is being conducted pursuant to the exemption of Rule 506 under Regulation D of the Securities Act of 1933, as amended.

Rule 506 allows you to sell securities interstate without having to register them or get approval with the Securities and Exchange Commission. Better still, Rule 506 offerings preempt the varying laws of all fifty states; therefore, in every applicable state, even in merit review states, the most the state can require of you is a fairly simple form to file along with a filing fee. They can't demand that you fulfill any other requirements. Within fifteen days after you accept a subscription agreement from your first investor in the offering, you'll just need to file a copy of Form D with the Securities and Exchange Commission—and there's no fee. And think about a nice side effect of the timing for filing the form: It needs to be filed within fifteen days after the first investment—file it immediately after the first one and you need only provide the information with respect to that single investor. That will save you a bundle of time trying to fill in information for everyone else. The SEC doesn't require—or even want—you to amend or add to Form D. Just make sure you do it on time. Meeting deadlines will become increasingly important for your business and its securities status. You don't want to start off looking ill-prepared and unprofessional.

There are three other significant points about Rule 506 that you should note. First, for purposes of federal law, the offering may have no more than thirty-five nonaccredited investors (for the moment, think basically millionaires versus nonmillionaires). Second, and related, is that in any given six-month period from the time an offering ends, the number of nonaccredited investors will be counted in the aggregate if you have more than one offering that is essentially similar in nature during the succeeding six months (this is called the integration rule). Thus, you need to be careful about the total number of nonaccredited investors that you may have now and in any initial private placement offering.

For the friends and family round at present, many, if not all, will probably be nonaccredited. So consider that although you need the cash to get the business going, don't exhaust all thirty-five allowed nonaccredited investors or have so many that it would hobble your next-round offering with the burden of having to find almost all accredited investors to sell enough stock at the higher price. Although the typical angel investor offering involves a small number of people, keep in mind that the money raised will have to last at least a good six months from the time it ends before you can initiate another offering without worrying about oversubscribing to nonaccredited investors. Also, your state may have even lower allowable limits on the number of nonaccredited investors you can have within that state. Nevada only allows twenty-five nonaccredited Nevada residents as investors, which means any of the ten more allowed by federal law would have to come from another state. Be sure to check about state regulation of nonaccredited investors as well.

There's a pretty good reason for this limit. Accredited investors can afford—at least in theory—to lose all the money invested without suffering extreme consequences in their personal lives. Nonaccredited investors are taking a bigger risk, and the government doesn't want you to rely on the aid of too many people who may not be as able to afford the risks of investing. Otherwise, they'd start to feel an increasing obligation to review and authorize your offering materials. To allow young businesses the opportunity to raise funds without too much government oversight, delays, and costs, is why this exemption from registration was created. So remember that the SEC is firm about the thirty-five nonaccredited investor limit and the six-month integration rule. These are at the heart of allowing this exemption, so be careful to live up to the spirit and letter of the law.

You'll need to explain to investors how they are classified, so here's a basic definition of accredited investors and a suggested definition for the types of people who could best afford the risk although not accredited:

An accredited investor is defined in Regulation D to include:

- A natural person (United States citizen or permanent resident—i.e., not an entity of any kind) whose individual net worth, or joint net worth with such person's spouse, exceeds $1 million at the time of purchase
- A natural person who has an individual income in excess of $200,000 in each of the two most recent years or joint income with that person's spouse in excess of $300,000 in each of those years and who reasonably expects to reach the same income level in the current year
- A business entity, not formed for the specific purpose of acquiring the units offered, with total assets in excess of $5 million
- An entity in which all of the equity owners are accredited investors

A nonaccredited investor is an investor who does not meet the income and asset test set out above. While there is no minimum income and asset test for a nonaccredited investor, it is a good idea, when considering offering securities to nonaccredited investors, to establish a minimum income threshold, for example, a yearly taxable income of $40,000 or more. In addition, certain states may impose different or additional suitability standards, which may be more restrictive.

Under Rule 506, the company may accept subscriptions from no more than thirty-five nonaccredited investors in total, per private placement offering. Remember also to consider states' laws when calculating the number of nonaccredited investors. As mentioned, Nevada only allows twenty-five per offering.

A crucial point to remember, however, is that the level of disclosure is significantly higher when nonaccredited investors are being solicited. A full private placement memorandum must be prepared, using the specific disclosure guidelines and headings promulgated by the SEC; and in addition, audited financial statements, no more than three months old, must be included with the private placement memorandum. Where a company can demonstrate significant hardship or expense in preparing a full set of audited financial statements, it is permissible to provide nonaccredited investors with an audited balance sheet only, but again, no more than three months old.

The third and final significant point about this exempt form of seeking investments is that when offering securities to nonaccredited investors under Rule 506, you are required to provide them with audited statements for some of the financial material. An audit, even a limited one like this, is going to be costly. A very few CPAs and accounting firms (and not the big ones) may consider receiving shares at least as partial compensation in exchange for their services, but this is not an option when being audited. The auditor cannot have an ownership interest in the company, which would obviously create conflict-of-interest problems. So you may need to set something aside from the outset for auditing expenses and, if possible, arrange to have part of the payment to be made to the auditor from proceeds of the offering.

Another important point to know: Unless you conduct a registered public offering (which you won't be doing in the early stages), there are restrictions on an investor's ability to transfer their interests to another. This is usually referred to as a Rule 144 restriction. Under Rule 144 of the Securities Act, no shares can be sold by an investor for one full year from the time they purchase their shares. During the second year, they are limited to selling shares equaling no more than 1 percent of the entire public float of the company's securities during any given three-month period. The public float means anyone other than people in controlling positions within the company, owners of 10 percent or more of the company's securities (a position known as a beneficial owner), and any affiliate of the company (i.e., another entity controlled by your company, in common control of your company, or in common control with your company over another company). After the second year, those investors whose shares are within the definition of the public float will have all restrictions on transfer lifted and the stock becomes fully marketable.

Shareholders not part of the public float remain subject to the 1 percent limit provision for so long as they remain in the positions that prevent them from being regarded as within the public float. If they cease to be in such positions, after three months from the time they meet the public float definition, they will then be treated as any other member in the public float.

So, on the certificates you issue, include a restrictive legend prominently on the front so that the corporation can show it has notified each investor of the Rule 144 restriction and has made sure anyone seeing the certificate will be alerted to the limitations on transfer. After the second year, you can replace restricted certificates with ones that have no restrictive legends. The following is such a legend commonly used:

> The securities covered hereby have not been registered under the Securities Act of 1933, as amended ("Act"), and may not be offered or sold within the United States or to or for the account or the benefit of U.S. Persons (i) as part of their distribution at any time or (ii) otherwise until one year after the later of the commencement of the offering of such securities or the closing date of the sale and transfer thereof, except in either case in accordance with Rule 144 under the Act. Terms used above have the meaning given to them by Rule 144.

Make sure you also discuss these restrictions within the documentation you give potential investors, and especially make a point of it (and the investor's understanding and acceptance of it) on the subscription agreement.

All this may seem like a lot of work at first, but after reviewing this material you'll find it isn't as overwhelming as it may appear at first glance. However, there's one more significant thing to make a point of right now, and this is really important: Skip or screw up any part of the several previous paragraphs on conducting an offering, and you may very easily find yourself in a great deal of trouble with the federal or state government—or both. From this point on, you're playing with other people's money, and obligations like the above will exist with every step of your business's existence.

It is important to again review the process for designating a lower price per share for angel investors than what you will be hoping to sell shares for in future offerings, as it requires a bit of advance calculation.

Think of the total number of shares you will want to have issued and outstanding after your first major private placement offering. Also think of the total funds you will need to raise including from that offering. Now back-track and figure in the percentage of founders' shares needed to keep some solid control over the stability of the corporation, your board of directors, and initial officers. Subtract that from the total shares, and the rest is available for the angels, the first major private offering down the road in six months, and some extra stock for a few other purposes.

Again, a good rule of thumb for the angel investor offering is to pour enough money into the coffers to get the corporation fully operational, to meet its initial goals, and to get revenue streams up and generating enough money to keep you afloat by the end of six months. That's a goal, but prepare in case revenues don't prove as fast and large as you'd hoped in that amount of time. You may also have to put off some projects for the time being, for almost certainly in six months you won't be able to do everything you hope for, although you can make reasonable projections for getting the business into shape and looking good for future investors. Also, recall the six-month integration limit for Rule 506, so put a short fuse as to when the angel investor offering will end, for it's from that time that the six-month integration rule will count. You'll probably need a good number of nonaccredited investors in the next offering, so try to get enough angel investor money to last through till then, cover the costs of the next offering (generally in the range of $10,000 for a first major private placement), and be able to take on another full thirty-five nonaccredited investors next time. Again, keep in mind that some states have lower limits on the number of their residents that can invest in a private placement.

Quite often, new businesses find themselves unable to generate enough capital through stock offerings alone. At this point, you may want to think about figuring in loans to help you get going. Without a strong background, bank loans are going to be tough to obtain, but you may wish to request information from the Small Business Administration, which can sometimes be a useful resource for ideas. You may have to sign promissory notes for loans and agree to sizable interest payments. Here, if possible, you may be able to create a promissory note that allows for an election of repayment either in cash or the company's securities in an effort to prove the company's worth to the creditor and issue stock rather than paying back large sums of money for a still fledgling business.

In any case with loans, try to get as much time and the lowest monthly payments you can. No matter how well you plan, finances are always tight for new businesses. You don't want to add creditors beating at the door to the other matters you'll need to devote your time and attention to. There is also a lending counterpart to private and public offerings, called a convertible debenture, but like those later equity offerings, structuring and marketing a convertible debenture offering is a costly and complicated process that is probably best left for debt financing as the company reaches a more mature stage.

In all issuances of shares, you'll need to hold a meeting of the board of directors during which the matters are discussed, the general elements of the offering are set forth, resolutions authorizing the same are given, and a resolution is passed directing the officers to take all necessary action to proceed.

At this point, you may be able to do much of this work without having to retain corporate and securities attorneys to put together the materials for founders and angels, but if you find yourself unsure, it's best to pay the money and have a professional make certain everything is done right. A few thousand dollars now might prevent you from the headaches of rescissions, lawsuits, state and federal investigations, and fines—virtually any and all of which will cost a lot more than a good attorney helping you at the start.

Which leads us to the next stage of securities. You've got your paperwork in order, a good business and financial plan, a solid set of founders, reliable officers and directors (or partners/managing members, as the case may be), and some much needed financing from the angels who've gotten you off the ground. It's now time for a reality check: If you don't retain legal counsel from now on, you could quickly find yourself sliding along the edge of disaster. No longer will it be Aunt Mabel's money and faith in you. No, now you are entering a world of investors who expect strong business judgment, serious answers to their concerns, and a reliable probability that their money will grow if invested with you. There are also a good number of sharks in this sea who are smelling for newcomers. They are ready to seize on any sign of uncertainty, hesitation, or inexperience, both in business and finance, either to get a high return for little investment or even to wrest control of the company right out from under you (recall the brief earlier mention of certain less scrupulous venture/vulture capitalists). Don't fall into the fear that everyone will be out to get you, but be realistic. From now on you're going to need lawyers—competent corporate counsel for objective assistance with the business, securities counsel to assist you with future, more complicated financing strategies, and both for maintaining protection of the corporation. Forget the lawyer jokes. A good corporate/securities lawyer is about to become among your business's most trusted friends.

Let's move on to your first private placement offering. This is going to require a good deal of time and effort, so begin preparing at least a couple of months before you hope to begin the offering. As stated earlier, a private placement generally costs something in the range of $10,000. Some law firms will only require a retainer of a few thousand dollars in a trust account to begin with and will draw the remainder of the bill from the proceeds of the offering if it seems probable that you'll raise significant sums not only to pay legal fees, but also to emerge with a large amount of money to support the company's short-term future plans over the next several months to a year. Not all attorneys are willing or able to defer payment, though, so be prepared with funds to cover legal counsel, accounting requirements, and printing fees.

One of the best ways to hold down the legal costs of the offering is to knock yourself out drafting and redrafting your business plan so that it flows smoothly and coherently, in a well-ordered outline, presenting a fair and accurate picture of the company, its results to date, and its hopes for the future. (Again, for more information see *The ABC's of Writing Winning Business Plans*.) If you do so, your securities attorney will not have to spend days or weeks drafting this material, but rather will be able to adjust the language into securities-speak, add additional legal legends, warnings, and discussions around your business plan, and thus be able to focus this costly attention on fine detail instead of doing the basics you could have done for yourself.

Taking the time to review and revise your business plan at regular intervals is also simply good business practice. It forces you to take a hard look at where things are, how well you are meeting expectations, what plans seem to work and what may need to be revised or dropped, and how to structure future activity and ever more realistic financial statements and planning.

There are strict limits about announcing, advertising, or paying anyone for seeking investors in private placements. Remember the key word: private. There can be no general solicitation of investors; in fact, it's important to keep knowledge of the offering very quiet and limited to those who need to know. Telling others can lead to problems of "attempting to create a market for securities," which is a big bad thing for both the SEC and most state purposes. This becomes of extreme significance at the point where shares become less restricted or unrestricted or publicly trading. Some people, including Martha Stewart, go to prison for insider trading. Even at an early stage, inside information is something to really guard against allowing to travel beyond those persons directly and of necessity involved in the offering. Accordingly, don't even mention it on your Web site, if you have one; individually number each private placement memorandum (the document you'll prepare with your securities attorney and accountants that houses the securities-oriented business plan, financials, other exhibits, and the subscription agreement); and require return of all materials should a potential investor choose not to subscribe. Keep a list of the private placement memorandums by consecutive number, who they are delivered to, and note the date of their return or the receipt of a subscription agreement.

But how do you find the investors in the first place? You'll need to demonstrate, if ever asked, that potential investors have some sort of prior relationship whereby they know who you are and inquired of their own volition if they may receive materials to consider investing in an offering of your stock. In fact, the subscription agreement will ask the potential investor to state how they found out about the offering. Sounds strange, right? How do you get someone to ask about an offering if you can't tell them it exists? For practical purposes, preexisting relationships are the main safeguard. The potential investor knows about and has been watching your company with interest. They have an inkling that an opportunity to invest may be coming soon, and they ask you—in writing!—for investment information when available. A new wrinkle in this process has entered the securities world with the advent of the Internet. You can't announce the offering, but someone who frequents your Web site may e-mail you (without being asked or encouraged to do so) and request information about investment opportunities. If there were ever a reason for not deleting an e-mail and keeping a hard copy in a safe place, this is it.

This limitation of not initiating new investor contacts, but rather only responding to potential investors who aren't informed of the offering itself in advance, is certainly frustrating to imagine. But consider how, if things have gone well, the growth and demonstrated early success of your company will lend a hand. A lot more people can inquire of their own accord now than you would have had reason to expect earlier on. You will have met them personally, sold them your product or service, and they may have even seen a mention of your company in the business section of the newspaper.

In fact, many people interested in investment opportunities make it a practice to keep an eye out for promising young businesses, and they frequently network themselves with other spheres of investors who find and observe young businesses for potential investment opportunities at a lower price by getting in early.

In addition, even with little or no idea that you're preparing for another offering, your own staff and prior investors may be familiarizing additional people among their own family, friends, and other acquaintances about the existence and status of your company. But remember they must keep a lid on any inside information such as a big contract that may be signed soon or even the preparation of the offering itself. Without you instigating direct interest in an offering, these people may be asked by others who are becoming familiar with your business through them to give them general company contact information to look into the possibility of investing someday themselves. And that's acceptable, so long as the potential new investor initiates the interest and your personnel and prior investors aren't suggesting the merits of an investment or directly encouraging someone to subscribe. They just provide a link—the offering, when it comes, will do the selling for itself.

There's one other method available for others to bring in potential investors, but be very careful and use it sparingly, if at all. A small finder's fee can be paid for introductions of potential offerees who are acquainted with current investors. The finder is very limited in acceptable action, however; he may only simply mention to the acquaintance that he's invested in the company and, if requested, can pass the potential investor's name and phone number or address along to the company. He can't do anything else that could even hint at being a sales pitch. He just passes along the contact information to the company, which does all the rest of the work without further involvement of any kind by the finder. The finder's name is simply added to the information records of private placement memorandums being sent out on request. If the person later chooses to subscribe, the finder may receive a fee for the introduction.

This fee is usually kept very small, a set figure or share equaling 1 percent to 3 percent of the amount invested. Finder's fees as high as 10 percent to licensed broker-dealers have been held allowable in some SEC opinions, but it's best not to get close to the edge.

There is no real limit on the number of private placement offerings that may be held. However, keep in mind the integration problems of thirty-five (or fewer in certain states) nonaccredited investors in any six-month period, and remember that every time you issue authorized shares the present ownership percentage of current shareholders (including the founders!) will be proportionately diluted, so don't go overboard.

After several years you may want to consider the next level, the Holy Grail for entrepreneurs: going public. For an excellent overview of that whole process, see *How Your Company Can Raise Money to Grow and Go Public* (Success DNA). For now, start working on that business plan. And in doing so make sure you have the right management . . .

Chapter 14

Know Who Your Directors and Officers Are!

You are raising money and things are looking bright. Until one of your big potential investors tells you that your management team consists of some well-known bad apples. He can't invest with them on board. And, he can't invest in you for allowing them in without having done a prudent background check.

You are devastated, but you've learned a huge lesson. You must know who your directors and officers really are.

What Are Directors and Officers and What Powers Do They Have?

As quick background, directors are individual persons appointed by the company's shareholders on a yearly basis at the annual shareholder meeting. Officers are positions such as president, secretary, treasurer, vice president, chief financial officer, and chief operating officer. They are appointed by the directors at the annual directors meeting (which follows immediately after the annual shareholder meeting).

Rich Dad Tips

- If you are going to run your own corporation you don't need to fill all the positions listed above. In Nevada and Wyoming, for example, one person can be the president, secretary, treasurer, and sole director.
- Even if it is just you running the company, you need to be mindful of and follow the duties listed below.

The directors of the company and, to a lesser extent, the officers hold an enormous amount of power and control over the actions of your business. They are responsible for the control and direction of the company. They can call meetings among themselves, sign contracts binding the company to various obligations, conduct purchases and sales of various assets, and incur debts in the name of your company. Directors can appoint and terminate the officers at any time, on a majority vote of the directors. Directors can also regulate the sale and transfer of the company's shares, including the price for purchases and sales, and they can control the company's bank account, including who may or may not sign checks. With that kind of power, investors are not going to turn money over to a board made up of bad apples.

Fiduciary Duty and Indemnification

In almost every jurisdiction, language is written into the governing corporation law which imposes a "fiduciary duty" on directors and officers to act at all times in the best interest of a company and its shareholders. This means that the directors and officers must act for the good of the company as a whole, as opposed to their own individual interests. They have a higher duty than themselves. Failure to follow this higher duty can result in personal liability.

To mitigate the risks involved with fiduciary duty, directors and officers may be indemnified against personal lawsuits brought by your shareholders or by third parties who have contracted with the company. Indemnification provisions in some states must be included in the articles; in other states, they must be in the bylaws. If a director or officer is personally sued for their acts on behalf of the company, an indemnification will allow them to seek reimbursement from the company for any claims and/or legal defense costs. As discussed in Chapter 11, companies may insure against such risks. As long as the acts in question do not involve an improper personal benefit or willful misconduct, indemnification may be appropriate. The irony for the company is that, while poor business judgment and bad decisions made by your directors and officers may not necessarily be breaches of fiduciary duty, they may have the effect of landing your company in a world of trouble, including lawsuits, liens, and debts. The company, through its indemnification, may then have no recourse against these decision makers, unless it goes to court to hold the directors judicially liable to the company.

Of course, indemnification only applies where directors and officers uphold their fiduciary duty. Where they do not—where directors mislead or commit fraud (for example, convincing the shareholders to sell all or a significant portion of the company's assets to what appears to be a separate company, but which is actually controlled by one or more of your own directors)—they may be found to have breached their fiduciary duty. Indemnification does not cover wanton or willful (bad) conduct or improper personal benefit.

Let's further explore the duties of directors:

Duty of Care

A director owes the company a duty of care. He must do what a prudent person would do with regard to their own business. There are several ways to breach the duty of care:

• *Nonfeasance (doing nothing).* With nonfeasance, a director is only liable if the breach of duty causes a loss. For example, if the director was an expert and the loss was caused by their lack of expertise, there would be a breach in the duty of care.

• *Misfeasance (doing something that loses money).* A director is not liable for misfeasance if he was prudent in his business judgment. This is referred to as the "business judgment rule." When determining whether a director used his best business judgment, you must inquire whether he or she carefully reviewed the course of action, sought out other options, and arrived at a decision supported by commonsense business judgment. If so, there is no breach of duty of care.

Duty of Loyalty

A director must act in good faith and with a reasonable belief that what he does is in the company's best interest. There are several ways in which a director can breach his loyalty:

• *Interested Director Transactions.* In an interested director transaction, a director or one of his relatives enters into a deal with the company such as a sale of property or a loan. An interested director transaction will be set aside unless the director can show either: (i) that the deal was fair to the company; or (ii) that disclosure was made and approval obtained from a majority of disinterested directors.

• *Competing Venture.* A director breaches his duty of loyalty if he competes directly and unfairly with the company. For example, a director cannot be on the board of a beauty school and start his own beauty school without independent board approval.

• *Corporate Opportunity.* A director breaches his duty of loyalty if he usurps a business opportunity from the company. A corporate opportunity is anything the company would be interested in pursuing. Before taking the opportunity himself, a director must inform the board and wait for the board to turn the opportunity down before proceeding. A company can be awarded damages for loss of a corporate opportunity, or a company can make the director sell the property to the company.

Which Directors Can Be Held Liable?

The general rule states that a director is presumed to have concurred with the board's action unless their dissent is noted in writing in the corporate minutes or in a registered letter to the company's corporate secretary. There are some exceptions:

• Directors absent from the meeting in which the action was approved or undertaken are usually not liable.

• Liability may be limited by a good faith reliance on any of the following: (i) financial statements by auditors; (ii) book value of assets; or (iii) an opinion of a competent employee or professional.

Directors and Officers Liability Insurance

Because of the risks associated with director or officer liability, many qualified professionals with assets to lose will insist that the company obtain directors and officers (D&O) liability insurance before they will agree to serve. In order to get the good apples, you're likely going to have to get a D&O policy.

As mentioned in Chapter 11, these policies differ widely, so be sure to consult with an insurance or other professional to make certain of your coverage. D&O insurance is not the easiest to obtain and the premiums may be high, in part because of the large claims associated with securities litigation. Insurers will look to the financial history and stability of the company, the background and reputation of the directors and officers, and a number of other factors.

A key element to consider when negotiating D&O coverage is the definition of the terms "fraud" and "dishonesty of the insured." In many cases, insurance companies will want to exclude such coverage, whereas those possibilities are the exact risks that the company is seeking to cover.

Another way an insurance company will deny coverage is by requiring that the directors and officers be listed by name on the policy. If someone leaves the company, their replacement name must be immediately placed onto the policy. While this requirement may easily be forgotten in the crush of daily business, failure to do so can mean that your new director or officer is not insured. In addition, if you are a new director or officer relying on D&O protection, ask for a copy of the policy with your name on it as an insured.

Finally, some policies will seek to not cover a company that is in bankruptcy. Of course, this is when the directors and officers need coverage the most. Be sure to negotiate that coverage to your satisfaction.

That final point raises an issue I sometimes see with clients who are about to serve on a board of directors or become an officer of a company. Generally, these people are cautious but many are lulled by the fact that the company will indemnify them. It must be noted that unless the company has money, indemnification is an empty promise. If the company is broke or bankrupt, it's not going to indemnify you for anything. You're on your own. So, unless there is a solid D&O policy in place or you are thoroughly involved in the company and see no immediate risk of being sued, be very careful. The company that indemnifies you may be giving you the sleeves off its vest.

Back to our main point: How will the backgrounds of your directors and officers affect potential investors and existing shareholders?

All potential investors into any type of company, be it a public, trading company with thousands of shareholders, or a private company with three shareholders, are entitled to receive certain information about the company and its directors, officers, and other management before investing. Included in this information requirement is the right to know whether any of these individuals have any criminal convictions, have been or are presently bankrupt, and whether they have been disciplined by the Securities and Exchange Commission or any state or other securities regulatory body for violation of securities laws. As you can imagine, this type of information can have a serious impact on potential investors and your ability to raise equity funds. Where this information is not provided to an investor prior to making the decision to invest in your company, the result can be financial penalties assessed by various securities regulatory authorities, as well as civil or even criminal proceedings being taken against your company for fraud and failure to disclose required information.

So, what does this all mean to you? That it is in your best interest to have some knowledge of the background and personal history of your directors and officers. In some jurisdictions, the local governing corporation law helps you by setting out certain requirements directors must meet. These requirements usually disallow individuals with criminal convictions or who are an undischarged bankrupt (that is, someone currently in bankruptcy) from acting as directors or officers. In other jurisdictions, directors requirements are little more than having a pulse.

Therefore, where corporation law does not adequately protect your company, you need to take your own affirmative steps. One suggestion is to have all directors and officers complete and sign a questionnaire when they are elected or appointed, which requires them to disclose relevant information and attest to its truth. With this, if there is a problem stemming from information that a director or officer did not disclose, you have a much better chance of successfully proving that your company made a reasonable effort to protect itself and its investors and shareholders, and deflect liability directly onto that individual director or officer (fiduciary duty, anyone?).

We have included a "Consent to Act as a Director," which also contains a brief questionnaire covering the most troublesome issues. You can modify this to suit your particular business endeavor, and you should, as a good point of practice, have directors and officers sign a new one every year following election or reelection, just to make sure your company stays current.

Consent to Act as a Director and Conflict-of-Interest Check

TO: _____(the "Company")

AND TO: The Board of Directors Thereof

I HEREBY CONSENT to act as director of the Company if appointed or elected, and to my reappointment or reelection from time to time unless and until this consent shall be revoked by me in writing, this consent to be effective from the date hereof.

Please answer the following questions. If your answer to any of these questions is "yes," please provide details on a separate sheet.

		Yes	No
(a)	I am under the age of 18 years.	☐	☐
(b)	I have been found to be incapable of managing my own affairs by reason of mental infirmity.	☐	☐
(c)	I am an undischarged bankrupt.	☐	☐

During the preceding 5 years I have:

		Yes	No
(a)	filed for personal bankruptcy or a company that I have been associated with as an officer or director has filed for bankruptcy.	☐	☐
(b)	been convicted of a criminal offense (excluding traffic violations and other minor offenses) or am the subject of any such pending action, inside or outside the United States.	☐	☐
(c)	been or currently am subject to any order, judgment, or decree (which has not been subsequently reversed, suspended, or vacated) of any court of competent jurisdiction permanently or temporarily enjoining, barring, suspending, or otherwise limiting my involvement in any type of business, securities, or banking activities.	☐	☐
(d)	been found by a court of competent jurisdiction (in a civil action), the Securities and Exchange Commission, any state securities agency, or the Commodity Futures Trading Commission to have violated a federal or state securities or commodities law or regulation (which judgment has not been reversed, suspended, or vacated).	☐	☐

During the preceding 5 years, I have acted as a Director or Officer of the following reporting* and/or nonreporting domestic or foreign companies:

During the preceding 5 years, I (or a company I am associated with) have entered into the following agreements with the Company, whereby I receive a direct or indirect benefit (including employment agreements, stock purchase agreements, incentive stock option agreements, etc.):

_____

_____

_____

I HEREBY UNDERTAKE to promptly notify the Company in the event of any change in my status.

DATED at _____, the ____ day of _____, 20__.

_____
(signature)

_____
(address)

*A reporting company is a company that files periodic financial and management reports with the Securities and Exchange Commission or other foreign securities regulatory agencies.

Consent to Act as a Director

If you answered "Yes" to any of the questions on page 1
(e.g., undischarged bankruptcies, felony convictions, or sanctions
by the SEC or any state securities authority), please provide details below.

_____

_____

_____

_____

_____

_____

_____

_____

_____

_____

_____

_____

_____

_____

_____

Chapter 15

How to Deal with All of the Employee Issues

You have a business plan and management team in place. Your angel round of financing has been placed and you have interest in your first round of funding. Now you need to hire employees.

There are four main issues to consider in this area. First, at the very start, you have to decide whether to hire employees or use independent contractors (be careful). Second, when hiring employees, you need to be familiar with what is involved in an employment agreement. Third, there are employment law issues you need to know. And finally, you need to decide what employee benefits you can offer.

Employee vs. Independent Contractor—Which Is Better?

Now that your company is incorporated and you're ready to begin operating, the next step is to think about employees, and how to fit them inside your business with the minimal amount of headache.

First up: Should you hire employees or engage independent contractors?

You know what it means to be an employee. Chances are you've probably been one. But once you step over to the employer side of the working relationship, it's a whole new ball game.

As an employee, your responsibilities include things like showing up for work on time, performing the duties assigned to you, and generally giving an honest day's work for an honest day's pay.

As an employer, however, you have to think about things like: payroll, remitting state and federal taxes, workers compensation premiums, health care plans and benefits, pension and 401(k) benefits, salary and performance reviews, paid holiday and overtime, vehicle allowances, sick and holiday time, assuming liability for certain acts of your employees (if they cause an accident driving the company van to make a delivery, guess who gets sued), severance pay, and on and on. Oftentimes this is going to effectively mean you either roll up your sleeves, train yourself, and go to it, or, alternatively, you bring someone in to do this for you. However, as a small start-up business, bringing someone in to manage your employee administration may not be economically possible. After all, you're just beginning and your efforts really need to be on growing your business.

The alternative is to turn away from a traditional employer-employee relationship to one of business—independent contractor. There are advantages and disadvantages to this type of scenario.

An independent contractor is just as it sounds. A contractor is someone who is contracted to perform services for someone else under a written agreement. The "independent" part of independent contractor means that you, as a party to a service contract, pay this individual a flat fee based on whatever terms you negotiate, and they assume all responsibility for their own taxes, health care premiums, workers compensation, and unemployment insurance. An independent contractor is specifically designated by law to not be an employee, and so your company takes on none of the obligations, liabilities, or responsibilities associated with traditional employer-employee relationships. You can also write specific indemnification clauses into your service contract, whereby you offset liability arising from certain acts of an independent contractor from attaching to your company. In many cases, people who are working as independent contractors have formed their own companies, in which case you would hire that company, and, by association, its employee(s), to perform whatever functions you agree to.

The drawback to this type of relationship comes mainly from IRS treatment of independent contractor relationships. Even though you and this individual have contracted out of the traditional employer-employee responsibilities and obligations, as far as the IRS is concerned, if an individual fits into certain criteria, then they are deemed to be an employee, regardless of contractual arrangements. In practical terms, this means that where an independent contractor fails to remit their taxes and statutory deductions out of the flat fee that you have negotiated to pay them, the IRS can and will come looking to you to make good if they consider the independent contractor to be classifiable as an employee.

Rich Dad Tips

- The IRS is using an electronic matching system to investigate companies that misclassify employees as independent contractors.
- If five or more workers are paid $25,000 or more on a company 1099 and they don't show any other sources of income, the company will be subject to an audit.

An idea of the criteria used by the IRS to determine whether employee or independent contractor status is appropriate follows:

Employee	*Independent Contractor*
• Works for you (the employer) 100 percent of their time, at least during the length of time it takes to achieve a specific goal.	• Works for you (the business owner) on a part-time basis, and may also be working for other companies or individuals at the same time.
• Hours and days of work are scheduled by you.	• Is given a goal and a deadline, but no specific schedule is set.
• Is trained by you, and must perform work in a particular fashion, sequence, or method.	• Is responsible only for the attainment of a goal, without specific requirements on how the goal must be achieved.
• Is provided with tools and materials, and must work on your premises.	• Provides own tools and materials, and may work from home, own location, or anywhere else.
• Must perform the work personally.	• May hire assistants or subcontractors to accomplish the goal.
• Is paid hourly, weekly, or monthly.	• Is paid on a per-project, commission basis, or invoices you for time worked.
	• Holds their own business licenses, permits, and other necessary legal requirements.

So, in order to make the argument that you are contracting with individuals on an independent contractor basis, you must ensure that, at a minimum, you enter into an independent contractor service agreement, and that independent contractors all submit invoices to your company to cover work they perform. If your contract with these individuals contains most or all of the points mentioned above, then you stand a better chance of successfully arguing that you are not an employer.

A sample independent contractor service agreement may be found at the end of this chapter, as well as a sample employment agreement.

Employment Agreements and Considerations

Employment agreements will likely feature prominently in a start-up company's business plan, especially in connection with your key management or technical employees.

Traditionally, there are two types of employment groups associated with start-up companies: regular employees and key employees. Regular employees work under you, or other management, have a minor to moderate level of responsibility, and are paid accordingly. On the other hand, key employees are those you need to get your business plan off the ground. They are highly skilled in either technology or business operations and are essential to your company. They are likely to receive a considerable amount of money for their services, or, in many start-up companies where cash is not available, they receive a large allocation of founders' shares in return for all or a part of their contributions. The relationship of key employees to your company is probably closer to that of a business partner or founder than it is to that of regular employees. Regular employees may also receive a stock allocation or option to purchase stock in your company, but it is usually a considerably smaller amount than that granted to your key employees.

For new companies, the use of carefully crafted employment agreements may be the only way that you can attract the talent you need to get your business off the ground. Highly knowledgeable individuals possessing extremely marketable skills have likely invested their own time and money to obtain those skills and knowledge, and will be looking to secure their own future and ensure fair compensation for their services. In these instances, it is quite likely that they will be looking for a significant stock allocation in addition to financial compensation.

Having employment agreements in place with your company's key employees may also be a condition of attracting venture capital. Prospective investors, especially those from whom you are seeking a large capital investment, will be looking to see that you have secured the talent required to put your business plan into effect. A new company with a great idea, but which is relying on a single person to put this idea into effect, and the single person in question is not under contract or obligated to stay with your company in any way, is not an attractive proposition for a potential investor.

A carefully crafted employment agreement can secure other things besides guaranteed service and peace of mind for investors. Through the use of confidentiality and noncompetition clauses, your company can be protected from employees selling your valuable information and processes to a competitor, or worse, breaking away to form a new company to compete directly with your company, based on ideas developed with your company and marketed at your company's existing customer base. Through the use of ownership clauses, you can ensure that the software or products you are paying people to develop for you remain your company's property.

Even in cases where you don't have any employees, and the bright shining idea that is your company is you, an employment agreement can still be desirable, or necessary. Remember, investors are investing in your company, not you personally, and, by investing in your company, are also purchasing a degree of control over how your company operates. Therefore, they will want some type of assurance that the products or technology you are developing belong to the company, and not to you. Another point to consider is how you are to be paid for your efforts. Having an agreed-upon amount that you will receive for the products and services you are contributing to your company is, again, reassuring to potential investors. It would not be prudent to invest in a company in which there was no guarantee that the products or services, which attracted such an investment in the first place, could not be removed at any time. It would be equally imprudent to invest in a company where there was no method to control what funds went to company development and what funds went into someone's pocket.

Who Should Sign an Employment Agreement?

As set out above, it is desirable to enter into employment agreements with all of your company's key employees. These should include (but are not limited to) yourself and your partners or other founders of your company, scientific personnel, software and hardware developers, financial officers, accountants, lawyers (if your company has in-house counsel), and sales managers (particularly those with in-depth knowledge of and significant contacts in your company's target industry).

What Should Go into an Employment Agreement?

What goes into an employment agreement will depend on whom your company is contracting with. However, there are certain basic elements that should be contained in every employment agreement:

JOB TITLE AND SCOPE OF DUTIES
What is this individual going to do for your company and how specific do you need to be?

Although a job title may on the face of it be fairly easy to apply, when considering what the scope of someone's duties will be, you must consider how specifically those duties should be set out, and whether you need to leave some room for a job to change and grow. A checklist of powers and duties traditionally assigned to various corporate officers is found in the materials at the end of this chapter. But be careful in relying upon only one format, and think through the powers and duties as they apply to your own situation. If the job title's scope is too narrow, the risk is that you will constantly be renegotiating your company's employment agreements, particularly in a start-up situation where the chances of positions expanding beyond their original scope are high. If the scope is too broad, however, the risk comes when you try to narrow the scope at a future date, particularly where you are looking to remove certain responsibilities from an employee. An employee who disagrees with having responsibilities removed may argue that the legal concept of constructive dismissal applies and take legal action against your company. (Constructive dismissal means making unilateral—i.e., one-sided—changes to an employee's position, duties, or wages—usually involving reduction or removal—that fundamentally alter his or her job.) Alternatively, an employee in this situation may argue that your company has breached the employment agreement and, by doing so, has nullified the entire agreement, including the portions relating to confidentiality and noncompetition. It is always a good idea to include in any employment agreement a clause that states that a company's board of directors is the final policymaker and may choose to amend employment duties as they see fit to best benefit the company as a whole.

Where the employment agreement being created is for you, as the founder, additional consideration needs to be given to ensure that you do not lose control over your company to incoming investors. You may wish to consider including a clause limiting the amount by which your position can be changed by the board of directors. You may also wish to establish a separate shareholder agreement with these individuals, which would cover other facets of your relationship with these investors, including control issues, veto powers, and so forth, and use that shareholder agreement to ensure that you do not wind up in a situation where you lose shareholder control over your company and then are terminated from your position within the company, effectively removing you entirely from the operation.

TERM OF THE EMPLOYMENT AGREEMENT

There are several ways to approach the idea of how long an employment agreement should last. With certain key employees, it may be best to limit the term of the employment agreement to a specific time, in which a specific project or goal is to be achieved. Alternatively, you may wish to make the employment agreement renewable annually or biannualy, depending on your company's specific requirements. Where you anticipate the employment relationship as being long-term and continuous, you may wish to allow for that in the employment agreement. You may also elect to add a clause to the agreement whereby the employment agreement is for an initial term of one year, and automatically renews for additional one-year terms until terminated by your company or the employee. It is generally preferable to have key employees contracted for a longer term, as opposed to a month-by-month basis, as, again, your company is trying to promote an image of stability to investors.

HOURS OF EMPLOY

In addition to setting out the job title and scope of duties, it is also important to note in the employment agreement that while an individual is working for your company, they are to devote their full time and attention to carrying out those duties. Again, you need to guard against becoming too narrow—for example, scientific and high-tech employees will oftentimes be involved in conferences and seminars, writing papers, and information exchanges with other members of their scientific community. If employees are not permitted time for these other opportunities, the risk exists that their knowledge will become stagnant and of less value to your company. On the other hand, an employee who is never at work isn't much help either. You need to consider where balance will be achieved, and tailor the employment agreement to each individual situation. You may wish to consider a clause limiting the amount of time that may be spent on these outside activities, or that attendance or participation in certain activities must be subject to prior consent by your company. This is particularly important in the case of part-time or consulting employees, who may work for several other organizations simultaneously. The more organizations an employee is working for simultaneously, the more difficult it becomes to properly ensure that your company's trade secrets, proprietary processes, and methods are not being transferred or modified to suit these other organizations.

PAID EMPLOYMENT EXPENSES, INCLUDING TRAVEL AND RELOCATION

If you are anticipating that an employment position with your company may require travel and/or relocation, it is important that this be addressed in the employment agreement. A proper schedule and method of reimbursement must be set out, and adhered to by both sides. If receipts and documentation are to be required for reimbursement, this must be made clear.

SALARY AND OTHER BENEFITS

In addition to the monetary portion of an employee's salary, there may be other benefits to consider such as stock allocations or options to purchase stock in the future, medical and dental health plans, pension plans, profit sharing arrangements, or paid vehicle allowances. It is a good idea, particularly in a start-up situation, where your company does not have significant cash on hand to pay large salaries, and is depending on stock allocations and options, to tie these to continuing service by employees, or upon milestones reached. A more detailed discussion on employee benefits is set out later in this chapter.

KEY MAN LIFE INSURANCE

It may be to the benefit of your company to consider life insurance on key employees, particularly in the case of a founders' employment agreement. Under such a policy, the company may be designated as beneficiary, or you may wish to consider having your company's investors as beneficiaries where the insured person is irreplaceable and your company not likely to succeed without them. Where such a clause is requested, though, you must ensure that the employee in question agrees to undergo any required medical examinations and perform such acts and sign any documents required to put such a policy into place.

ASSIGNABILITY

Any employment agreement should contain a clause allowing your company to assign the employment agreement to an affiliate, associate, subsidiary, or successor company to your company. You do not want to be in a situation where your company is being purchased by another company but a key employee whose services are essential to your company refuses to work for the successor company.

CONFIDENTIALITY AND NONCOMPETITION

As discussed earlier, it is vital for start-up companies to protect their intellectual property, patents, trade secrets, products, methods of production, and business model from being either provided to existing competitors, or poached by your own employees into new spin-off operations. An employment agreement should be fairly specific as to what is considered confidential information, and should also set out a clause whereby an employee acknowledges that breaching this confidentiality clause could leave him or her open to prosecution by your company.

Noncompetition, on the other hand, must be tailored a bit more specifically. For example, hiring a software engineer to write a certain piece of software for your company does not mean that this person may realistically be barred from ever writing another piece of software for another company, even if that company is in a similar business venture. What your company may be able to do, however, is set a reasonable time and/or geographical limit before that individual is permitted to engage in conduct that could be seen as in competition to yours, either directly, by creating their own start-up business, or indirectly, by working for a competitor, and potentially utilizing all of the knowledge gained at your company to assist the competition. It is important, however, when considering this provision to obtain proper legal advice on what is considered reasonable and what is considered excessive. Most courts hold that, as a matter of public policy, it is good for society for people to work. And so the courts are not fond of employers who try to limit, in draconian fashion, future activities of employees. For example, a requirement whereby a former employee is not permitted to engage in their profession for several years following termination of their employment with your company, or where they are not permitted to work in your company's state and six surrounding states, will likely be overturned by a court, and may even result in penalties being assessed against your company. You cannot prevent an employee from practicing his trade, especially where knowledge and skills have been obtained over a lengthy time prior to employment with your company. You can, however, seek to minimize, to a reasonable degree, what that employee can do with the knowledge gained during their employment with your company.

DEVELOPMENT AND OWNERSHIP OF INVENTIONS, TRADE SECRETS, AND NEW BUSINESS IDEAS

Again, as set out above, where your company is engaging individuals to help it develop a business, expand on an idea, and create new products, services, or ideas for your company, it is important that all parties be clear on who owns what. An employment agreement should have a section requiring an employee to acknowledge that ideas, inventions, and improvements created by that employee which (1) relate to your company's existing, proposed, or contemplated business, or actual or anticipated research; (2) result from work done by the employee, using your company's equipment, including software platforms; and (3) result from the employee's access to your company's trade secrets, assets, information, and so on, belong to the company, and not the employee. You should also follow up this clause with a clause requiring an employee to specifically assign all of his or her right, title, and interest in and to such idea, invention, or improvement to your company.

TERMINATION

It's going to happen, sooner or later. The best way to protect your company from future wrongful dismissal lawsuits is to set out a termination clause, identifying the circumstances under which an employee can be terminated, how much notice is required, or what appropriate payment in lieu of notice will be. In this clause, you should set out a "neutral termination" section, whereby either you or the employee can choose to terminate the employment relationship for no cause, by providing each other with sufficient written notice. A section allowing for "natural termination" should also be included, whereby either party can choose not to renew the employment agreement following the completion of its term. There should also be a "for cause termination," in which you set out specifically what is unacceptable conduct and what will result in immediate termination or termination on sufficient notice. It is also a good idea to set out a section dealing with what would constitute a breach of the employment agreement by your company, which should typically be limited to failure to pay salary.

Where the employment agreement is being drafted to cover you, as a founder, you may wish to include other events that would constitute a breach by your company, including fundamental changes to your job responsibilities and functions mandated by the board of directors that would constitute constructive dismissal.

In situations where stock allocations have been made, or more particularly, in situations where options to purchase stock have not been exercised, or have not entirely vested, it must be made clear what happens to unexercised or unvested portions. ("Vesting" is the term used to describe how ownership of shares is transferred in a situation where a stock grant is made over a period of time. For example, a yearly allocation of 120 shares per year, vesting on a monthly basis, would mean that ten shares per month would vest into an employee's name. Accordingly, should this employee leave after six months, a total of sixty shares would have vested in his name, and he would lose his entitlement to the remaining sixty shares.) In addition, you may wish to consider a clause whereby all stock sold to an employee during the course of their employment is subject to repurchase by your company, at a favorable price, or at the purchase price. A repurchase clause is found most commonly in privately held company situations, where it is in a company's best interests to have shares held by as few shareholders as possible.

You may also wish to consider a repurchase formula in employment agreements entered into between you, as a founder, with your company, particularly in instances where you are being bought out by investors. Alternatively, if your company is considering going public, then you, as founder, may wish to add a clause allowing you to retain your shareholdings and liquidate them into the public market following the completion of the going-public process. It may be advantageous to you to try to tie a stock repurchase formula to a noncompete clause in a founder employment agreement.

Another point for a founder to consider including in an employment agreement is a requirement for a valuation of your company's business to be performed prior to investors seeking to buy out your interest and terminate your working relationship with your company. Having a valuation conducted by a third party ensures that your shareholding and contribution may be fairly valued, and you get fully compensated for the time and effort you have put into building your company.

A sample founder/key employee employment agreement is found in the materials at the end of this chapter in addition to the sample employment agreement and independent contractor service agreement (discussed earlier in this chapter).

Employment Law Primer

We talked briefly in the "Employment Agreements and Considerations" section above about certain things your company should and shouldn't do in order to avoid being the subject of a wrongful or constructive dismissal lawsuit by former employees. The following is a very brief primer on fundamental employment law concepts to give you an idea of what exactly you are getting yourself into. As with everything else in this book, this section is not meant to take the place of proper legal advice, nor is it overly detailed. It is meant simply to cover the major laws in place surrounding the employer-employee relationship.

FAIR LABOR STANDARDS ACT (FLSA)

This is a federal-level law, which governs things like minimum wage, equal pay, overtime, child labor, and what records a company is required to keep regarding its employees. The FLSA covers companies who engage in commerce, production of goods for sale, handling, selling, or moving of goods with a minimum gross sale value of $500,000 (whether or not the goods were manufactured by them). The FLSA also covers all companies, regardless of what they do, if such companies engage in interstate commerce, which is essentially meant as a catch-all category, as it is very unlikely that a company would be able to purchase all of its raw materials and supplies, make sales, and conduct advertising and marketing strictly within its state boundaries.

Assuming that the FLSA applies to your company, minimum wage requirements will apply. The minimum wage is set by the federal government from time to time. Certain states and even cities have their own wage rates, which may be higher than the federal minimum wage. If you are operating a business where employees receive tips, you may claim that up to 50 percent of their minimum wages may be paid by way of the tips they receive, but you must be able to prove that overall, wages and tips included, your employees receive at least the minimum wage.

Overtime is also payable, once an employee has worked more than forty hours in a workweek. Overtime is traditionally calculated to be 1.5 times the employee's regular wage, but there are exceptions to this rule, depending on the employee's specific classification. Before modifying the traditional 1.5 calculation, it is best to contact the U.S. Department of Labor to determine whether you have any employees who can be reclassified at a lower rate.

With respect to coffee and lunch breaks, the rule of thumb is, where the break is twenty minutes or less in length, the time is considered to be on the clock, and payable by the company. On the other hand, meal breaks of thirty minutes or longer in length are not considered payable, as long as the employees are relieved of all duties during this time, and are not required to remain on the job and eat at their desks or workstations.

The FLSA also provides that employees receive a Form W-2 on a yearly basis, which is a record of hours worked, wages received, and statutory deductions made. So good record keeping is essential, as you must be able to produce these records, complete and intact, should the Department of Labor come looking.

Child labor laws are strictly regulated under the FLSA. Children under the age of sixteen are generally prohibited from being employed, although there is an exception for children of a business owner. In addition, children are prohibited from performing hazardous work such as mining, or from being around hazardous work sites, such as heavy manufacturing or machining, transportation, warehousing, or construction.

CIVIL RIGHTS ACT OF 1964 (CRA)

The CRA is another federal law, which guards employees from being the target of discriminatory practices by an employer, including discrimination based on race, color, gender, religion, or national origin. A subsection of the CRA deals with the treatment of pregnant women in the workplace, prohibiting employers from using someone's pregnancy as a reason to deny her a job, or removing her from a job at a certain stage of pregnancy, unless that employee is physically unable to perform the work due to her pregnancy. Sexual harassment is covered under the CRA, requiring an employer to provide a safe, harassment-free workplace. The CRA also provides for protection from retaliation by an employer against an employee who raises a complaint, as well as protection for any other employees assisting an employee with a discrimination complaint.

AGE DISCRIMINATION IN EMPLOYMENT ACT (ADEA)

As employment law has advanced significantly through the past few decades, the ADEA was written to cover those individuals who were found to not be covered by the CRA. Prior to the enactment of the ADEA, age had never been considered an applicable factor upon which to base a claim of discrimination. However, massive changes in the workplace led to situations where qualified individuals were denied employment because younger, cheaper, and less qualified help was available, or, individuals over a certain age were prohibited from applying for certain positions that had been reserved for younger individuals. The ADEA provides that companies may not discriminate against individuals in either hiring or firing, where age is a motivating factor. In addition, the ADEA also provides that a company generally may not force a person to retire, although there are certain compulsory retirement provisions applicable to executives who are sixty-five years or older and have held an executive-level position for a minimum of two years preceding their retirement.

AMERICANS WITH DISABILITIES ACT (ADA)

Another entry into the employment law forum is the ADA. Under the ADA, individuals with disabilities such as blindness, deafness, speech impediments, cerebral palsy, epilepsy, muscular dystrophy, multiple sclerosis, AIDS, cancer, heart disease, diabetes, mental retardation, and emotional illness are protected from discriminatory hiring and firing practices by employers. However, in order to rely on the ADA, disabled persons must be able to show that they are qualified as well as physically capable of performing the work required, or would be capable of performing it with reasonable accommodations and adjustments by an employer (e.g., installing ramps for wheelchair access). On the other hand, where an employer can show that employing the individual in question would be enormously costly, in terms of modifications required, to the point where the cost of hiring the employee would far outstrip the value of the work to be performed, then an exemption to the ADA may be available.

OCCUPATIONAL SAFETY AND HEALTH ACT (OSHA)

The OSHA was enacted to protect employees from being forcibly exposed to harmful substances while working. While the OSHA is not applicable to businesses with standard office environments, it is applicable to industries such as manufacturing, restaurant, agriculture, medical by-products and waste, and the like. Employers are required to provide a safe and healthy working environment, and to minimize the risk to their employees, through the use of protective equipment such as masks or breathing apparatus, or through the design of the workplace itself, e.g., proper installation of exhaust/ventilation systems.

WORKERS COMPENSATION

Even with the best efforts on the part of an employer and its employees, accidents in the workplace will happen. Workers compensation is designed to protect employees from being impoverished due to their inability to work following a work-related accident. It requires an employer to take certain steps, which include (a) obtaining an insurance policy to cover workplace accidents (the most popular method of complying with workers compensation requirements); or (b) establishing individual self-insurance funds, either on an employer-by-employer basis, or in collective groups of employers. Employers who do not have adequate workers compensation coverage may find themselves the subject of a lawsuit if an employee is left unprotected following a workplace-related accident. As workers compensation is not applicable to independent contractors or subcontractors, it is important to be clear, when preparing any sort of employment agreement or independent contractor service agreement, regarding what the exact status of the would-be employee will be. Courts do not look favorably upon employers who attempt to reclassify employees as independent contractors to avoid paying workers compensation benefits.

EMPLOYEE POLYGRAPH PROTECTION ACT OF 1988 (EPPA)

An act for every situation, a situation for every act. Under the provisions of the EPPA, subjecting job applicants and employees to lie detector testing, although a novel way of interviewing, is illegal, unless it falls under a specialized exemption, for example, employees who will be dealing with certain controlled substances.

ELECTRONIC COMMUNICATIONS PRIVACY ACT OF 1986 (ECPA)

Wiretapping or other monitoring of an employee's conversations and actions while on the job is illegal without the express consent of the employee. So, for situations where you will want to visually monitor employees (as in banks or jewelry stores), or monitor by telephone (telemarketing, customer service, and so on), you will need to clearly explain what you are doing and obtain their consent ahead of time.

FAMILY AND MEDICAL LEAVE ACT (FMLA)

Under the provisions of the FMLA, employees may take up to twelve weeks per year of unpaid leave for medical reasons or to deal with family problems. The act covers employees seeking leave for childbirth or adoption, caring for an immediate family member with a serious health condition, or being unable to work due to a serious health condition. Employees are required to provide thirty days' notice prior to taking leave under the FMLA, although obviously this will not always be possible, given the nature of the family or medical emergency.

Again, we remind you, this is a brief overview to introduce you to certain employment-related issues that may arise in your company. It is not, nor is it intended, to be complete or to replace proper legal advice and assistance.

Employee Benefit Plans

An employee benefit plan can be a crucial element in attracting the talent that your company needs to grow and thrive. Oftentimes in the case of start-up companies, there is limited cash flow, and so a degree of flexibility and creativity is called for to make up for this.

Employee benefits may be broadly defined into two distinct areas— traditional benefits, such as health and dental plans, pension plans, vacation and sick allowances; and equity benefits, such as stock option grants, incentive stock option plans, profit sharing formulas, and performance bonuses. When considering how to implement employee benefit plans, it may be to your company's advantage to consider two separate plans, one covering the traditional benefits, which will be available to all employees, and the second one covering equity benefits, which may be available to select employees only.

The following is a brief overview of elements to consider including in your company's employee benefit plan. We have divided these elements into the traditional and equity sections. Because of the various tax implications involved in many elements of an employee benefit plan, we recommend that you not attempt to implement one into your company without individual legal and financial advice from your lawyers and accountants.

TRADITIONAL BENEFITS

Health Insurance Plans

Health insurance plans may be purchased through most insurance companies, in varying levels of coverage. Elements of a health insurance plan may include HMO coverage, dental and vision coverage, short-term and long-term disability coverage, life insurance, prescription reimbursement, cafeteria-style medical plans, and emergency hospitalization coverage. The levels and complexity of packages offered vary widely, and it will require some time and effort on your part to review and consider the most appropriate plan for your company. Monthly premiums for coverage may be paid wholly by your company, or apportioned to some degree between your company and its employees.

Health insurance plans are tax deductible for your company, and are tax deductible for most employees as well. However, as previously mentioned, 2 percent or greater shareholders of an S corporation must pay taxes on the value of health benefits received. Be sure to work with your tax advisor to make certain you are capturing all the allowable deductions in this area.

Tax-Qualified Retirement Plans

A tax-qualified retirement plan is an employer-funded plan, whereby the company makes contributions on behalf of its employees, usually to a separate entity that then manages and invests the funds. The payments by the company into the plan are tax deductible at the time of payment, and do not become taxable until the employee withdraws the funds, at which time the employee is responsible for payment of the taxes. While from a taxation point of view this type of plan is attractive to a company, due to the tax deductible status of the contributions, it is subject to detailed government regulations, review, and continued monitoring by both the IRS and the Department of Labor.

Section 401(k) Plan

A Section 401(k) plan allows for employees participating in certain tax-qualified retirement profit sharing or stock bonus plans to elect whether to receive company contributions in cash or to have them paid into a tax-qualified plan. Monies or shares paid into an employee's Section 401(k) plan are tax-deferred until withdrawal, and are then taxed at the holder's normal rate. Alternately, monies paid into a Roth 401(k) plan are taxed on the way in, but tax free on the way out of the plan at retirement. (Given several years or more compounding, this may be the best way to go.) In addition, a company may also negotiate with employees to enter into a salary reduction agreement, whereby an employee elects to have yearly salary raises, bonuses, and other compensation paid directly into their Section 401(k) plan, thus decreasing their taxable income. Companies favor these arrangements as it allows them to reduce payroll tax contributions.

Supplemental Compensation Benefits

These are additional benefits from which employees may make a selection, with their premium rates being adjusted accordingly, based on the benefits they select. Supplemental compensation benefits may include things like interest-free loans, company car (for use on company business only), financial or retirement planning and counseling, or fitness or other club memberships.

EQUITY-BASED BENEFITS

Equity shares are one of the most attractive benefits a start-up company is able to offer. Where your company has a sound business idea and a likelihood of success, the chances are good that your company's shares will increase in value, perhaps significantly. Therefore, a person receiving a share allocation as a part of their compensation potentially stands to make a profit from the sale of their shares in the future, or, alternatively, stands to benefit from shareholder dividends realized from the profits of your company. While the chances of success and profitability are not guaranteed, the potential to make significant profit is there, and, ultimately, may be higher than the employee would have received had they been receiving straight, market-value cash compensation for their services.

Equity compensation can take many forms, including outright grants of stock, and grants of incentive stock options (the grant of a right to purchase stock in the future). In many instances, equity stock granted using one or more of these methods may be subject to special capital gains treatment, and can therefore minimize the tax impact on employees.

Stock Purchase Plans

The simplest of all methods to provide employees with equity stock, a stock purchase plan provides a method whereby employees may purchase shares in your company, either at market value or at a discount. It is important, however, from a psychological and motivational viewpoint, to keep some type of link between employment performance and the stock purchase plan, for example, by offering employees interest-free loans to purchase stock. It is in your company's best interests to encourage a sense of motivation and participation among employees, as opposed to being merely passive shareholders. In addition, to provide incentive for your company's employees to stay with your company, you may wish to consider imposing a vesting schedule on all stock purchases. A vesting schedule provides that an employee must remain employed for a designated period in order to receive full ownership rights to all of the stock purchased. Where an employee ceases employment with a company prior to completing the agreed-upon vesting period, they must then sell a portion of their purchased shares back to the company, on a pro rata basis, or, they may have to forgo receiving future allotments of shares due to their termination. By using a vesting schedule, your company can maintain a tighter shareholder base, as well as provide an incentive for employees to remain with your company.

Incentive Stock Option Plan

An incentive stock option plan is similar to a stock purchase plan, except that instead of actually purchasing stock, employees are granted a right to purchase stock during a set period of time, usually at a discounted price from the current market value. Employees may, therefore, choose whether or not to exercise all or a part of their option, depending on the market value of the company's shares, or other factors. Exercise of an incentive stock option is not mandatory. In addition, depending on the type of plan initiated, there may be no tax consequences to the employee until the option is actually exercised and the stock purchased.

Rich Dad Tips

- In a small-company setting do not even mention the possibility of setting up a stock option or other benefit plan if you do not intend to offer one.
- Your employees will hold you to such a promise and will only be angered—perhaps to the point of litigation—if such a plan is not implemented.

The foregoing is a very brief overview of elements to consider when contemplating an employee benefits plan, and is not meant to substitute in any way for proper legal and financial advice. Prior to implementing any sort of employee benefit plan into your company, you should first make sure that you have discussed all elements to be included with your legal and financial advisors.

Following is a list of skills and qualities that are required and/or desirable in all of your corporate management, and particularly in your company's CEO and president:

- Managerial skills, including group management; motivational, organizational, and delegation skills; ability to develop, direct, and control staff; strategic and analytical thinking, problem solving, and creativity; technical expertise.
- Social and communication skills, including verbal and written communications, presentation, negotiation, cooperation, listening, and empathy.

- Personal qualities such as enthusiasm, initiative, drive for achievement and results, as well as being self-motivated, stress-tolerant, and a calculated risk taker.

Guideline of Powers and Duties and Required or Desirable Skills for Various Corporate Officer Positions

Chief Executive Officer

- Has general supervision over the company
- Presides at all corporate meetings
- Is often also the chairman of the board
- Has the power to sign all corporate documents, share certificates, and other instruments except where, by law, the president must sign
- Is often made an ex officio member of all standing committees

President

- May also be the chief executive officer
- May substitute for the chairman of the board in his or her absence
- Power is limited to matters that arise within the ordinary course of business and are in the best interests of the company, including, but not limited to: calling special meetings of shareholders; fixing compensation paid to officers; appointing and removing officers; setting out the duties of subordinate officers
- Has implicit powers with respect to carrying out authorized acts on behalf of the company
- Has authority to perform any act that the directors authorize and ratify, unless powers are restricted in the company's charter, articles, or bylaws
- Unauthorized legal acts may be ratified subsequently by the directors

Vice President

- Acts as assistant to the president
- Is often assigned an important role in corporate administration
- Assumes president's power and duties and acts in his or her place in the event of president's absence, death, or incapacity (but, in some cases, will require prior approval of the directors to carry out certain acts)
- Has no other powers by virtue of the office; without express or implied authority, cannot manage or bind the company
- Designated by seniority in situations where a company has multiple vice presidents

Corporate Secretary

- Keeps corporate books and has charge of corporate seal (if company has one)
- Has additional powers (assigned by president or directors), which may include: preparing shareholder lists for annual meetings; maintaining and recording entries in stock ledger; signing corporate documents and instruments
- Authority determined primarily by character of corporate business and relative powers of other officers
- Powers may overlap with those of treasurer, controller, or auditor

Treasurer

- Usual powers include: care, custody, and maintenance of corporate funds and securities; maintenance of books of accounts and records; preparation of financial statements; disbursement of corporate funds
- Has powers delegated to it by directors, committees, or by direction of president/CEO
- Is often appointed to finance committee and as advisor to other officers in financial matters

General Manager

- Has authority to perform acts necessary in the usual and ordinary course of company's business
- Specific functions vary with size and nature of business, and as delegated by directors, committees, or president/CEO
- Authority may be limited to general management over specific portions of the business, such as manufacturing or sales

Controller

- Is chief accounting officer with powers including, but not limited to: maintenance and audit of company's financial records; preparation of financial statements; supervision of company accounting practices
- Works with audit committee, outside auditors, creditors, and corporate counsel

Assistant Officers

- Perform specific duties assigned by directors and other senior officers
- May substitute for senior officers during absences (in order of seniority)

Founder/Key Employee Employment Agreement

THIS EMPLOYMENT AGREEMENT (the "Agreement") is made as of _____,
20__

BETWEEN:

[YOUR COMPANY], a [state of incorporation] Corporation with a registered
office address at [address—you can also use your business address]

(the "Company")

OF THE FIRST PART

AND:

[INDIVIDUAL NAME], an individual, who resides at [Address]

(the "Founder/Key Employee")

OF THE SECOND PART

WHEREAS:

(a) [Founder only] The Company, the Founder, and [Names of Investors] (the
"Investors") have executed a Subscription Agreement and a Stockholders
Agreement (the "Stockholders Agreement"), each dated [date], pursuant
to which, amongst other things, the Investors purchased for the amount
of [amount], a total of [number of shares or securities purchased] of the
Company and the Founder purchased [number of shares owned by
Founder] shares of Common Stock, par value of $ [found in your Articles of
Incorporation, usually minimal, e.g., $0.001 or $0.01] per share;

(b) The Company is in the business of _____ (the "Business")
and the [Founder/Key Employee] is acknowledged as a leading expert in
the Business;

(c) [Founder only] The parties acknowledge that the Founder's knowledge
and experience are unique and essential to the Business and that certain of
the Company's investors (the "Investors") have been induced to invest in
the Company by reason of the Founder's knowledge and experience;

(d) The Company wishes to formalize its agreement with the [Founder/Key
Employee] as to his provision of services and knowledge to the Company,
by engaging the services of the [Founder/Key Employee] as its [Job Title,
e.g., President, Chief Executive Officer, etc.], and the [Founder/Key
Employee] has agreed to be engaged by the Company in this fashion;

NOW, THEREFORE, in consideration of the mutual promises, covenants, terms,
and conditions herein, and for other good and valuable consideration, the receipt
and sufficiency of which are hereby acknowledged by the parties, the parties
agree as follows:

1. Agreement to Employ. The Company agrees to employ the [Founder/ Key Employee] as its [Job Title] and the [Founder/Key Employee] agrees to be employed in this capacity, upon the terms and conditions hereinafter set forth.

2. Term. This Agreement shall commence on the date hereof and shall terminate as of the earlier of:

   (a) [six months, one year, five years, etc.] (the "Initial Term") unless either the Founder or the Company notifies the other that he or it elects to extend the term hereof for an additional [number of years of Term extension] (the "Renewal Period"), such notice to be given within ninety (90) days before the end of the Initial Term hereof or within ninety (90) days before the end of each successive Renewal Period;

   (b) the death of the [Founder/Key Employee]; or

   (c) thirty (30) days after notice is given by one party to the other after a material breach of this Agreement, by either party; or

   (d) [for Founder] thirty (30) days after notice is given by one party to the other after a material breach of this Agreement [or of the Stockholders Agreement], by either party.

   The exercise of the right of the Company or the [Key Employee] to terminate this Agreement pursuant to subsection 2(c) shall not abrogate the rights and remedies of the terminating party in respect of the breach giving rise to such termination. The Company shall only be deemed to have materially breached this Agreement and the terms of the Founder's employment if it fails to comply with Section 3 hereof or the proviso in the second sentence of Section 4 hereof in all material respects.

   [or, for Founder] The exercise of the right of the Company or the [Founder] to terminate this Agreement pursuant to subsection 2(c) shall not abrogate the rights and remedies of the terminating party in respect of the breach giving rise to such termination. The Company shall only be deemed to have materially breached this Agreement and the terms of the [Founder's] employment if it fails to comply with Section 3 hereof or the proviso in the second sentence of Section 4 hereof in all material respects.

3. Compensation. For all services rendered under this Agreement:

   (a) (i) the Company shall pay the [Founder/Key Employee] a base salary of [amount], per annum, in equal monthly or semimonthly installments. Such salary shall be reviewed and adjusted annually, on the anniversary date of this Agreement during the Initial Term, or on the yearly anniversary date of each successive Renewal Term, to accommodate any change in the cost-of-living index for the region as compiled by the Department of Labor. The Board of Directors shall review, on an annual basis, the [Founder/Key Employee]'s salary with a view to increasing it if, in the sole judgment of the Board of Directors, the earnings of the Company or the services of the Founder merit such increases;

   (ii) if the [Founder/Key Employee] has been disabled for a period of at least [how long?] consecutive days, the Company may elect, upon notice to the [Founder/Key Employee], to pay the [Founder/Key Employee] [how much?] of the compensation the [Founder/Key Employee] would otherwise be entitled to pursuant to clause (i) above and shall thereupon have no further obligation under Section 3(d) or (e) hereof. Disability shall mean the [Founder/Key Employee]'s inability, due to sickness or injury, to perform effectively their duties hereunder.

(b) During the Initial Term, the [Founder/Key Employee] shall be entitled to incentive compensation, payable by the Company within thirty (30) days after delivery to the [Founder/Key Employee] (which delivery shall be no later than [how long?] months after the end of each fiscal year of the Company) of the Company's annual audited financial statements, as follows: (i) [percentage of gross/net profits attained by the Company] or (ii) [formula or accomplishments agreed to between the parties]; subject to a yearly maximum limit of incentive compensation of [how much?] per annum.

(c) If this Agreement is terminated or the Company notifies the [Founder/Key Employee] in respect of the disability provision set out in 3(a)(ii) above, incentive compensation in respect of the fiscal year of such termination or in which such notice is given shall be computed as if such termination had not occurred and the [Founder/Key Employee] shall be paid an amount equal to the product of the incentive compensation to which they would otherwise have been entitled, multiplied by a fraction having a numerator equal to the number of days in such year preceding the date of termination and a denominator equal to 365; provided that the [Founder/Key Employee] shall not be entitled to any amounts pursuant to this Section 3(c) if this Agreement is terminated pursuant to Section 2(c) prior to the date of payment of such amount.

(d) During the term of this Agreement, the [Founder/Key Employee] shall be entitled to participate in any employee benefit plans or programs of the Company, if any, to the extent that his tenure, salary, age, health, and other qualifications make him eligible to participate, subject to the rules and regulations applicable thereto. Such additional benefits shall include, subject to the approval of the Board of Directors, full medical, dental, and income insurance, [how many?] weeks of paid vacation, and qualified pension and profit sharing plans.

(e) The Company will furnish the [Founder/Key Employee], without cost to him, a Company-owned or -leased automobile of the make and model authorized by the Company's policy, and life insurance in the amount of at least [how much?].

(f) The [Founder/Key Employee] shall be entitled to reimbursement of all expenses incurred by him in the performance of his duties, subject to the presenting of appropriate receipts and documentary evidence in accordance with the Company's policy.

4. Duties. So long as the Company has not notified the [Key Employee] of termination pursuant to Section 3(a)(ii) above, the [Key Employee] is engaged initially with the title and functions of [Job Title, e.g., President and Chief Executive Officer] of the Company and, subject to the direction of the Board of Directors, shall perform and discharge well and faithfully the duties which may be assigned to him from time to time by the Company in connection with the conduct of its business. Nothing herein shall preclude the Board of Directors of the Company from changing the [Key Employee]'s title and duties, if such Board has concluded, in its reasonable judgment, that such change is in the Company's best interest. If the [Key Employee] is elected or appointed a director or officer of the Company or any subsidiary thereof during the term of this Agreement, the [Key Employee] will serve in such capacity without additional compensation.

4. [or, for Founder] Duties. So long as the Company has not notified the [Founder] of termination pursuant to Section 2 above, the [Founder] is engaged initially with the title and functions of [Job Title, e.g., President and Chief Executive Officer] of the Company and, subject to the direction of the Board of Directors, shall perform and discharge well and faithfully the duties which may be assigned to him from time to time by the Company in connection with the conduct of its business. Nothing herein shall preclude the Board of Directors of the Company from changing the [Founder]'s title and duties, if such Board has concluded, in its reasonable judgment, that such change is in the Company's best interest; PROVIDED HOWEVER, that at all times during the term of this Agreement, the [Founder] shall be employed as a senior executive of the Company with appropriate and commensurate compensation, title, rank, and status. If the Founder is elected or appointed a director or officer of the Company or any subsidiary thereof during the term of this Agreement, the [Founder] will serve in such capacity without additional compensation.

5. Extent of Service. So long as the Company has not notified the [Founder/Key Employee] of termination pursuant to Section 2 above, the [Founder/Key Employee] shall devote his entire time, attention, and energies to the business of the Company and shall not, during the term of this Agree-

ment, be engaged (whether or not during normal business hours) in any other business or professional activity, whether or not such activity is pursued for gain, profit or other pecuniary advantage; but this shall not be construed as preventing the [Founder/Key Employee] from:

(a) investing his personal assets in businesses which do not compete with the Company in such form or manner as will not require any services on the part of the [Founder/Key Employee] in the operation or the affairs of the companies in which such investments are made and in which his participation is solely that of an investor;

(b) purchasing securities in any corporation whose securities are regularly traded PROVIDED THAT such purchase shall not result in his collectively owning beneficially at any time, five percent (5%) or more of the equity securities of any corporation engaged in a business competitive to that of the Company; and

(c) participating in conferences, preparing or publishing papers or books, or teaching, so long as the Board of Directors approves of such activities prior to the [Founder/Key Employee]'s engaging in them. Prior to commencing any activity described herein, the [Founder/Key Employee] shall inform the Board of Directors of the Company in writing of any such activity.

6. Disclosure of Information.

(a) The [Founder/Key Employee] represents and warrants to the Company that Exhibit "A" hereto sets forth:

(i) all rights, in respect of the [Founder/Key Employee]'s engaging in any business activity (whether or not for profit), of former employers, clients, principals, partners, or others with whom or for whom the [Founder/Key Employee] has performed services since [when?]; and

(ii) all of the business activities (whether or not for profit) of the [Founder/Key Employee] applicable to periods after the time such services were performed.

(b) The [Founder/Key Employee] recognizes and acknowledges that the Company's trade secrets and proprietary information and processes, as they may exist from time to time, are valuable, special, and unique assets of the Company's business, access to and knowledge of which are essential to the performance of the [Founder/Key Employee]'s duties hereunder. The [Founder/Key Employee] will not, during or after the term of their employment by the Company, in whole or in part, disclose such secrets, information, or processes to any person, firm, corporation, association, or other entity for any reason or purpose whatsoever, nor shall the [Founder/Key Employee] make use of any such property for his own purposes or for the benefit of any person, firm, corporation, or other entity (except the Company) under any circumstances during or after the term of his employment, provided that after the term of his employment these restrictions shall not apply to such secrets, information, and processes which are then in the public domain (provided that the [Founder/Key Employee] was not responsible, directly or indirectly, for such secrets, information, or processes entering the public domain without the Company's consent). The [Founder/Key Employee] agrees to hold as the Company's property, all memoranda, books, papers, letters, formulas, and other data and all copies thereof and therefrom, in any way relating to the Company's businesses and affairs, whether made by him or otherwise coming into his possession, and on termination of his employment, or on demand of the Company, at any time, to deliver the same to the Company.

7. Inventions. The [Founder/Key Employee] hereby sells, transfers, and assigns to the Company or to any person or entity designated by the Company, all of the right, title, and interest of the [Founder/Key Employee] in and to all inventions, ideas, disclosures, and improvements, whether patented or unpatented, and copyrightable material, made or conceived by the [Founder/Key Employee], solely or jointly, or in whole or in part, during or before the term hereof (but after [date]) which:

(a) relate to methods, apparatus, designs, products, processes, or devices sold, leased, used, or under construction or development by the Company or any subsidiary; or

(b) otherwise relate to or pertain to the business, functions, or operations of the Company or any subsidiary; or

(c) [optional] arise in whole or in part from the efforts of the [Founder/Key Employee] during the term hereof.

The [Founder/Key Employee] shall communicate promptly and disclose to the Company, in such form as the Company requests, all information, details, and data pertaining to the aforementioned inventions, ideas, disclosures, and improvements; and, whether during the term hereof or thereafter, the [Founder/Key Employee] shall execute and deliver to the Company such formal transfers and assignments and such other papers and documents as may be required of the Founder to permit the Company or any person or entity designated by the Company to file and prosecute the patent applications and, as to copyrightable material, to obtain copyright thereon. Any invention by the [Founder/Key Employee] within [how many?] year(s) following the termination of this Agreement shall be deemed to fall within the provisions of this section unless provided by the [Founder/Key Employee] to have been first conceived and made following such termination.

8. Covenant not to Compete.

(a) During the term hereof and, unless this Agreement is terminated pursuant to Section 2(d) hereof, for a period of [how long?] year(s) thereafter, the [Founder/Key Employee] shall not compete, directly or indirectly, with the Company, interfere with, disrupt, or attempt to disrupt the relationship, contractual or otherwise, between the Company and any customer, client, supplier, consultant, or employee of the Company, including, without limitation, employing or being an investor (representing more than five percent (5%) equity interest) in, or officer, director, or consultant to, any person or entity which employs any former key or technical employee, whose employment with the Company was terminated after the date which is one year prior to the date of termination of the [Founder/Key Employee]'s employment therewith. An activity competitive with an activity engaged in by the Company shall include becoming an employee, officer, consultant, or director of, or being an investor in, or owner of, an entity or person engaged in the business then engaged in by the Company.

(b) It is the desire and intent of the parties that the provisions of this Section shall be enforced to the fullest extent permissible under the laws and public policies applied in each jurisdiction in which enforcement is sought. Accordingly, if any particular portion of this section shall be adjudicated to be invalid or unenforceable, this Section shall be deemed amended to delete therefrom the portion thus adjudicated to be invalid or unenforceable, such deletion to apply only with respect to the operation of this Section in the particular jurisdiction in which such adjudication is made.

(c) Nothing in this Section shall reduce or abrogate the [Founder/Key Employee]'s obligations during the term of this Agreement under Sections 4 and 5 hereof.

9. Remedies.

(a) The parties hereto acknowledge that the damages suffered by the Company and the Investors from the [Founder/Key Employee]'s breach of this Agreement by his continued neglect of his duties in Section 4 or 5 is not ascertainable. Accordingly, if the [Founder/Key Employee] breaches Section 4 or 5 hereof by continuously neglecting his duties in either of said sections, the Company and the Investors (in proportion to the ownership of the Company's securities) shall be entitled to liquidated damages from the [Founder/Key Employee] in the amount of $_____.

(b) If there is a breach or threatened breach of the provisions of Sections 5, 6(b), 7, or 8 of this Agreement, the Company shall be entitled to an injunction restraining the [Founder/Key Employee] from such breach.

Nothing herein shall be construed as prohibiting the Company from pursuing any other remedies for such breach or threatened breach.

(c) If this Agreement is terminated pursuant to Section 2(d) hereof, the [Founder/Key Employee] shall not be required to mitigate damages otherwise obtainable from the Company hereunder.

10. Insurance. The Company may, at its election and for its benefit, insure the [Founder/Key Employee] against accidental loss or death and the [Founder/Key Employee] shall submit to such physical examination and supply such information as may be required in connection therewith.

11. Relocation/Location of Performance.

(a) The parties acknowledge that the [Founder/Key Employee] [is/may be] required to change his place of residence to perform his obligations under this Agreement. The Company agrees that, should relocation become necessary, it shall pay all of the costs and expenses of the [Founder/Key Employee] and his family connected with such relocation, including reasonable moving and travel expenses and reasonable temporary dwelling costs (for a period not to exceed 60 days), [and costs associated with purchasing and selling a permanent place of residence], all such expenses not to exceed [how much?].

(b) The [Founder/Key Employee]'s services will be formed in the [where?] area. The [Founder/Key Employee]'s performance hereunder shall be within such area or its environs. The parties acknowledge, however, that the [Founder/Key Employee] may be required to travel [extensively?] in connection with the performance of his duties hereunder.

12. Assignment. This Agreement may not be assigned by any party hereto, PROVIDED THAT the Company may assign this Agreement in connection with a merger or consolidation involving the Company or a sale of substantially all its assets to the surviving corporation or purchaser, as the case may be, so long as such assignee assumes the Company's obligations thereunder.

13. Notices. Any notice required or permitted to be given under this Agreement shall be sufficient in writing and sent by registered mail to the [Founder/Key Employee] at the address set out above or to the Company at the address set out above, to the specific attention of [who is the primary contact at the Company?].

14. Waiver of Breach. A waiver by the Company or the [Founder/Key Employee] of a breach of any provision of this Agreement by the other party shall not operate or be construed as a waiver of any subsequent breach by the other party.

15. Entire Agreement. This Agreement contains the entire agreement of the parties. It may be changed only by an agreement in writing signed by a party against whom enforcement of any waiver, change, modification, extension, or discharge is sought.

IN WITNESS WHEREOF, the parties hereto have executed this Agreement as of the day and year first above written.

[COMPANY]

By

[Sign above, type name here], President

[FOUNDER/KEY EMPLOYEE'S NAME], an Individual

Signature

Independent Contractor Service Agreement

THIS INDEPENDENT CONTRACTOR SERVICE AGREEMENT (the "Agreement") is made as of [month/day/year]

BETWEEN:

[YOUR COMPANY], a [state of incorporation] Corporation with a registered office address at [address—you can also use your business address]

(the "Company")

OF THE FIRST PART

AND:

[INDIVIDUAL NAME], an individual, who resides at [Address]

("[Name]")

[OR, where you are contracting with an individual through their own company]

[NAME of CONTRACTOR'S COMPANY], a [State of incorporation] Corporation with an address for service of [address of Contractor's company],

AND

[NAME OF INDIVIDUAL], an individual who resides at [Address]

("[Corp. Name]" and "[Indiv. Name]," respectively)

OF THE SECOND PART

WHEREAS:

(a) The Company is in the business of [describe briefly the main aspects of your operations] (the "Business");

(b) The Company wishes to engage the services of [Name of Independent Contractor] as its [Job Title], and [Name of Independent Contractor] has agreed to be engaged by the Company in this fashion;

[OR, WHERE YOU ARE CONTRACTING WITH A COMPANY, USE THE FOLLOWING CLAUSE]

(b) The Company wishes to engage the services of [Name of Individual Independent Contractor] in his capacity as the principal of [Name of Corporate Independent Contractor], to act as [Job Title] for the Company, and [Corp. Name] and [Indiv. Name] have agreed to be engaged by the Company in this fashion;

(c) the Company and [Corp. Name or Indiv. Name] have agreed that, as compensation for the services to be provided by [Corp. Name or Indiv. Name], the Company shall pay [Corp. Name or Indiv. Name] the amount of [set out your payment details, including options to purchase stock or stock to be issued as a portion of consideration], on the terms and conditions set forth herein;

NOW, THEREFORE, in consideration of the mutual promises, covenants, terms, and conditions herein, and for other good and valuable consideration, the receipt and sufficiency of which are hereby acknowledged by the parties, the parties agree as follows:

1. **Term**. This Agreement shall be for an initial term of [i.e., one year, six months, etc., or for the length of time it will take to accomplish a specific task] (the "Term"). This Agreement may be renegotiated for such additional Terms, on such terms and conditions as may be agreed between the parties. This Agreement, or any successive agreement(s), shall remain in full force and effect unless terminated by either party in writing, in accordance with the provisions of Section 9 of this Agreement.

2. **Duties to Be Performed**. The specific duties to be performed by [Corp. Name or Indiv. Name] on behalf of the Company are as follows:

   • [set out in point form or in narrative form what duties and responsibilities you are contracting with this individual to perform]

   (collectively, the "Duties").

   The [Corp. Name or Indiv. Name] may work such hours and days as are required to complete the Duties and which are agreed to by the parties, and may perform the Duties at either the Company's premises or such other premises as may be possible, given the nature of the Duties.

   • [Where applicable to your company, consider adding this clause]

   [Corp. Name or Indiv. Name] shall be wholly responsible for supplying such tools and equipment as may be required to carry out the Duties, and shall be permitted to engage such assistants or subcontractors as may be required to perform the Duties. Where the [Corp. Name or Indiv. Name] engages assistants or subcontractors to assist in carrying out the Duties, the [Corp. Name or Indiv. Name] shall be solely responsible for the payment and supervision of such assistants or subcontractors, including the responsibility to remit any payroll taxes or statutory deductions on behalf of such assistants or subcontractors as may be required.

3. **Additional Duties**. [Corp. Name or Indiv. Name] may perform such additional duties for the Company as may be requested by the Company and agreed to by [Corp. Name or Indiv. Name].

4. **Remuneration**. The Company shall pay to [Corp. Name or Indiv. Name] total remuneration of [set out total amount to be paid under this Contract, including any stock to be issued or stock options to be granted], (the "Remuneration"), during the Term of this Agreement. The Remuneration

shall be paid in equal [monthly? biweekly? weekly?] installments, on the [when? 15th and 30th?, 1st and 15th, etc.] day of each month [or, where payment is to be made in a lump sum amount, "The Remuneration shall be paid by way of a lump-sum payment, on or before the final day of the Term, or earlier, as the parties may agree."]. [For either installment or lump sum payments, add the following:] [Corp. Name or Indiv. Name] shall be responsible for submitting interim [monthly? weekly? biweekly?] invoices to the Company during the Term [or, . . . shall provide the Company with an invoice covering the Remuneration for the Duties to be performed on or before [date].]

5. Should this Agreement be terminated prior to the completion of the Term, as provided for in Section 9 below, the Remuneration to be paid to [Corp. Name or Indiv. Name] shall be paid on a pro rata basis, as provided for in Section 10 below.

6. *No Employment Relationship.* The parties expressly agree that [Corp. Name or Indiv. Name] or any subcontractors or assistants engaged by [Corp. Name or Indiv. Name] shall be considered an Independent Contractor to the Company, and that no employment relationship shall be formed by the provision of the Duties by [Corp. Name or Indiv. Name] or such subcontractors or assistants as may be engaged by [Corp. Name or Indiv. Name]. Neither [Corp. Name or Indiv. Name] nor any subcontractors or assistants engaged by [Corp. Name or Indiv. Name] shall have any claim whatsoever under this Agreement or otherwise against the Company for vacation pay, sick leave, retirement benefits, Social Security, workers compensation, disability, unemployment insurance benefits, or any other employee benefits, all of which shall be the sole responsibility of [Corp. Name or Indiv. Name]. The Company shall not withhold on behalf of [Corp. Name or Indiv. Name] or any subcontractors or assistants engaged by [Corp. Name or Indiv. Name] to carry out the Duties, any sums for income tax, unemployment insurance, Social Security, or any other withholding pursuant to any law or requirement of any government agency, and all such withholdings and remittances shall be the sole responsibility of [Corp. Name or Indiv. Name]. [Corp. Name or Indiv. Name] shall indemnify and hold the Company harmless from any and all loss or liability arising with respect to any of the foregoing benefits or withholding, including the failure of [Corp. Name or Indiv. Name] to remit any benefits or withholdings on behalf of itself or any subcontractors or assistants engaged by [Corp. Name or Indiv. Name] to carry out the Duties. Furthermore, [Corp. Name or Indiv. Name] agrees to reimburse the Company for any withholdings or benefits which the Company is required to pay to any regulatory authorities arising as a result of the failure of [Corp. Name or Indiv. Name] to remit such payments on their behalf.

7. ***Confidentiality.*** The parties agree that during the course of performing the Duties, [Corp. Name or Indiv. Name] may receive confidential information with respect to the Business of the Company. [Corp. Name or Indiv. Name] expressly agrees at all times to maintain the confidentiality of all such confidential information provided and follow such appropriate procedures as may be put into place by the Company to ensure that no confidentiality rights of the Company are abridged during the Term of this Agreement or at any time following the expiration or termination of this Agreement.

8. ***Costs of Legal Proceedings.*** Should the Company be required to commence legal proceedings against [Corp. Name or Indiv. Name] with respect to enforcement of the confidentiality provision of this Agreement or with respect to a breach of the confidentiality provision of this Agreement resulting in damages to the Company being incurred, then the Company shall be entitled to recover from [Corp. Name or Indiv. Name] its reasonable costs of such action, including attorneys' fees and expenses.

9. ***Termination.*** This Agreement may be terminated as follows:

   (a) by either party, for any reason, upon the provision of thirty (30) days' notice in writing; or

   (b) by the Company, upon [Corp. Name or Indiv. Name] breaching the confidentiality provision set out in Section 7 above, upon twenty-four (24) hours' notice in writing.

   Any written notice to be provided from one party to the other shall be delivered by either registered mail or courier delivery, to the addresses of the parties as set out below, or to such other address as the parties may from time to time advise the other, in writing:

   To the Company: To [Corp. Name or Indiv. Name]:

   _____

   _____

   _____

With a copy to its legal counsel: [optional]

10. ***Pro-Rated Remuneration upon Termination.*** Upon termination of this Agreement pursuant to the provisions of Section 9 above, the Remuneration will be pro-rated to the date of termination of the Agreement.

11. ***Waiver.*** No waiver of all or any portion of this Agreement is enforceable unless in writing and signed by such waiving party, and any waiver shall

not be construed as a waiver by any other party or of any other or subsequent breach.

12. *Indemnification.* [Corp. Name or Indiv. Name] agrees to indemnify and defend the Company against, and hold the Company harmless from, any and all claims, actions, suits, proceedings, costs, expenses, damages and liabilities, including attorney's fees and costs, resulting from, or arising out of, or connected in any way with any act or omission of [Corp. Name or Indiv. Name] under this Agreement or [Corp. Name or Indiv. Name]'s failure to comply with the provisions of this Agreement.

13. *Entire Agreement.* This Agreement supersedes any and all other agreements, either oral or in writing, between the parties hereto with respect to the subjects discussed herein, and contains the entire agreement between the parties relating to the subject matter.

14. *Amendments.* This Agreement may not be amended except by the mutual consent of the parties hereto, such consent to be provided in writing.

15. *Governing Law.* The parties expressly agree that this Agreement shall be governed by the laws of the United States of America and the State of [State where Company is located]. Each party to this Agreement consents to the exclusive jurisdiction of the state and federal courts sitting in [County where Company is located] County, [State where Company is located], in any action on a claim arising out of, under, or in connection with this Agreement.

16. *Assignment and Binding Effect.* Neither this Agreement nor any of the rights, interests or obligations hereunder shall be assigned by either party hereto without the prior written consent of the other party hereto, except as otherwise provided herein. This Agreement shall be binding upon and shall inure to the benefit of the parties hereto and their respective officers, directors, administrators, permitted successors, assigns, and/or delegates.

17. *Integration and Captions.* This Agreement includes the entire understanding of the parties hereto with respect to the subject matter hereof. The headings herein are solely for convenience and shall not control the interpretation of this Agreement.

18. *Legal Representation.* Each party has been represented by independent legal counsel in connection with this Agreement, or each has had the opportunity to obtain independent legal counsel and has waived such right, and each party shall be responsible for obtaining its own tax counsel at its own expense.

19. *Construction.* Each party acknowledges and agrees that it has had the opportunity to review, negotiate, and approve all of the provisions of this Agreement.

20. ***Cooperation.*** The parties agree to execute such reasonable necessary documents upon advice of legal counsel in order to carry out the intent and purpose of this Agreement as set forth herein.

21. ***Fees, Costs, and Expenses.*** Each of the parties hereto acknowledges and agrees to pay, without reimbursement from the other party, the fees, costs, and expenses incurred by it with respect to this Agreement, including the cost of obtaining independent legal advice with respect to entry into this Agreement.

22. ***Consents and Authorizations.*** Upon the execution of this Agreement, the parties acknowledge and agree that they each have the full right, power, legal capacity, and authority to enter into this Agreement, and the same constitutes a valid and legally binding agreement and obligation of each party in accordance with the terms, conditions, and other provisions contained herein.

23. ***Gender and Number.*** Unless the context otherwise requires, references in this Agreement in any gender shall be construed to include the other gender, references in the singular shall be construed to include the plural, and references in the plural shall be construed to include the singular.

24. ***Severability.*** In the event that any one or more of the provisions of this Agreement shall be deemed unenforceable by any court of competent jurisdiction for any reason whatsoever, this Agreement shall be construed as if such unenforceable provision had never been contained herein and the remaining provisions of this Agreement shall remain enforceable and in full effect.

25. ***Counterparts and Execution by Facsimile.*** This Agreement may be executed in counterpart and/or by facsimile, each of which shall constitute a duplicate original and all of which shall constitute the entire agreement.

IN WITNESS WHEREOF, the parties hereto have executed this Agreement as of the day and year first above written.

[YOUR COMPANY]

By:

[Type Name], President

[Where Independent Contractor is an Individual:]

[Name of Independent Contractor], an Individual

Signature

[Where Independent Contractor is a corporation:]

[NAME OF CORPORATE INDEPENDENT CONTRACTOR]

By:

[Type Name and Title below signature line]

And By:

[Type Individual's name here], as an Individual

Employment Agreement

THIS EMPLOYMENT AGREEMENT (the "Agreement") is made as of _____, 20__

BETWEEN:

[YOUR COMPANY], a [state of incorporation] Corporation with a registered office address at [address—you can also use your business address]

(the "Company")

OF THE FIRST PART

AND:

[INDIVIDUAL NAME], an individual, who resides at [Address]

(the "Employee")

OF THE SECOND PART

WHEREAS:

(a) The Company is in the business of _____ (the "Business");

(b) The Company wishes to engage the services of the Employee as its General Manager of Operations, and the Employee has agreed to be engaged by the Company in this fashion;

(c) The Company and the Employee have agreed that, as compensation for the services to be provided by the Employee, the Company shall pay the Employee an amount equivalent to twenty-five percent (25%) of the Company's net profits, on the terms and conditions set forth herein;

NOW, THEREFORE, in consideration of the mutual promises, covenants, terms, and conditions herein, and for other good and valuable consideration, the receipt and sufficiency of which are hereby acknowledged by the parties, the parties agree as follows:

1. ***Agreement to Employ.*** The Company agrees to employ the Employee as its [Job Title?] and the Employee agrees to be employed in this capacity.

2. ***Employment Term.*** The term of this Agreement shall be for a [?? monthly, yearly ??] period, commencing on the date of this Agreement and terminating on [date?].

[Alternatively, if it is to continue for successive periods, consider the following clause:

This Agreement shall be for an initial term of [??? months/years] and shall automatically renew for additional [how long? month/year terms] unless terminated by either party in writing, in accordance with the provisions of

Section 11 of this Agreement.]

3. ***Duties to be Performed.*** The specific duties to be performed by the Employee on behalf of the Company are as follows:

   [List the duties you are hiring this individual to perform for you]

   (collectively, the "Duties").

4. ***Additional Employment Duties.*** The Employee may perform such additional duties for the Company as may be requested by the Company and agreed to by the Employee.

5. ***Remuneration.*** The Company shall pay to the Employee [monthly/yearly/hourly?] gross remuneration of [amount, as well as stock or options to purchase stock], (the "Remuneration"). The Employee shall receive the Remuneration on a [monthly/weekly/biweekly?] basis, on the [1st and 15th?/every other Friday?] of each month.

6. Should this Agreement be terminated prior to the completion of the Term, as provided for in Section 11 below, the Remuneration to be paid to the Employee shall be paid on a pro-rata basis, as provided for in Section 12 below.

   [Clause 7 may be customized to apply to your specific situation].

7. ***Vacation Time and Medical Leave.*** Following completion of the first year's continuous employment, the Employee will be entitled to receive paid vacation time of two (2) calendar weeks. Paid vacation time entitlement will increase as follows:

   (a) following completion of the second year of continuous employment—two (2) calendar weeks per year;

   (b) following completion of the third and fourth years of continuous employment—three (3) calendar weeks per year;

   (c) following completion of the fifth and subsequent years of continuous employment—four (4) calendar weeks per year.

   The Employee shall also be entitled to [how many?] days of paid medical leave per calendar year. Unused medical leave [may?may not?] be banked for use in subsequent years.

8. ***Employment Relationship.*** The parties expressly agree that the Employee shall be considered an employee of the Company, and that an employment relationship has been entered into. As such, the Company will be responsible for deducting and remitting, from the gross Remuneration due to the Employee, all required statutory deductions, including but not limited to: federal and/or state income tax, unemployment insurance, Social Security, and health benefit premiums as may be offered by the Company.

9. *Confidentiality.* The parties agree that during the course of performing the Duties, the Employee may receive confidential information with respect to the Business of the Company. The Employee expressly agrees at all times to maintain the confidentiality of all such confidential information provided and follow such appropriate procedures as may be put into place by the Company to ensure that no confidentiality rights of the Company are abridged during the Term of this Agreement or at any time following the expiration or termination of this Agreement.

10. *Costs of Legal Proceedings.* Should the Company be required to commence legal proceedings against the Employee with respect to enforcement of the confidentiality provision of this Agreement or with respect to a breach of the confidentiality provision of this Agreement resulting in damages to the Company being incurred, then the Company shall be entitled to recover from the Employee its reasonable costs of such action, including attorneys' fees and expenses.

11. *Termination.* This Agreement may be terminated as follows:

    (a) by either party, for any reason, upon the provision of [how many days'/months'?] notice in writing; or

    (b) by the Company, upon the Employee breaching the confidentiality provision set out in Section 9 above, upon [how many days'/weeks'/hours'?] notice in writing.

Any written notice to be provided from one party to the other shall be delivered by either registered mail or courier delivery, to the addresses of the parties as set out below, or to such other address as the parties may from time to time advise the other, in writing:

To the Company: To the Employee:

                                   _____

                                   _____

                                   _____

With a copy to its legal counsel: [optional]

12. *Pro-Rated Remuneration upon Termination.* Upon termination of this Agreement pursuant to the provisions of Section 11 above, the Remuneration will be pro-rated to the date of termination of the Agreement.

13. *Waiver.* No waiver of all or any portion of this Agreement is enforceable unless in writing and signed by such waiving party, and any waiver shall not be construed as a waiver by any other party or of any other or subsequent breach.

14. *Entire Agreement.* This Agreement supersedes any and all other agreements, either oral or in writing, between the parties hereto with respect to

the subjects discussed herein, and contains the entire agreement between the parties relating to the subject matter.

15. *Amendments.* This Agreement may not be amended except by the mutual consent of the parties hereto, such consent to be provided in writing.

16. *Governing Law.* The parties expressly agree that this Agreement shall be governed by the laws of the United States of America and the State of [State where your business operates]. Each party to this Agreement consents to the exclusive jurisdiction of the state and federal courts sitting in [County and State where your business operates], in any action on a claim arising out of, under, or in connection with this Agreement.

17. *Assignment and Binding Effect.* Neither this Agreement nor any of the rights, interests or obligations hereunder shall be assigned by either party hereto without the prior written consent of the other party hereto, except as otherwise provided herein. This Agreement shall be binding upon and shall inure to the benefit of the parties hereto and their respective officers, directors, administrators, permitted successors, assigns, and/or delegates.

18. *Integration and Captions.* This Agreement includes the entire understanding of the parties hereto with respect to the subject matter hereof. The headings herein are solely for convenience and shall not control the interpretation of this Agreement.

19. *Legal Representation.* Each party has been represented by independent legal counsel in connection with this Agreement, or each has had the opportunity to obtain independent legal counsel and has waived such right, and each party shall be responsible for obtaining its own tax counsel at its own expense.

20. *Construction.* Each party acknowledges and agrees that it has had the opportunity to review, negotiate, and approve all of the provisions of this Agreement.

21. *Cooperation.* The parties agree to execute such reasonable necessary documents upon advice of legal counsel in order to carry out the intent and purpose of this Agreement as set forth herein.

22. *Fees, Costs, and Expenses.* Each of the parties hereto acknowledges and agrees to pay, without reimbursement from the other party, the fees, costs, and expenses incurred by it with respect to this Agreement, including the cost to obtain independent legal advice with respect to entry into this Agreement.

23. *Consents and Authorizations.* Upon the execution of this Agreement, the parties acknowledge and agree that they each have the full right, power, legal capacity, and authority to enter into this Agreement, and the same

constitutes a valid and legally binding agreement and obligation of each party in accordance with the terms, conditions, and other provisions contained herein.

24. ***Gender and Number.*** Unless the context otherwise requires, references in this Agreement in any gender shall be construed to include the other gender, references in the singular shall be construed to include the plural, and references in the plural shall be construed to include the singular.

25. ***Severability.*** In the event that any one or more of the provisions of this Agreement shall be deemed unenforceable by any court of competent jurisdiction for any reason whatsoever, this Agreement shall be construed as if such unenforceable provision had never been contained herein and the remaining provisions of this Agreement shall remain enforceable and in full effect.

26. ***Counterparts and Execution by Facsimile.*** This Agreement may be executed in counterpart and/or by facsimile, each of which shall constitute a duplicate original and all of which shall constitute the entire agreement.

IN WITNESS WHEREOF, the parties hereto have executed this Agreement as of the day and year first above written.

[YOUR COMPANY]

By:

[Sign above, Type Name here], President

[EMPLOYEE'S NAME], an Individual

Signature

Chapter 16

How to Use a
Buy-Sell Agreement

A buy-sell agreement is used by the owners of a small closely held business entity to cover the buyout of shares upon death, divorce, disability, or withdrawal of an owner. You generally would not see such an agreement with a publicly traded company because, subject to any restrictions, the shares are freely tradable.

But in a smaller company, where people are working closely together and have to get along, many will want to control who gets to own shares in the company.

Consider the following:

Case No. 19—Herman, Chloe, and Matty

Herman, Chloe, and Matty formed a corporation and contributed into it an awesome technology that was going to change the way e-commerce was done. They incorporated AweTech, Inc., in Wyoming and issued Herman 250,000 shares, Chloe 100,000 shares, and Matty 50,000 shares based upon their relative contributions. Herman wanted AweTech, Inc., to institute a buy-sell agreement for very personal reasons. He was the lead developer of this once-in-a-lifetime technology, and was having problems with his new wife, Bambie. He was sensing after all of six weeks of married life that she was a gold digger out for his future prospects. They lived in a community property state whereby half of what the business grew to become would be hers. And in the event of a divorce settlement where she received shares, having her as a shareholder of the company, with her loud and flashy know-nothingness, would be a major embarrassment. A buy-sell agreement, he knew, could address his concerns.

Chloe also wanted a buy-sell agreement. She was a very serious technician and had married her opposite. Dieter was a surfer, a rocker, and a slacker. She loved him for these qualities but knew that he had no business being anywhere near a technical enterprise.

Matty was willing to go along with the group on a buy-sell agreement. He was with them for the experience, which he saw as more of a résumé builder and not a windfall opportunity. He was not married and had no real emotional or business allegiance to the company, so signing another document did not bother him.

AweTech, Inc.'s attorney prepared a fifty-page buy-sell agreement covering every possible contingency with a multitude of terms, conditions, and boilerplate (standard) provisions too lengthy to be reprinted here. Nevertheless, several key sections along with the spousal consent are given below in order to understand what later happened at AweTech, Inc.

At Herman's insistence they established a book value for the purchase price of the shares. And they bought insurance so the corporation would have money to buy the shares.

AweTech, Inc., Buy-Sell Agreement

Section Five—Events Triggering a Buyout Right

A. *Death.* Upon the death of an individual Shareholder, the Corporation and/or remaining Shareholders shall have an option to purchase in accordance with the procedures set forth herein, all (but not less than all) of the decedent's shares at the book value of the corporation.

B. *Disability.* In the event an individual Shareholder is employed by the Corporation in a capacity as an officer, employee, consultant, or director and becomes disabled, as defined below, the Corporation and/or remaining Shareholders shall have an option to purchase, in accordance with the procedures set forth herein, all (but not less than all) of the disabled Shareholder's shares, and all other shares in the Corporation owned by such individual Shareholder, whether such Shareholder is the owner of record or merely the beneficial owner of such shares, at the book value of the corporation.

Definition of Disability. A Shareholder is disabled for purposes of this Agreement if he: (1) has been declared legally incompetent by a final court decree (the date of such decree being deemed to be the date on which the disability occurred); (2) receives disability insurance benefits from his/her State Industrial Insurance System or any disability income insurance policy maintained by the Corporation for a period of twelve (12) consecutive months; or (3) has been found to be disabled pursuant to a Disability Determination. A "Disability Determination" means a finding that the Shareholder, because of a medically determinable disease, injury, or other mental or physical disability, is unable to perform substantially all of his regular duties to the Corporation and that such disability is determined or reasonably expected to last at least twelve (12) months. The Disability Determination shall be based on the written opinion of the physician regularly attending the Shareholder whose disability is in question. If a majority of the members of the Board of Directors of the Corporation disagree with the opinion of this physician (the "First Physician"), the Corporation may engage, at its own expense, another physician (the "Second Physician") to examine the Shareholder. If the First and Second Physicians disagree on the disability of the Shareholder, they shall choose a third consulting physician (whose expense shall also be borne by the Corporation), and the written opinion of a majority of these three (3) physicians shall, except as otherwise provided in this Subsection, be conclusive as to the Shareholder's disability. The date of any written opinion conclusively finding the Shareholder to be disabled is the date on which the disability will be deemed to have occurred. If there is a conclusive finding that the Shareholder is not disabled, the remaining Shareholders shall have the right to request additional Disability Determinations, provided they agree to pay all the expenses of the Disability Determinations and do not request an additional Disability Determination more frequently than once every six (6) months. In conjunction with a Disability Determination, each Shareholder hereby consents to any required medical examination, and agrees to furnish any medical information requested by any examining physician and to waive any applicable physician-patient privilege that may arise because of such examination. All physicians except the First Physician must be board-certified in the speciality most closely related to the nature of the disability alleged to exist.

C. *Termination of Employment.* If any individual Shareholder is employed by the Corporation on a part-time or full-time basis as an officer, employee, director, or consultant, and ceases to be employed by the Corporation for any reason other than death or disability, whether the termination results from retirement because of age under a retirement policy adopted by the Corporation that applies to the Shareholder, voluntary termination of employment, termination of employment by the mutual consent of the Shareholder and the Corporation, or termination by the unilateral act of the Corporation for cause, with cause being defined as (i) a final nonappealable conviction of or a plea of guilty or nolo contendere by the Shareholder to a felony or a misdemeanor involving dishonesty or other criminal conduct against the Corporation or any affiliate of the Corporation, (ii) the Shareholder's continual breach of his duties and obligations arising under an employment contract with the Corporation or continued breach of any written policy, rule, or regulation of the Corporation or any affiliate of the Corporation for a period of at least five (5) days following receipt of written notice from an officer of the Corporation of any affiliate of the Corporation specifying such breach, or the receipt by the Shareholder of three (3) or more such notices in any twelve (12) month period. The Corporation and/or remaining Shareholders shall have an option to purchase, in accordance with the procedures set forth herein, all (but not less than all) of the terminated Shareholder's shares, and all other shares in the Corporation owned by such individual Shareholder and his spouse, if any, whether such Shareholder and his spouse are the owner of record or merely the beneficial owners of such shares, at the book value of the corporation.

D. *Transfers by Operation of Law.* In the event any Shareholder: (a) files a voluntary petition under any bankruptcy or insolvency law or a petition for the appointment of a receiver, or makes an assignment for the benefit of creditors; (b) is subjected involuntarily to such a petition or assignment or to an attachment or other legal or equitable interest with respect to his or her shares in the Corporation and such involuntary petition, assignment, or attachment is not discharged within thirty (30) days after its effective date; or (c) is subjected to any other possible involuntary transfer of his shares in the Corporation by legal process, the Corporation and/or other Shareholders shall have the option to purchase, in accordance with the procedures set forth herein, all (but not less than all) of the shares that are subject to the involuntary transfer, for the book value of the corporation.

E. *Divorce.* If, at the time of their divorce, both spouses are Shareholders in the Corporation and the court awarding the divorce does not order all the shares owned by one spouse to be transferred to the other spouse as part of the divorce decree or any property settlement incorporated into the divorce decree, then: if only one of the spouses is, at the time of the divorce decree, employed by the Corporation as an officer, employee, director, or paid consultant, the shares owned by the other spouse shall be offered for sale at the book value of the corporation as follows:

(a) The spouse who is an employee of the Corporation shall have a first option to purchase some or all of the shares in question. This option must be exercised within twenty (20) days after the entry of the divorce decree.

(b) The Corporation shall have a second option to purchase the shares in question not purchased pursuant to Paragraph (a). Within twenty (20) days after the date the Corporation's Secretary receives written notification of the divorce and the purchase right granted by this Subsection, the Corporation will call a special Board of Directors meeting, to be held not more than forty (40) days after the call, to decide whether the Corporation should purchase any of the shares not purchased by the employee-spouse. The option to purchase must be approved by the affirmative vote of the holder of a majority of votes entitled to be cast at the meeting, excluding the vote of the selling spouse. The Corporation shall, within twenty (20) days of this Shareholder meeting, notify the spouse required to offer shares for sale, in writing, whether it has or has not exercised its option to purchase. If the Corporation exercises the option to purchase, it may allocate some or all of the shares it agrees to purchase to one or more of the remaining Shareholders or other persons if all the Directors who voted in favor of the purchase approve the allocation.

The shares of the spouse required to offer shares for sale pursuant to this subsection that are not purchased pursuant to paragraphs (a) and (b) shall continue to be subject to the terms and conditions of this Agreement.

* * *

SPOUSAL CONSENT

Each of the undersigned, being the spouse of a Shareholder who has signed this Agreement, hereby acknowledges that he or she has read and is familiar with its provisions of the AweTech, Inc., Stock Transfer Restrictions and Buy-Sell Agreement dated _____, 20__, and agrees to be bound thereby and to join therein to the extent, if any, that his or her joinder may be necessary. The undersigned hereby agrees that his or her spouse may join in any future amendment or modification of this Agreement without any further signature, acknowledgment, agreement, or consent on his or her part; and further agrees that any interest which he or she may have in the shares of stock in the Corporation owned directly or beneficially by his or her spouse shall be subject to the provisions of this Agreement.

Six months after signing the buy-sell agreement a terrible thing happened. Chloe became disabled in a car accident. While she was going to be able to live a somewhat comfortable life, she would never be able to work again. She fit the definition of disability in the buy-sell agreement. The corporation decided to use the insurance money to buy Chloe's 100,000 shares for their book value of $1.00 per share.

Surprising everyone, Dieter emerged from his slackerdom and challenged the valuation of the shares. It was way too low, he argued. He knew the company was worth far more than $1.00 per share. He argued that the $100,000 AweTech, Inc., was going to pay for Chloe's shares was less than a tenth of their true value. Book value was the lowest measure of shares a company could use. It did not take into account the fair market value of their patent, which was worth many times more on the open market. He argued that an independent appraisal by a CPA could be prepared to gauge the true value of the company.

But Dieter had been a slacker when he signed the spousal consent. His signature was on the document agreeing to a buyout based on book value. He and Chloe were obligated to accept $100,000 for their shares.

With Chloe no longer with the company, Matty grew less interested and more and more easily frustrated by Herman's demanding management style. One day Matty blew a fuse and lashed out at Herman. He quit his job in a very loud and obnoxious way, a story he regaled his friends with over beers that night. He did not care. The company was going public soon and he would get his millions when he cashed in his shares.

Matty had forgotten all about signing the buy-sell agreement. He only re-called it the next day when Herman demanded his stock certificate for 50,000 shares back in exchange for a check of $50,000. Matty hired a lawyer to argue that the share value was worth at least $500,000. But Matty had signed the agreement consenting to a book value valuation. Quitting his job three months before the public offering cost Matty a lot of money.

Herman was now the only founder left. But he still had a problem. Bambie. He knew it would never work out. He was constantly embarrassed by her and now more convinced than ever that all she wanted was his money.

He filed for divorce. She hired the biggest divorce-shark attorney she could find. The attorney threatened to prove that she had signed the buy-sell agreement under duress and was not properly counseled as to its mean-ing or contents. He argued that book value was a standard that no court would uphold in caring for the future of a material community component to the success of the business. He threatened to show pictures of Herman involved in unnatural acts.

Herman's attorney withstood the assault but realized they had to settle. A compromise was reached where Bambie received a property settlement based on the difference between the shares' book value and their soon to be public value. Herman was satisfied with the settlement. Without the buy-sell in place he (or the corporation) would have had to pay top dollar for all the shares.

The others were not so happy. By setting the shares at less than their fair market value they had been negatively affected by the buy-sell. A lesson learned.

Rich Dad Tips

- Always have the terms of a buy-sell agreement reviewed by your own independent attorney.
- Remember, the corporation's attorney represents the company—not you as an individual.
- For more information and useful forms see "Buy Sell Agreements" at www.successdna.com.

Chapter 17

Protecting You and Your Business from Scams

An important but often overlooked component of being a successful business owner or investor is the ability to spot all of the scam artists out there. Yes, you can give yourself a pat on the back for ignoring the latest Nigerian e-mail scam. But with that minor celebration complete, we must return our attention to being ever vigilant and on guard against the next scam headed our way.

In this chapter we shall review some of the business and tax schemes promoted by a multitude of con artists. It is important in all of this to remember the origins of the phrase "con artists." The "con" in not short for "convict," as in a criminal person. Instead, it is short for "confidence," as in a confidence man, a person of great sincerity who engenders the trust and confidence of their victim. So when you are dealing with a con artist remember that you are not dealing with someone who looks and sounds like a criminal. It's not that easy. You need to know that you are dealing with someone who looks and sounds like a professional. A confidence man is a person of great skill and charm. A confidence man is a person you would be pleased to take home to have dinner with your grandmother, and she would be duly impressed until, like you, she lost her life's savings.

And why is all of this so important? Simply put: You can't afford to be the next victim. Many of us only get one shot at building our own business or getting started on our first real estate investment. Nothing can ruin your dreams faster than getting drawn into a scam that sucks out your money, time, and enthusiasm. If an established business loses a few thousand dollars in a scam it might hurt a little and someone may lose their job. However, if a fledgling business or new investor losses a few thousand dollars, it may bring about the end of the enterprise and quite possibly the loss of one's life savings.

Asset Protection Scams to Avoid

Ironically, while we counsel asset protection to protect your savings, there are asset protection scam artists out to drain your savings account. As is true with every other type of business, there are plenty of so-called asset protection advisors out there who are nothing more than confidence men ready to take advantage of unsure entrepreneurs. The following is a cautionary tale from one of our clients who was kind enough to share her story so that other business owners can avoid the same mistakes.

Case No. 20— Pamela

Pamela Jones is a successful business owner in her early fifties. Pamela had earned two Ph.D.'s and considered herself a well-educated, bright, capable woman. She owned her own home as well as a small acupuncture business and hoped that she would be able to invest in some rental properties in the near future. Pamela had been told by several people that she needed to incorporate to protect herself from liability. She had a vague understanding of what that meant, but being a savvy businessperson and knowing that we live in a highly litigious society she realized isolating personal liability from the liability of her business was a good idea.

Her brother, Steve, a well-respected businessperson in his own right, recommended a company that he had used to incorporate his landscaping business, a company we shall call Asset Protection of Las Vegas, or APLV. They seemed like a highly reputable group who knew what they were talking about and could be trusted to give good advice. They certainly had very expensive color brochures. She contacted them and set up an appointment for a consultation.

Pamela's APLV advisor appeared very polished and interested in her situation. She was drawn in by his sincerity. Pamela explained what she thought she needed. Maybe an S corporation, she suggested, having heard that was a good way to protect yourself. Her consultant was concerned for her future and explained to her that to properly protect herself she needed to create layers of protection. Her limited liability companies should be owned by S corporations, which would then be advised by limited partnerships, which would be managed by an additional corporation and so on and so forth. Pamela tried to follow along and comprehend all of the fancy legal jargon. She didn't really comprehend the advice she was being given, but she did understand their overriding point that she needed to be very afraid for her protection. In her confusion and concern she thought, these guys are the experts. She wouldn't expect them to know how to do acupuncture. Why should she become an expert on asset protection?

Pamela wanted to be responsible and do the right thing to protect the small estate that she had accumulated. However, she didn't really want to jump into this complex business scheme her APLV consultant was smoothly encouraging. She went there thinking she needed a corporation and her APLV advisor was telling her she needed six to eight different entities if she really wanted to be protected.

Pamela ended the consultation by telling her advisor that she needed to think it over before she erected her business empire, but she did want to begin forming an S corporation for her small acupuncture business. Her advisor quoted her a price of $1,500 and she authorized the charge to her Visa card. Believing she was making a savvy business decision, she left the office feeling great. She even paused to commend herself on being smarter than all the other sole proprietors out there who didn't take care of this sort of thing until it was too late.

Two days later while trying to purchase a latte at her favorite coffee shop, Pamela's card was declined. She was not a frivolous spender and always kept a good account of her money. She called Visa and found out she was charged $15,000 by Asset Protection of Las Vegas. It was obviously a mistake. Somehow an extra zero had been added on to her authorized $1,500 charge. She immediately called APLV to tell them of the error. To her complete shock she was informed by the office person assigned to handle incoming calls that she was charged for exactly what she had authorized. In fact, they had a legal binding contract where she had authorized the purchase of three

S corporations, three LPs, and two LLCs, along with a myriad of other fees and charges that she had agreed to pay.

Trying to maintain her composure, Pamela explained that she did not authorize the charges. She had authorized the purchase of one S corporation for $1,500 and she wanted the remaining money refunded immediately. She was politely but firmly told that it was too late to refund her money. She had authorized the charges and APLV had already begun working on her entities. Pamela demanded to speak to the owner of the firm. This time, in a voice layered with condescension, the assistant informed her that he was not available to speak at that time, but she would be happy to have him contact her when he was available.

Pamela hung up the phone in total disbelief. Not only was she being ripped off and given the run-around, but she had been referred to this company by her own brother. She immediately called him and proceeded to explain what had transpired. Steve told her not to worry. He had worked with Asset Protection of Las Vegas many times. He would call them right away and get it straightened out.

Steve had been a longtime client of APLV and knew the owner personally. While acknowledging he wasn't a lawyer, Steve felt the man knew his stuff. Steve called the office and asked to speak with the owner. He was also told that he was unavailable and would be called back when he was available.

Several days later Pamela received a call from the owner of Asset Protection of Las Vegas. To her utter disbelief, he explained to her that there was no mistake. She had authorized the charges, they had begun working on her file, and furthermore, the plan that she had purchased was exactly what she needed if she wanted protection. Pamela explained that she was only an acupuncturist with one piece of property. She had heard about asset protection and limited liability and she merely wanted to set up one corporation. Eight separate entities was way more than she needed or could afford. The more she explained the more she realized that the owner had no intention of refunding her money. Instead, he insisted on trying to convince her that this was what she needed if she wanted to be protected.

Pamela was fed up and demanded a complete refund of all her money. She stated she wanted nothing to do with the company ever again and she intended to report them. Surprisingly, the owner offered a compromise. They would refund half of her money if she agreed to have them set up four entities instead of eight. Pamela was adamant. She no longer wanted to do any business with the company and once again demanded her money back. The owner hung up on her.

After three weeks of unreturned calls, Steve traveled to the Asset Protection of Las Vegas offices with several other prominent businesspeople to see the owner in person. They told him that if Pamela did not get a full refund they would pull all of their business from APLV as well as place a call to a close personal friend who was the editor at the local newspaper about the firm's unethical business practices. Finally realizing the damage and loss of money that would befall his business, the owner relented and agreed to fully refund the money back to Pamela. Although she did receive a full refund, it took over seven weeks from the date of her appointment to get her money back. If not for the fact that APLV would have lost a substantial amount of business, they may have never refunded the money.

Pamela was fortunate. But how many others have been scammed and never received a refund? (If you have been scammed, please e-mail your story to scamwatch@successdna.com.)

You must be diligent about who you are trusting to assist you with your asset protection plan. Some companies charge a little more, some a little less. But you must ask yourself: When your life's savings or the future of your business is at stake do you really want to work with a company because they are initially the cheapest, or are the best at preying on your fears, or have the best closing technique? Are you dealing with this company because they have pitched you on a tax deductible trip to Las Vegas? (Is such a trip really necessary or important to your wealth building?) Be sure to deal only with ethical advisors who have your best interests at heart.

$99 INCORPORATION

You need to know that there are a number of other corporate information scams in the marketplace. A popular one is the $99 incorporation. For just $99, they claim you will be bulletproofed and asset-protected. C'mon down. We'll set you right up.

We have tested such services to see how they could possibly do all the work necessary to completely and properly form and document a corporation or LLC for just $99. These providers fall into two camps.

The first camp does the minimal work needed to form an entity. They file the articles. That's it. Once you pay the $99 they will no longer take your phone calls or questions. Eventually you will be sent a document with a state seal on it indicating that you are incorporated.

But you will not be sent the minutes, the bylaws, or any issued stock, all of the other components necessary to be a complete corporation. Of course, if you hadn't read this book, you would probably think in your blissful ignorance that for just $99 you were protected. You are not.

The second camp uses the $99 as a come-on. They offer an à la carte menu in which the $99 is just for the filing of the articles. The bylaws are another $350. The meeting minutes are $250, and so on. By the time you are done they have gained your confidence and that $99 has ballooned up to $2,000 to $3,000 for just one entity.

By contrast, our firm charges a flat fee of $695 (plus state filing fees, which vary from state to state) for a complete package. Three or more entities are $595 each, plus state filing fees. (Check in the back of this book to see how you can save $50 per entity.) While we realize there are many choices out there, including your existing attorney, we would be pleased to have you as a client.

NEVADA OFFICE PACKAGE

As well, we won't sell you on one of the bigger scams out there: the Nevada Office Package.

Many providers of Nevada corporations will misrepresent Nevada law to you during their sales process. They will tell you that if you set up a Nevada corporation the state's law requires you to have a Nevada office presence, which they conveniently provide for $3,000 a year.

Please be assured: There is no Nevada law requiring your corporation, LLC, or LP to maintain an office in the state. Yes, you need a resident agent to accept service process. But that is just $125 per year. For thousands of dollars you don't need a receptionist answering your phone or a phony office with a plaque on the door. Save your money. Deal with reputable companies who are not out to deplete your resources.

Tax Scams to Avoid

Just as with asset protection there are a number of tax evasion scams you must avoid. But before we start this discussion let's get a little political philosophy out of the way. I am all in favor of structuring my affairs in any way possible to reduce taxes. I attempt only to pay the absolute minimum in taxes. I believe that if governments ceased their politically expedient, nonsensical, and insanely wasteful spending patterns I would pay a lot less in taxes. That said, I follow the rules. I don't yet have the time to try to change the rules, so I follow them. And in doing so I realize that if absolutely everyone followed the rules, like most of us do, we would also all pay less in taxes. The burdens of the tax cheats and the tax evaders fall on the rest of us. So in writing about tax scams to avoid I do so not as a lapdog of the IRS but rather as an angry witness to the fact that the scams take money out of my pocket in the form of higher taxes.

With that stated, let's hear from the IRS.

"Taxpayers shouldn't let their guard down," former IRS commissioner Mark W. Everson warns. "Don't get taken by scam artists making outrageous promises. If you use a tax professional, pick someone who is reputable. Taxpayers should remember they are ultimately responsible for what is on their return even if some unscrupulous preparers have steered them in the wrong direction."

The Internal Revenue Service has recently issued a guidance list of forty frivolous positions that taxpayers (or more precisely "nonpayers") have attempted in the past. The IRS released this list to put the public on notice that these positions have no basis for validity in existing law. Tax returns containing these will be rejected. Furthermore, taxpayers attempting to use these positions on their returns could be subject to penalties from $5,000 to $25,000, along with other civil penalties based on tax underpayments.

It is important to note that the following is not an exhaustive list of all positions that the IRS has deemed frivolous. The penalty can also be assessed on a tax return that contains a position not included in this list, "yet reflects a desire to delay or impede the administration of Federal tax laws."

Here are some of the frivolous positions that the IRS has warned the public will not work:

1) Compliance with the Internal Revenue laws is voluntary or optional and not required by law, including arguments that:
   a) Filing a federal tax or information return or paying tax is purely voluntary under the law, or similar arguments.

b) An employer is not legally obligated to withhold income or employment taxes on employees' wages.

c) A taxpayer may "untax" himself or herself at any time or revoke the consent to be taxed and thereafter not be subjected to Internal Revenue taxes.

d) Because filing a tax return is not required by law, the IRS must prepare a return for a taxpayer who does not file one in order to assess and collect tax.

(e) A taxpayer may lawfully decline to pay taxes if the taxpayer disagrees with the government's use of tax revenues.

(f) Only certain types of incomes are taxable; for example, income that results from the sale of alcohol, tobacco, or firearms, or from transactions or activities that take place in interstate commerce.

2) Federal income taxes are unconstitutional or a taxpayer has a constitutional right not to comply with the federal tax laws for one of the following reasons:

a) The First Amendment permits a taxpayer to refuse to pay taxes based on religious or moral beliefs.

b) The requirement to file a tax return is an unreasonable search and seizure contrary to the Fourth Amendment.

c) Income taxation, tax withholding, or assessment of taxes is a "taking" without due process of law in violation of the Fifth Amendment.

d) Mandatory or compelled compliance with the Internal Revenue laws is a form of involuntary servitude prohibited by the Thirteenth Amendment.

3) A "reparations" tax credit exists, including arguments that African-American taxpayers may claim a tax credit on their federal income tax returns as reparations for slavery or other historical mistreatment and that Native Americans are entitled to an analogous credit.

4) A taxpayer's wages are excluded from Social Security taxes if the taxpayer waives the right to receive Social Security benefits.

5) A taxpayer may lawfully avoid income tax by sending income offshore, including depositing income into a foreign bank account.

6) A taxpayer is allowed to buy or sell the right to claim a child as a qualifying child for purposes of the Earned Income Tax Credit.

Of course, we all wish that one or more of these arguments would work. Then we would all be free from taxation. But then, wait a minute: If we all did this, who would pay for the roads and the free cheese?

So a key question to ask when faced with one of these scams is: What if every taxpayer took advantage of it? If the answer is that the U.S. Treasury would promptly be depleted, you know to steer clear. You should also know that the IRS really has no sense of humor when it comes to collecting taxes. Even when the positions taken are downright laughable.

Alongside the frivolous tax positions mentioned above are the tax scams promoted by, once again, confidence men who first gain your trust and then your money. All too often these folks will disappear, leaving you not only out their expensive fees but owing the IRS huge amounts in back taxes, penalties, and interest.

Know that as far as the IRS is concerned, ignorance is no excuse. If you are caught with fraudulent activity on your tax return, you may be punished just as harshly as the person who prepared the return, even if you didn't know about the fraud. Again, be careful who you are going to for advice regarding your asset protection and tax preparation needs.

The following are some of the schemes that the IRS urges taxpayers to avoid:

1. *Abusive Roth IRAs.* Taxpayers should be wary of advisors who encourage them to shift undervalued property to Roth Individual Retirement Arrangements. In one variation, a promoter has the taxpayer move the undervalued common stock into a Roth IRA, circumventing the annual maximum contribution limit and allowing otherwise taxable income to go untaxed.

2. *Phishing.* A technique used by identity thieves to acquire personal financial data in order to gain access to the financial accounts of unsuspecting individuals. These mostly Internet-based criminals pose as representatives of a financial institution and send out fictitious e-mails or place phone calls in an attempt to trick people into providing confidential information. Oftentimes consumers will be directed to official-looking Web sites where they will be asked to provide their Social Security or credit card number as well as their password. It is important to note that the IRS does not call taxpayers (or send out e-mails) about issues relating to their accounts. If you have any

concern whether the person who called you is really from the organization they claim to be hang up and call the company directly to confirm.

3. *Disguised Corporate Ownership.* Asset protection is one of the most valuable tools available to us. However, some "asset protection advisors" promote setting up corporations and other entities to disguise ownership so as to evade taxes. Once formed, some of these anonymous entities are used to facilitate underreporting of income, nonfiling of tax returns, money laundering, and other financial crimes. Once again, be wary of any advisor suggesting that you set up an entity for any fraudulent purpose. These people are not asset protection advisors. They are instead scamsters trying to rope you into their scheme of separating you from your money.

4. *Return Preparer Fraud.* The IRS warns taxpayers to look out for dishonest tax preparers. These unethical preparers make their money by skimming a portion of their client's refunds and charging inflated prices for their services. Many of these tax preparers lure new clients by promising large tax refunds. Some of them advocate filing fraudulent claims for refunds on items such as fuel tax credits from previous years, or inflated telephone excise tax credits. You should choose carefully when selecting who you will go to for tax advice. Remember, you are ultimately responsible for your tax return, even if someone else prepares it.

5. *Trust Abuse.* Another scam involves the constitutional, common law, or pure trust. Con men prey on people's distaste for the IRS by offering boxes of documents "guaranteed" to hide your profits through layers of trusts. These "advisors" charge a great deal of money for these trusts, and then disappear. When the IRS catches on to this scheme the fact that you relied upon an advisor to set up your trusts is no defense. The IRS position is that you should have known better than to try and evade taxes in this manner. Anyone with a pulse should know that a series of trusts which can completely eliminate your tax obligation is a fraud. (Again, if it were true, everyone would do it and all government functions would halt.) When the hustler and your money are gone you are going to owe a huge amount of money in taxes, penalties, and interest to the IRS. Some people will never recover from the damage.

This is only a small sample of the various scams that exist in the marketplace. The absence of a particular scheme from the previous list should not be an indication that the IRS is not aware of it or not taking steps to prosecute it, or that you need not avoid it. For additional information regarding some of the newest scams businesses are encountering, go to www.successdna.com/scams.

As an investor and business owner it is your responsibility to look out for yourself. Seek out quality advisors for your team. Steer clear of those who play on your fears and greed. Never be afraid to challenge someone who advocates strategies that are questionable or overly expensive. Never be afraid to get a second opinion on such strategies. With vigilance you can protect not only your assets but your standing as well.

Chapter 18

What Happens at the End

Because hopes are high upon creating a business, people often avoid thinking about what will happen if the business comes to an end. But the subject of dissolution is one that should not be ignored. Planning ahead by understanding some basic principles of dissolution is important. Whether you go out of business or enter into a relationship with another business where your existing business dissolves, there are procedures that must be prepared for from the start. What follows are considerations concerning consequences related to the dissolution of various business entities. And, as discussed in this chapter's final section, dissolution may not be appropriate.

Limited Partnership

In a limited partnership, the partnership agreement should include express provisions for dissolution, liquidation, termination, and winding up of the partnership. Dissolution of the partnership means the triggering moment when provisions for winding up and liquidation shall begin; termination occurs only upon the conclusion of all such activities.

When designing the partnership agreement, a variety of possible triggering events should be considered that could allow for or require dissolution. Dissolution provisions for short-term activities may specify an exact date when the partnership will dissolve. More frequently, provisions invoke dissolution:

• When a final general partner leaves the partnership, unless a majority— or greater percentage—of the remaining limited partners are allowed a brief time to keep the business and find a new general partner;
• If the business does not achieve expected financing goals within a given period of time;
• Upon a judicial decree;
• If it is found that the partnership's status is unlawful; or
• Upon the sale of substantially (over 90 percent) all assets and other property of the business.

Commonly, an express provision requires the prior written consent of the limited partners before a general partner can initiate the dissolution of the partnership. Alternatively, provisions may require unanimous written consent of all general partners in addition to a majority of limited partners. Additionally, if a general partner is in default without meeting the deadline and conditions to cure the default, a provision in the partnership agreement can allow a nondefaulting general partner and, typically, a minimum of a majority of the limited partners to elect to dissolve the partnership at once.

An express provision should state the order of operations for the winding-up phase of the business upon dissolution, during which a brief but sufficient amount of time is allowed for liquidation of assets, a final accounting, and the closing of the business's books. Unless dissolution is invoked by a judicial decree, which will state who will be in charge of the winding-up process, the general partner(s) ordinarily take on the task unless, where no general partner is left, the limited partners may jointly conduct the winding-up process. Your state will very likely require a form to be filed with the appropriate authority.

Sometimes state law specifies the order in which liquidation proceeds are distributed, but many states also allow the partnership agreement to control such distribution if the agreement specifies reasonable provisions. A common pattern is first to pay all creditors, other than partners who may have made loans to the business, whose debts are to be paid. Those partner debts get paid second. Finally, if money is left, profit and loss is computed for the taxable year during which liquidation is taking place. Distributions are then made according to each partner's capital account balance (providing the balance is positive). Usually all distributions must be made by the end of the taxable year in question or within a period specified by law (often, ninety days after the date set for liquidation).

But what if there's a deficit? Generally, if, after the calculations described above, there is a deficit in a general partner's capital account, that general partner will have until the end of the applicable distribution period to furnish sufficient funds to eliminate that deficit from the books before they are closed. Limited partners may be protected from restoring funds to eliminate any deficit in their account because the idea itself is counter to the fundamental principle that limited partners are protected from the business's liabilities. This needs to be provided for specifically in the partnership agreement with provisions for loss limitations and offsets for qualified income with respect to limited partners.

Limited Liability Company

Limited liability companies are also subject to rules covering dissolution specific to this type of entity. As discussed earlier in this book, the statutory provisions for LLCs vary from one state to another and, because the LLC remains a somewhat newer phenomenon, not a great deal of guidance can be found in case law supporting the fine points involved. Thus, you'll need to be very careful about determining what rules apply in the state where you form the LLC. Here are some frequently specified provisions (but, again, you'll need to check your own state's requirements and guidelines for LLCs):

• Dissolution requires advance approval by a vote for dissolution passed by at least a majority percentage of membership interests (sometimes a larger percentage is specified in the articles of organization or operating agreement).

• There are limitations on a member's ability to have his capital contribution returned upon termination or withdrawal (often a unanimous vote of members is required to allow lower values to be set for a membership interest differing from capital contributions of other members), and even where allowed under an operating agreement, liability for capital contributions existing at the time when a debt is undertaken may allow for continued rights of a creditor even after membership ceases with respect to that part of the capital contribution. Also, unless allowable with a specific provision in the operating agreement, members usually cannot withdraw capital contributions before the process of dissolution and winding up has been completed.

• Note that corporate members may endure dissolution and winding up of their own entities, in which case such an event in some states may cause the LLC to dissolve as well, unless the remaining members purchase the interest and have an agreement to continue the LLC (again, at least a majority of membership interests are required to do so).

• Much like limited partnerships, LLCs often have similar triggering events for dissolution: a specific date upon which the LLC is to end; sale of the LLC's assets; judicial decrees; or a vote for dissolution by at least a majority percentage of membership interests (sometimes a majority of members or a unanimous vote by all eligible voting members). Also, death, dissolution, withdrawal, or any other event that renders a member's position untenable may require dissolution (with similar requirements of votes to continue operating, and with similar requirements to provide for the company's future as discussed above with respect to limited partnerships).

• The winding-up process is conducted by the managing member or, if the managing member is in default or has left the LLC, then by the remaining members. The LLC can't do any other business at that point other than address itself to matters directly related to winding up. Almost always, notice of the dissolution must be given to all of the LLC's creditors and others with a legal interest at stake (such as a plaintiff with a judgment against the LLC) as well.

• The order of payment, included—and sometimes modifiable—in the articles of organization or operating agreement, begins with payment to all creditors of the LLC; next, the costs involved in the liquidation process (including reasonable compensation fees for those undertaking the job of winding up); then a reserve account if there are any other expected needs (a potential debt that may become due or a lawsuit that has yet to reach a judgment); repayment of any loans to the LLC made by its own members; and finally, distribution of remaining funds to members (as with limited partnerships, similarly calculated according to positive account balances). Again, a judicially decreed dissolution will usually set forth the details of the process within the declaratory documents.

- Deficits are not normally subject to further contributions by members, although, if provided for in the articles or operating agreement, a member whose capital contribution was not received or was insufficient may be reachable to the amount still owing by the other members. Usually this is provided for prior to dissolution, but if properly documented as ongoing, it may be possible to reach the member after the dissolution. Nearly all LLCs give no remedy by members versus other members if insufficient funds are available at the point where member distributions would occur. Only the company's own assets are at stake unless, where applicable, an agreement to the contrary allows members to look to others for reimbursement or even indemnification or contribution of that member's liabilities.

Corporation

For a corporation, dissolution requires the approval of the board of directors and the shareholders. In most jurisdictions, when the approvals are obtained, the corporation (and in most states, LLCs and LPs too) must file with the state certifying the dissolution has been approved along with a list of the directors who will wind up the affairs.

The directors then collect monies owed, sell real and personal property, and generally settle the corporate accounts. After paying expenses, costs, and all general and special liens, the directors pay any other debts due. If not enough money is available, the debtors receive a pro rata distribution. If any funds remain after the payment of debts and expenses, the shareholders are then paid according to their priority. Recall that preferred shareholders may have a liquidation preference over common shareholders.

It is important to be cautious in this process. If the directors distribute money to a shareholder without properly paying a creditor they may be held personally liable.

In some states a holder of a specified percentage of the issued stock (in Nevada, for example, it is 10 percent) may apply to the local court for an order dissolving the corporation and appointing a receiver to wind up its affairs. This is known as involuntary dissolution, and if you are hit with it you are going to need an attorney. Note that you, as an officer, director, or shareholder, cannot legally represent the corporation in pro per (without a lawyer) as an individual. A corporation, as a separate legal entity, can only be represented in court by an attorney.

The circumstances in which a court will appoint a receiver include:

- Willful violation of the corporate charter;
- Corporate insolvency or inability to pay debts;
- Abandonment of the business;
- Fraud or mismanagement by the directors; or
- Corporate assets in danger of loss or waste.

A receiver is an independent third party, like a bankruptcy trustee, who will take over the affairs of the company, investigate any claims, and report back to the court. A receivership should be avoided at all costs because (1) you lose control of your company; (2) receivers (and the lawyers they get to hire) can be very expensive; and (3) receivers are not always 100 percent objective. There is a good chance that all parties involved will be upset with how things turn out in a receivership. You are better advised to try to work things out.

But Why Dissolve?

A final point on dissolution. As mentioned, the directors (or trustees in some states) charged with winding up the affairs of a dissolved corporation can be held personally liable for a failure to pay creditors. In some cases, the directors were unaware of the creditor claims, paid the remaining corporate monies to the shareholders, and several years later were held personally liable to the unknown creditors. Likewise, once dissolved, a lawsuit against the corporation may instead be brought personally against the directors.

You need to carefully review whether you want to be in that position.

An option to consider: Do not dissolve the company. If there are claims lurking out there, and no great monies to distribute to the shareholders anyway, keep the corporation intact. In Wyoming for example, to keep the corporation alive is only $50 a year to the state and a little more for a resident agent and annual federal tax return. There is no state tax return to worry about in Wyoming. Keep your shield up for several years, until the statute of limitations for bringing claims has run out. And even then, do not file dissolution papers with your secretary of state but rather just stop paying the annual renewal fees. In most states your charter will be revoked, but you can pay extra fees and reinstate it for two or three years after revocation, buying you even more time and protection.

It is hard to understand why some people are in such a rush to dissolve their entities. They were formed to limit liability and provide asset protection. If they have done any kind of business at all, they need to be left on the corporate rolls for as long as possible to carry out the objectives of their formation.

Chapter 19

Some Miscellaneous Traps and Thoughts

You have learned quite a bit reading this book. You now know how informed businesspeople and investors use good entities to shield their assets and protect their business.

Before we close there are three additional tax traps to review. They serve as a closing reminder that what the IRS sees as too beneficial to the taxpayer it will attempt to rule out.

Personal Service Company

A personal service company is defined as any company where substantially all of the activities involve the performance of services in the fields of health, law, engineering, architecture, accounting, actuarial science, performing arts, or consulting. Further, a personal service company is a corporation whereby personal services are substantially performed by employee-owners. An employee-owner is any employee who owns more than 10 percent of the outstanding stock of the corporation.

The corporate tax rate for a personal service company is a flat 35 percent, without a graduation of tax rates as in a regular corporation. The purpose is to prevent people who perform personal services from claiming lower corporate tax rates than they would ordinarily have to pay as an individual.

Personal Holding Company

A corporation is a personal holding company when (1) at any time during the last half of the tax year more than 50 percent in value of its outstanding stock is owned, directly or indirectly, by or for not more than five individuals, and (2) at least 60 percent of adjusted ordinary gross income for the tax year is personal holding company income. Personal holding company income consists of passive types of income: interest, dividends, royalties, and rents. The kind of income we all like to have because you do not have to work every day to earn it.

There are extremely complicated rules associated with personal holding company income. So see your accountant. What you need to know here is that if you do not distribute the income from a personal holding company to yourself, the corporation can be assessed with a 39.6 percent tax on top of its normal tax rate. Again, the purpose is to ensure that taxes are paid on this income as if the individual had to pay it at individual rates.

Accumulated Earnings

Accumulated earnings are past profits, the previously taxed income reduced by any capital gain, within a C corporation. They are the retained earnings held by the corporation without any capital gains reflected and the monies that the company needs for the future to operate and expand its business.

The problem is that the IRS likes to see those profits distributed to shareholders, where they can tax them again. They do not want you using them for such mundane and prudent needs as working capital or retaining them as a reserve in case of an economic downturn. And so every C corporation with accumulated earnings greater than $250,000 (or $150,000 for personal service companies) is at risk of being taxed an additional 39.6 percent on top of regular corporate tax rates.

As one would suspect, this is a greatly litigated issue. Courts have generally supported business owners who claim that retained earnings are needed for future expansion, additional inventory, and other legitimate business needs. But beware of this provision. If it becomes an issue for you, consult your tax professional. As with all the advice you have received in this book, be sure to review it with professionals competent to give you the advice you need to succeed.

While there are a number of traps out there for the unsuspecting, like the ones above, they should not deter you from your business and asset protection objectives. As we have discussed throughout the book, with a team of professional advisors assisting you, all of the various traps (and there aren't that many) are easily avoided.

In selecting and building a group of advisors be sure to work with people you like and trust. You are going to want your attorney, accountant, graphic designer, engineers, consultants, and other professionals you bring in to be team players. There should be no room for individuals who are egocentric, abrasive, negative, or nonresponsive. Your team members should be able to work with you and the other team members to achieve a common goal—protecting and advancing your business interests. This is not that much to ask, especially since you are paying these people.

To that end, consider interviewing for your professional team. Meet with several accountants, attorneys, and other service providers to get a feel for them and their practice. Ask specific questions such as how much their fees are and what their level of experience is in certain areas. Be a comparison shopper. For example, our firm charges $695 plus state filing fees for a complete corporate (or LLC and LP) package, including articles of incorporation, bylaws, minutes of shareholder and directors meetings, and issuance of stock. Any attorney who charges $1,000 or more (and some charge $2,000 to $5,000) for this service may not be the right person for you.

And, like any coach or manager, feel free to replace members of your team if they are not performing for you. If, for example, your accountant won't return your phone calls for weeks at a time you may want to start looking for someone who's more responsive.

By building and cultivating a team of professionals that care about you and your business, you will be able both to concentrate on your core goals and succeed in the future.

Of course, your advisory team can only take you so far. The true source of your success is going to come from within you. The choices and decisions you make, the means by which you approach your business, and the ways in which you deal with people and situations will all be determinative factors in your achievement. The balance you strike between the obligations of work, family, and community will also be important.

Please also remember to focus on working smarter, not harder. As

Robert Kiyosaki's rich dad taught him, by using the same strategies the rich use to your advantage you too can become wealthy.

All the strategies discussed herein—the use of corporations, LLCs, and LPs, the strategic utilization of Nevada and Wyoming entities, and maximizing the use of the tax code to your advantage—can be implemented easily and without great expense. They are all present to help you achieve your greatest dreams and goals.

Good luck.

About the Author

Garrett Sutton, Esq., is the bestselling author of *Own Your Own Corporation, The ABC's of Getting Out of Debt, The ABC's of Writing Winning Business Plans, How to Buy and Sell a Business* and *Real Estate Advantages* in Robert Kiyosaki's Rich Dad's Advisors series. Garrett has over twenty-five years experience in assisting individuals and business to determine their appropriate corporate structure, limit their liability, protect their assets and advance their financial, personal and credit success goals.

Garrett and his law firm, Sutton Law Center, have offices in Reno, Nevada, Jackson Hole, Wyoming and Sacramento, California. The firm represents hundreds of corporations, limited liability companies, limited partnerships and individuals in their real estate and business-related law matters, including incorporations, contracts, and ongoing business-related legal advice. The firm continues to accept new clients.

Garrett is also the owner of Corporate Direct, which since 1988 has provided affordable asset protection and corporate formation services. He is the author of *How to Use Limited Liability Companies and Limited Partnerships*, published by SuccessDNA, which further educates readers on the proper use of entities.

Garrett attended Colorado College and the University of California at Berkeley, where he received a B.S. in Business Administration in 1975. He graduated with a J.D. in 1978 from Hastings College of Law, the University of California's law school in San Francisco. He has appeared in the *Wall Street Journal, The New York Times* and other publications and is the radio host of the nationally syndicated *Wealth Talk America*, which is archived at www.successdna.com.

Garrett is a member of the State Bar of Nevada, the State Bar of California, and the American Bar Association. He has written numerous professional articles and has served on the Publication Committee of the State Bar of Nevada.

Garrett enjoys speaking with entrepreneurs and real estate investors on the advantages of forming business entities. He is a frequent lecturer for small business groups as well as the Rich Dad's Advisors series.

Garrett serves on the boards of the American Baseball Foundations, located in Birmingham, Alabama, and the Reno-Nevada based Sierra Kids Foundation.

For more information on Garrett Sutton and Sutton Law Center, please visit his Web sites at www.sutlaw.com, www.corporatedirect.com, and www.successdna.com.

Video Learning, Free Resources and more. . .

Visit

Resources   Videos   Stories

use now   watch now   vote now

Join now and receive the following free reports:

Homestead Exemption Chart
Federal Exemptions
Bankruptcy Chart
State Exemptions for IRA's
IRS National Standards

and more. . .

More Books by Garrett Sutton. . .

How to Buy and Sell a Business reveals the strategies used by successful entrepreneurs to acquire and cash out business investments. Written in a clear and easily understandable style, How to Buy and Sell a Business provides the necessary knowledge to avoid the pitfalls and overcome the obstacles in order to achieve a winning transition.

The ABC's of Writing Winning Business Plans illustrates how to:
Focus your vision for the business
Format your plan to impress
Use your business plan as a tool
Deal with competition
Attract the funding you need
Identify strengths and weaknesses
Draft a plan for real estate
Understand your financials

More Books by Garrett Sutton. . .

Real Estate Advantages is for *first-time* as well as *seasoned* real estate investors. It reveals the tax and legal loopholes available and most important, how they can be used together to not only maximize your income - but accelerate your income from real estate investing.

The ABC's of Getting Out of Debt reveals the strategies for avoiding and overcoming bad debt, as well as using good debt to your advantage. *The ABC's of Getting Out of Debt* illustrates how to:

* Beat the lenders at Their Own Game
* Understand Your Credit Report
* Repair Your own Credit
* Master the Psychology of Debt
* Deal with Debt Collectors
* Avoid Credit Scams
* Win with Good Credit
* Take Charge of Your Finances

Where Can I Receive More
Legal Information?

For free information on a variety of legal topics, visit the Sutton Law Center Web site at: www.sutlaw.com.

Obtain free downloads, including:

Winning With Trademarks

and

Winning with Franchises.

Bestselling Books by
Robert T. Kiyosaki & Sharon L. Lechter

Rich Dad Poor Dad
What the Rich Teach Their Kids About Money
that the Poor and Middle Class Do Not

Rich Dad's CASHFLOW Quadrant
Rich Dad's Guide to Financial Freedom

Rich Dad's Guide to Investing
What the Rich Invest In that the Poor and Middle Class Do Not

Rich Dad's Rich Kid Smart Kid
Give Your Child a Financial Head Start

Rich Dad's Retire Young Retire Rich
How to Get Rich Quickly and Stay Rich Forever

Rich Dad's Prophecy
Why the Biggest Stock Market Crash in History is Still Coming...
And How You Can Prepare Yourself and Profit From it!

Rich Dad's Success Stories
Real-Life Success Stories from Real-Life People
Who Followed the Rich Dad Lessons

Rich Dad's Guide to Becoming Rich Without Cutting Up Your Credit Cards
Turn "Bad Debt" into "Good Debt"

Rich Dad's Who Took My Money?
Why Slow Investors Lose and Fast Money Wins!

Rich Dad Poor Dad for Teens
The Secrets About Money – That You Don't Learn In School!

Rich Dad's Escape from the Rat Race
How to Become a Rich Kid by Following Rich Dad's Advice

Rich Dad's Before You Quit Your Job
Ten Real-Life Lessons Every Entrepreneur Should Know
About Building a Multi-Million Dollar Business

Rich Dad's Increase Your Financial IQ
Get Smarter With Your Money

www.richdad.com

Bestselling Books by
Rich Dad's Advisors

Sales Dogs
by Blair Singer
Reveal the Five Simple but Critical Revenue - Generating Skills

Own Your Own Corporation
by Garret Sutton
Don't Climb the Corporate Ladder, Why Not Own the Corporate Ladder?

How To Buy & Sell A Business
by Garrett Sutton
Strategies Used by Successful Entrepreneurs

The ABC's of Real Estate Investing
by Ken McElroy
Learn How to Achieve Wealth and Cash Flow Through Real Estate

The ABC's of Building A Business Team That Wins
by Blair Singer
How to Get Rich Quickly and Stay Rich Forever

The ABC's of Getting Out of Debt
by Garrett Sutton
Strategies for Overcoming Bad Debt, as Well as
Using Good Debt to Your Advantage

The ABC's of Writing Winning Business Plans
by Garrett Sutton
Learn to Focus Your Plan for the Business and Format Your Plan to Impress
About Building a Multi-Million Dollar Business

The Advanced Guide to Real Estate Investing
by Ken McElroy
How to Identify the Hottest Markets and Secure the Best Deals

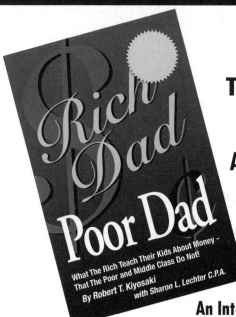

The New York Times writes:

"Move over, Monopoly®...

A new board game that aims
to teach people how to get rich
is gaining fans
the world over!"

WHY PLAY GAMES?

Play often and learn
what it takes to
get out of the Rat Race—
for good!

Games are **powerful learning tools** because they enable people to experience 'hands-on' learning. As a **true reflection of behavior,** games are a **window to our attitudes,** our **abilities to see opportunities,** and **assess risk and rewards.**

Each of the CASHFLOW® games creates a forum in which to evaluate life decisions regarding money and finances and immediately see the results of your decisions.

CASHFLOW Clubs

The Benefits of Joining
a CASHFLOW Club

Invest Time Before You Invest Money

The philosophy of The Rich Dad Company is that there are only two things you can invest: time and money. We recommend you invest some time studying and learning before you invest your money. The CASHFLOW games offer the opportunity to learn and 'invest' with 'play money' – before you invest real money.

Meet New Friends from Around the World

When you visit or join a CASHFLOW Club (or play the CASHFLOW games on line) you'll meet like-minded people – from all over the world. The world is filled with people with negative attitudes, know-it-all attitudes and loser attitudes. The type of person a CASHFLOW Club attracts is a person who is open minded, wants to learn and wants to develop his or her potential.

Have Fun Learning

Learning should be fun! Too often financial education is dull, boring and fear-based. Many financial experts want to educate you on how risky investing is and why you should trust them. That is not the Rich Dad philosophy on learning. We believe that learning should be fun and cooperative and lead you toward becoming smarter about money so you can tell the difference between good and bad financial advice.

Find a CASHFLOW Club near you:
www.richdad.com

Rich Dad's Wisdom:
The Power of Words

Words are gasoline for your brain. If you improve your financial vocabulary, you will become richer and richer. The good news is: words are free. Which proves, once more, that it does not take money to make money. To expand your vocabulary beyond the financial terms in the glossary you'll find on the Rich Dad web site you might consider acquiring a dictionary of financial terms. When you look up financial words on a regular basis (or look up the definition of a term you hear but do not understand) you may find yourself becoming richer and richer.

An example of the power of words: When people advise you to get out of debt, do they know what they are talking about?

> When you buy a bond, you are buying debt. For example, a U.S. T-bill is a bond – an IOU from the U.S. government. So when you buy a bond you are buying debt…debt that is an asset to you and a liability to the government. So debt can be good. Some of the richest people in the world (as well as financial institutions) get richer because they invest in debt.

When a banker says your house is an asset…ask yourself: Whose asset is it? By definition, assets put money in your pocket and liabilities take money from your pocket. When you look at your bank's financial statement, you can better see whose asset your home really is…

To improve your brain's financial power…improve your financial vocabulary. Words are fuel for your brain!
